MW00778224

HISTORY IN TRANSIT

Other Works by Dominick LaCapra

Emile Durkheim: Sociologist and Philosopher
History and Criticism
History and Memory after Auschwitz
History, Politics, and the Novel
History and Reading: Tocqueville, Foucault, French Studies
Madame Bovary on Trial
A Preface to Sartre
Representing the Holocaust: History, Theory, Trauma
Rethinking Intellectual History: Texts, Contexts, Language
Soundings in Critical Theory
The Bounds of Race: Perspectives on Hegemony and Resistance (edited)
*Modern European Intellectual History: Reappraisals and New
    Perspectives* (edited with Steven L. Kaplan)
Writing History, Writing Trauma

HISTORY IN TRANSIT: EXPERIENCE, IDENTITY, CRITICAL THEORY

Dominick LaCapra

CORNELL UNIVERSITY PRESS

ITHACA AND LONDON

Copyright © 2004 by Cornell University

All rights reserved. Except for brief quotations in a review, this book, or parts
thereof, must not be reproduced in any form without permission in writing from
the publisher. For information, address Cornell University Press, Sage House, 512
East State Street, Ithaca, New York 14850.

First published 2004 by Cornell University Press
First printing, Cornell Paperbacks, 2004

Printed in the United States of America

Library of Congress Cataloging-in-Publication Data

LaCapra, Dominick, 1939–
  History in transit : experience, identity, critical theory / Dominick LaCapra
    p. cm.
Includes bibliographical references and index.
  ISBN 0-8014-4254-0 (alk. paper)—ISBN 0-8014-8898-2 (pbk. : alk. paper)
  1. History—Psychological aspects. 2. History—Philosophy. 3. History—Social
aspects. 4. Personality and history. 5. Psychohistory. I. Title.
  D16.16.L32 2004
  901'.9—dc22

                                                                    2003021658

Cornell University Press strives to use environmentally responsible suppliers and
materials to the fullest extent possible in the publishing of its books. Such materials
include vegetable-based, low-VOC inks and acid-free papers that are recycled,
totally chlorine-free, or partly composed of nonwood fibers. For further
information, visit our website at www.cornellpress.cornell.edu.

Cloth printing   10 9 8 7 6 5 4 3 2 1
Paperback printing   10 9 8 7 6 5 4 3 2 1

For my graduate students

In significant ways, this book queries the views expressed in the following quotations:
Many realities are subject to the law of all or nothing. (1937)

The least explained of all the "mysteries," TRAGEDY, like a festival given in honor of horror-spreading time, depicted for gathered men the signs of delirium and death whereby they might recognize their true nature. (1938)

I propose to admit, as a law, that human beings are only united with each other through rents or wounds. . . . Men, assembling for a sacrifice and for a festival, satisfy their need to expend a vital excess. The sacrificial laceration that opens the festival is a liberating laceration. The individual who participates in loss is obscurely aware that this loss engenders the community that supports him. (1939)

The sensibility that goes to the furthest limits moves away from politics and, as is the case for the suffering animal, the world has at a certain point nothing more to it than an immense absurdity, closed in on itself. But the sensibility that looks for a way out and enters the path of politics is always of cheap quality. . . . The tens of thousands of victims of the atom bomb are on the same level as the tens of millions whom nature yearly hands over to death. One cannot deny the differences in age and in suffering, but origin and intensity change nothing: horror is everywhere the same. The point is that, in principle, the one horror is preventable while the other is not is, in the last analysis, a matter of indifference. (1947)

—Georges Bataille

CONTENTS

Acknowledgments
ix

Introduction
1

CHAPTER ONE
Experience and Identity
35

CHAPTER TWO
History, Psychoanalysis, Critical Theory
72

CHAPTER THREE
Trauma Studies: Its Critics and Vicissitudes
106

CHAPTER FOUR
Approaching Limit Events: Siting Agamben
144

CHAPTER FIVE
The University in Ruins?
195

Epilogue
249

Index
271

ACKNOWLEDGMENTS

I would like to thank Jane Pedersen, Scott Spector, and an anonymous reader for their careful readings and suggestions. I would also like to thank fellows at the Society for the Humanities and participants at the School of Criticism and Theory over the past few years for their readings and discussions of several chapters. In addition I thank present and former graduate students at Cornell University with whom I have discussed issues germane to this book, especially Ben Brower, Federico Finchelstein, Tracie Matysik, Ryan Plumley, Camille Robcis, Richard Schaefer, David "Brook" Stanton, Judith Surkis, and Jeremy Varon. I thank Ryan Plumley for his assistance in preparing the index.

A version of chapter 4 was published in *Witnessing the Disaster: Essays in Representation and the Holocaust*, ed. Michael Bernard-Donals and Richard Glejzer (Madison: University of Wisconsin Press, 2003).

A version of chapter 5 was published in *Critical Inquiry* 25 (autumn 1998).

HISTORY IN TRANSIT

Introduction

History is always in transit, even if periods, places, or professions sometimes achieve relative stabilization. This is the very meaning of historicity. And the disciplines that study history—both professional historiography and the other humanistic or interpretive social-scientific disciplines addressing it—are also to varying degrees in transit, with their self-definitions and borders never achieving fixity or uncontested identity. From a historical perspective, the very idea of the end of history might seem to be a nonhistorical absurdity. It may, however, refer to the hoped-for or feared, utopian or dystopian, transcendence of history in some intemporal or (post)apocalyptic beyond, whether outside time or somehow suspending, if not putting a stop to it. The so-called end of history may also constitute an ideological attempt to remain fixated at an existing historical condition, such as a market economy and limited political democracy.[1] In these senses, it informs us about a phantasmatic structure of desire and its possible effects, but it becomes a cultural symptom posing as a general theory—a symptom attesting to the prevalence of postapocalyptic sensibilities or self-understandings—when it pretends to conceptualize historicity or historical processes in general.

History in the sense of historiography cannot escape transit unless it negates itself by denying its own historicity and becomes identified

---

[1] This is clearly the case with Francis Fukuyama's *End of History and the Last Man* (London: Macmillan, 1992).

1

with transcendence or fixation. This transitional condition affects the very meaning of historical understanding; it requires a continual rethinking of what counts as history in the dual sense of historical processes and historiographical attempts to account for them. The notions of transit and transition do not imply either relativistic skepticism or an overall teleology for history or historiography but instead a willingness to rethink goals and assumptions, including the very meaning of temporality, as a structural feature of historicity itself. Any "defense" of history that negates or forecloses historicity, including the historicity of the historical discipline, amounts to an attempt to immobilize the discipline in a manner that denies or marginalizes the forces making up its internally contested structure and emergent possibilities or goals; it also defensively denatures dialogical encounters with voices and forces that challenge its present constitution. A dialogical encounter with a challenge may not only change existing historical practices; it may lead to a rethinking that legitimates certain of them that are able to withstand critical scrutiny, at times situating them in a larger conception of historical understanding. Professionalization itself involves an attempt to stabilize the movement of historical understanding through normative limits, and hence poses, in its own way, the (ethicopolitical) problem of normative limits and that which exceeds them, perhaps prefiguring newer articulations of historical understanding and even of the discipline of history in its variable relations to other disciplines and intellectual ventures such as those represented in the humanities and social sciences.

The transition and transformation of historical understanding require recurrent attempts to think through problems bearing on one's conception of the relation between the present and the past in their import for possible futures. The form of writing that may best enable close, engaging, supple encounters with a series of problems is the essay. What follows is an interacting set of essays addressing certain problems, notably with respect to experience, identity, normativity, the extreme or limit event, and the interaction between history and critical theory, notably psychoanalysis understood not as an escapist psychotherapy or as an ideologically saturated substitute for philosophy but as a form of critical theory with explicitly evaluative and sociopolitical dimensions.

One of my objectives is to gain greater clarity about the concept of experience, especially in its implications for historical understanding.

In the last decade or so, historians have turned or returned to the question of experience, particularly with respect to nondominant groups and such problems as memory in its relation to history. The experiential turn has led to an increased interest in oral history and its role in recapturing the voices and experience of subordinate groups that may not have left sufficient traces in official documents and histories. At least in certain quarters, the turn to experience has also led to an awareness of the importance of "traumatic" history and what occurs in those living through the limit or extreme events attending it. And it has prompted attempts to read the archives differently by interrogating how they have been constructed and maintained, even their very silences, for traces of the experience and outlook of seemingly voiceless or underrecorded groups, for example, by analyzing inquisition registers or records with an eye to re-creating the lives and worldviews of various groups, from peasants and millers to priests and nuns. Hence much attention has been given to microhistory, which focuses on small or face-to-face groups, as in Emmanuel Le Roi Ladurie's acclaimed *Montaillou* (1975) or Michel de Certeau's powerful and insufficiently recognized *Possession at Loudun* (1970), or even on the experience of an individual, as in the now famous case of the once mute, inglorious Menocchio in Carlo Ginzburg's *Cheese and the Worms* (1976).[2] More recently, the experiential turn has also directed attention to the problem of the status and nature of testimony that does not simply convey information about events but bears witness to experience, notably in the difficult case of extreme occurrences and traumatic experience.[3]

[2] On the latter book, see my *History and Criticism* (Ithaca: Cornell University Press, 1985), chap. 2. De Certeau's *Possession at Loudun* (trans. Michael B. Smith [Chicago: University of Chicago Press, 1996]) is especially interesting for the way it combines archival research and an engagement with the past involving the historian's strongly "cathected" transferential relations with protagonists and problems, notably de Certeau's relation to the exorcist Surin, where one may at times even detect elements of uncontrolled projective identification. De Certeau in this book undertakes perhaps his most compelling attempt to relate history and psychoanalysis in a micrological, close study of the past.

[3] See, for example, Saul Friedlander, *Nazi Germany and the Jews*, vol. 1, *The Years of Persecution 1933–1939* (New York: HarperCollins, 1997); and Lawrence Langer, *Holocaust Testimonies: The Ruins of Memory* (New Haven: Yale University Press, 1991) as well as my own discussion in *Representing the Holocaust: History, Theory, Trauma* (Ithaca: Cornell University Press, 1994), chap. 6, and *Writing History, Writing Trauma* (Baltimore: Johns Hopkins University Press), chap. 3.

Beyond professional history, experience is of course a crucial issue in psychoanalysis and in phenomenological and existential approaches to philosophy. The incentive of both Edmund Husserl and Martin Heidegger, whatever their differences, was to reclaim lived experience as an object of philosophical reflection, an ambition taken up by such different thinkers as Henri Lefebvre, Maurice Merleau-Ponty, Jean-Paul Sartre, and Emmanuel Levinas. And experience has become a concern in other disciplines, such as literary criticism and cultural studies, at times prompting an ethnographic orientation in research (a long-standing dimension of important approaches to history as well). It is a crucial concern in various "minority" studies attempting to elicit the experience and possible modes of agency of the oppressed. Experience is central to the question of identity, whether one sees the latter as unified or at least as having a core, or as radically split, fragmented, decentered, and disseminated. At times "experience" threatens to become a hollow shibboleth, especially when what begins as populism turns into an indiscriminate method-ology, and one affirms the need to recover lost popular voices in cases marked by insufficient evidence of any sort and the tendency to com-pensate for such insufficiency through unrestrained speculation, pro-jective identification, and ventriloquism. In any event, "experience" is a frequently invoked but undertheorized concept both in history and in related disciplines or discourses, and much remains to be done in its critical examination and use and in elucidating its relation to structural as well as institutional analyses of society, culture, and the complex vicissitudes of trauma. These problems may be seen as raising questions about the scope and grasp of experience from "above" and "below."

Experience should not, however, be isolated or abstracted from other significant questions in research, analysis, and understanding. Indeed the interaction of experiential and other-than-experiential dimensions of history and social life is the broader issue raised by the turn to experience. What is it that escapes experience yet may still have experiential effects? How does experience interact with lan-guage and with signifying practices in general? Do concepts always leave ungrasped a residue of experiential remainders, and are these remainders particularly insistent and disconcerting in the case of excessive, traumatic, limit experiences? How does traumatic memory or the posttraumatic symptom relate to memory as critically controlled recollection, and is memory in either sense a reliable guide in representing events? What kinds of experience help in resisting trauma or in working through its aftermath? Is affect a crucial dimension of experience and is it related to historical understanding that is not simply objectifying? How may normatively unbound affect, notably in modes of compulsive repetition, disorient and possibly reorient experience and social life? How is experience, including affectivity, shaped and regulated, particularly by forms of normativity, including ritual? How is it related to subject positions and identity? Do different groups, including scholars and other occupational groups in disciplines or even subdisciplines, have different normative and identity-forming experiences—experiences they need to have had in order to count as a recognizable and accepted member of the group? How is experience a component of a politics or an ethics of recognition? Is the intense interest in experience and identity to some extent symptomatic of the feeling that modern or "modernized" experience has been drained or commodified and that identity, including its viable normative articulation, has become increasingly elusive or open to question?

Identity is probably best understood as a problematic constellation or more or less changing configuration of subject positions. And subject positions themselves are not necessarily fixed or complacent (even when they become fixations). For example, the child of a Nazi has received a burdensome "legacy" and at times a name (Martin Bormann, say) that carries connotations and even conveys narratives that are difficult to live down. If someone with such a subject position did not attempt to come to terms explicitly with his or her positionality, or claimed that subject positions are ineluctably and universally undecidable or indeterminate, one might suspect evasiveness. This is not to say that someone in this position inherits the guilt of a parent or even that anyone has a definite, prescriptive idea of what coming to terms with such a "legacy" should be. Nor is it to deny the significance of ambiguous cases in the twilight or gray zone of perpetrator-victims and more or less complicitous bystanders. But it is to say that in certain respects people are implicated in a past (hence are not simply contingent singularities [self-]created ex nihilo) and at some level are subject to experiences that require an attempt to situate themselves historically and work with and through that situatedness. And it is also to resist rashly generalizing the gray zone into a night in which everything becomes levelingly ambiguous or gray on gray. Indeed certain relatively determinate subject positions may not be all that comfortable or complacent, and the universalization of a notion of the self as utterly indeterminate, of identity as altogether fluid or disarticulated, and of history as sheer contingency and disjunctive event (or singular epiphany) is itself a dubious absolutization, the inverted mirror image of the chimeras of a totally stable self, a fully determinate identity, and a continuous, forward-flowing or progressive history.[4] It is also significant that descendants of perpetrators and victims may have a basis for coming empathically together to deal with events that divided their parents or ancestors, for they experience a psychic burden regarding events for which they are not responsible but for which they may nonetheless feel in some sense answerable.

Personal and especially collective identity has emerged as a particularly pressing problem for nondominant groups, and it too has stimulated research that gives special weight to testimonies, diaries, autobiographies, and other experiential sources. It has also been related to so-called identity politics wherein a group's subject position or constellation of subject positions becomes a crucial if not the paramount consideration in political and, more generally, social activity. A dominant group, at least insofar as its position is not subjected to basic challenge, need be less concerned about its often unmarked identity, and it typically assumes that its experience is normative (even "normal"), setting the standard of authenticity for others. Indeed subject positions and identities may always have been crucial for social and political action in ways that vary over time, space, and

[4] For an often insightful treatment of important issues that extend beyond the role of photography, see Ulrich Baer, *Spectral Evidence: The Photography of Trauma* (Cambridge: MIT Press, 2002). Unfortunately, Baer extends a valid critique of the conventionalizing overcontextualization of unsettling or traumatic events into a misleading binary opposition between historical understanding in general (at times simply associated by Baer with complacent identity and naïve certainty) and intransigently deconstructive, militantly antihistorical, quasi-transcendental, disjunctive, indeed postapocalyptic (and presumably truly political and future-oriented) insight. In Baer's analysis, the rather indiscriminate invocation of notions of testimony, bearing witness, and enactment (for example, with respect to Georges Bataille's "fascination with . . . photographs of trauma" [p. 178]) tends to preclude or foreclose any critical analysis (however tentative or self-questioning) of the complex relations between symptomatic, participatory, or even celebratory acting-out and various attempts to work through problems, including the analysis of how certain issues are framed and addressed.

social location, and the current concern with identity politics, whether pro, con, or mixed, may be only the most recent and self-conscious manifestation of a broader phenomenon. One type of identity politics has received little consideration and, to my knowledge, has not even been given a distinctive name—what I would term disciplinary identity politics. It is a specific form of professional and intellectual identity that often covertly informs analyses or critiques of other phenomena, notably, more readily recognizable forms of identity politics based on such factors as race, ethnicity, gender, sexual orientation, or religious affiliation. I try to provide a critical map of identity in its relation to experience in the first chapter of this book, where I also raise the possibility of a revised understanding of objectivity.[5]

There may well be resistance to critical reflection about "experience" and its relation to identity insofar as these concepts are polemically invoked to declare the bankruptcy or uselessness of all theory and the "pragmatic" need to get beyond theorizing. Instead of dismissively amalgamating and stereotyping all theoretical approaches as little more than spinning one's logical (or paralogical) wheels in the void, we might ask, more pointedly, how theory is specifically understood or deployed and what may be its critical potential, especially insofar as it is consistently related to historical, ethical, and sociopolitical problems rather than opposed to them in binaristic or radically dissociative terms. Yet, while cashiering or moving beyond theory is a specious and even sociopolitically and ethically suspect move (a certain pragmatism is premised on large-scale accommodation to a status quo), those discussing and debating the issues

[5] In a discussion of the implications of recent film studies (notably those of Eric Rentschler and Linda Schulte-Sasse) for the work of historians, Scott Spector argues that experience and identity constitute crucial and challenging dimensions of a newer interdisciplinary approach to ideology broader than that taken by historians who restrict themselves to the study of official doctrine and institutional practice. See his "Was the Third Reich Movie-Made? Interdisciplinarity and the Reframing of 'Ideology,'" *American Historical Review* 106 (2001): 460–84. Invoking views of Slavoj Žižek and Louis Althusser, he states that "a discussion of liberalism is somehow partial if it does not consider the ways in which the ideology becomes internalized or active in its subjects—it must tackle the question of *how subjects experience themselves* as 'free individuals.' . . . Ideology, in this sense, is not a set of (false) ideas that are believed to a greater or lesser degree by historical subjects. Rather, it is the field in which those subjects are given identity; it is inseparable from their sense of where they stand in relation to others in society, as well as in relation to state and family" (481). My first chapter tries to raise some significant critical and theoretical questions with respect to this understanding of ideology.

addressed in this book are thinking in the aftermath of the great onrush of theoretical initiatives usually labeled poststructural or postmodern. There is even a temptation to compound the "posts" in one's thinking (is there a post-poststructuralism?) and to become ever more "meta" in approaching problems. (As a well-known saying has it, every day in every way we are becoming "meta" and "meta.") Practitioners of various disciplines are also working after some version of the linguistic turn, which itself was bound up with the turn to theory and recently has been conjoined or conflated with it by those who would turn away from both. In exploring various theoretical approaches and trying to defend certain variants or dimensions of them, one may obviously recognize the importance of language without being "pantextualist" or denigrating other signifying practices. Indeed such recognition should be accompanied and actively contested by sensitivity to what exceeds or undercuts language or signification while nonetheless requiring their renewal and rearticulation. One form of the "post" mentality with which I nonetheless take issue is the postapocalyptic, which has been widespread in theoretical circles in the recent past. When it becomes a dominant or accentuated mode of thought, a postapocalyptic orientation tends to create what I term a sense of enlightened disempowerment—a kind of elaborately theorized fatalism or, at best, a tragic sense often associated with an inchoate, endless desire for unheard-of change or the totally "beyond," which may itself not get beyond aimless agitation, blank utopianism, or blind hope.

In the second chapter I turn in a more sustained manner to psychoanalysis. My interest in psychoanalysis is revisionary and critically self-reflexive (which should not be confused with self-referential or totalizing). I try to take from psychoanalysis certain concepts and frames of reference that may be of importance in rethinking both historical understanding and critical theory. This is a limited but, I think, significant project and I am not terribly concerned about whether I am being Freudian, Lacanian, Kleinian, or whatever. Nor do I devote energy to the speculative attempt to determine the intricate flows of affect or libido in the inner psychic plumbing. With respect to the perspective I try to develop, the value of psychoanalysis is in what it does to provide a better, theoretically informed (but not monomaniacally theory-driven or theoreticist) approach to historical understanding in relation to social and political problems on the one hand, and related disciplines or fields such as the social sciences, philosophy, literary criticism, and cultural studies on the other. From this perspective, I try to raise critical questions for other perspectives, notably a conception of theory or philosophy that is ahistorical or for which history simply serves as a repository of illustrations, contingencies, exempla, or "signs." And those working within the perspectives I criticize may well have thought-provoking questions to raise in return that will indicate the limitations of the arguments I make. One issue that has received much attention recently and which I have addressed in my recent work is the role of trauma in experience, notably in its relation to extreme events in history. I continue this attempt here, and it extends into the next two chapters.

I would make special mention of the fact that one crucial use of psychoanalysis here is to provide a critical theory of experience. But my approach is different from many recent tendencies epitomized in the important, influential work of Slavoj Žižek. In contrast to such tendencies, I do not put forward a pure or even predominantly symptomatic reading of all cultural texts or artifacts, at times in relatively indiscriminate terms that override the problem of specificity, whether it be the specificity of art or of historical phenomena such as concentration camps or the Holocaust itself. While recognizing the symptomatic dimension as well as the role of the phantasmatic in all cultural phenomena, I question any homogenizing notion of desire and would distinguish among phenomena (including texts and other artifacts) on the basis of the specific combination in them of symptomatic, critical, and possibly transformative processes and effects.[6] Cultural texts or phenomena are compromise formations in various ways and in a specific sense that does not restrict the notion of compromise formation to an exclusively symptomatic level of operation. Indeed this sense points to a constellation of forces involving unconscious and conscious processes in which repression or dissociation would not be the only force at play and in which processes of working-through might also be active and, within limits, effective.

I would relate the symptomatic dimension of phenomena to their tendency to act out or compulsively repeat symptoms and transfer-

[6] This line of argument continues and further develops views expressed in my earlier work, including *"Madame Bovary" on Trial* (Ithaca: Cornell University Press, 1982), *Rethinking Intellectual History: Texts, Contexts Language* (Ithaca: Cornell University Press, 1983), *History and Criticism*, and *Representing the Holocaust*, esp. chap. 1.

ential relations. More critical and transformative processes would counteract the compulsive repetition (as well as the unqualified "enjoyment" or ecstatic enactment) of symptoms through significant variations or changes that rework problems, including social and political problems, and would indicate a possible role for agency in intervening in developments. This distinction between acting-out and working-through cannot be mapped directly onto that between mass or popular and elite or high culture. Its application to any given text, artifact, or other phenomenon would be a matter of inquiry and argument.

While one may argue that no cultural phenomenon transcends or fully masters symptomaticity or transferential repetition, the most symptomatic artifacts would be those that are most ideologically saturated, propagandistic, dogmatic, or formulaic, for example, racist tracts or rallies in which there would be few self-critical (or self-deconstructive) tendencies, and (nonprojective or nonapologetic) critique would explicitly have to draw on resources or bring in considerations not significantly active in the artifacts or phenomena in question. By contrast, more critical and self-critical artifacts or phenomena signal or even foreground (however subtly) their own symptomatic dimensions and engage processes that offer perspective on these dimensions and may provide the wherewithal for their critique, at times indicating transformative possibilities. The latter possibilities could be termed situationally transcendent in that they work (or play) with and through problems (including those transmitted from the past) and do not leap beyond them in some unmediated rupture. Any break or major disjunction would be at most a dimension of a complex dynamic, often coming retrospectively (*nachträglich*, or *après coup*) after an arduous process has been largely accomplished, and one recognizes the distance covered or even the caesura effected. In this sense, artifacts or phenomena putting critical and transformative processes into play cannot be understood only as functions, symptoms, or legitimating reinforcements of contexts precisely because they respond to or rework them in ways that make—not simply mark or represent—a historical difference.

Moreover, significant cultural artifacts offer in a particularly accentuated manner a variable articulation or combination of critical and transformative work (or play) on pertinent contexts, along with a strangeness, alterity, or opaque and enigmatic dimension that is in excess both of contexts and of the delimited sociopolitical work on them. This extremely defamiliarizing and uncanny dimension evokes the question of the sublime, understood as a displacement of the sacred or a transfiguration of the traumatic (which has also been a cardinal dimension of sacralization). It points to a certain "transcendence," perhaps most accentuated recently in art, that is other than merely situational, without necessarily being subject to hypostatization as the perennial or universal. One issue, however, is whether one should fixate on the uncanny dimension of phenomena to the exclusion or denigration of other considerations (including sociopolitical critique). A related issue is whether "sublime" effects and ecstatic elation are best sought in politics, collective action, or even commentary on the extreme or traumatic experience of others—or whether they should be located, without being simply domesticated (or "territorialized"), insofar as possible in art, religion, and certain activities affirmed and accepted by those involved in them but not imposed on others. In any event, one "psychoanalytic" view of art in the modern period might be to see it nonreductively as a relatively "safe" but often disconcerting haven or special site for exploring the symptomatic acting out and the attempt to work or play through extreme events and problems, including their role in enigmatic or opaque areas of experience that cannot be reduced to solvable puzzles or "cured" in the interest of full ego identity or untrammeled intersubjective communication.

The third chapter on trauma and its vicissitudes is a *mise au point* of my thinking about approaches to trauma and the posttraumatic. At times it returns to points made in my earlier publications that have been misunderstood and tries to clarify and extend them, and at times to elaborate them in different directions. One of the key arguments of this chapter proposes a sociocultural Lamarckianism involving the "inheritance" of acquired characteristics through interacting processes of acting out (or compulsively repeating) posttraumatic symptoms and working through them, including educational and critical processes. I also attempt to elucidate a nonreductive, sociopolitically and critically inflected notion of working-through that cannot be dismissively conflated with totalization, closure, unproblematic identity, therapeutic cure, or a return to "normality."

The problem of the link between trauma and limit events extends into the following chapter, a case study focusing on Giorgio

Agamben's treatment of Auschwitz. Agamben has emerged as one of the major voices in recent critical theory. I do not provide a comprehensive assessment of his impressive body of work. I focus on his important book, *Remnants of Auschwitz*, and provide a critical analysis of its interpretive and discursive strategies directed toward the aftermath of a traumatic limit event. In certain significant ways Agamben's thinking on Auschwitz is the culmination of some prominent tendencies in recent critical theory, for example, in Theodor Adorno and Jean-François Lyotard. Interestingly, Agamben says little about his own subject position and experience with respect to the problems he treats. One question is whether Agamben is Jewish or of Jewish ancestry and whether relatives of his were victims of the Holocaust. Another question is whether the answer to this question would or should have any bearing on a critical appreciation of his work—a question to which there is no easy or simple answer but one that is prompted by the concern for experience, subject position, and identity in relation to thought. In any event, Agamben's subject position in terms of a Jewish "heritage" has, I think, no significant or perhaps even detectable role in his *Remnants of Auschwitz* or in the other works I mention that are relevant to reading and interpreting it. If I am correct, this point is itself of interest in reading and responding to his work, for it indicates how such questions are bracketed or suspended in widespread conceptions of philosophy or theory. (Indeed, one of the alluring "consolations" of both extremely abstract, quasi-transcendental theory or philosophy and highly formalized areas, such as mathematics or even certain types of poetry, is their protective distance from experience and its empirical involvements.)

It is also noteworthy that Heidegger is probably the most important intellectual reference point for Agamben, yet Agamben does not try to sort out the relations or nonrelations between Heidegger's philosophical and political orientations, notably the implications of his notorious postwar silence, or at most equivocal remarks, concerning Auschwitz.[7] More generally, I argue that philosophy and theory in Agamben are most importantly quasi-transcendental and postapocalyptic. Auschwitz is apocalyptic for Agamben, and it discloses in its starkest form (in the *Muselmann*) a thoroughly disorient-

[7] For one attempt to do this, see my "Heidegger's Nazi Turn," chapter 5 of *Representing the Holocaust*.

ing dimension of the human being and simultaneously gives rise to the need for a radically new ethics and politics. Yet in Agamben's conceptualization of the new, history, including experience, is voided of specificity and counts at best as an instantiation of transhistorical theoretical concerns and postapocalyptic apprehensions. The *Muselmann*, the most abject being in the camps, who was seen by other victims as one of the living dead, marks an epochal caesura or disjunction in history and simultaneously becomes a figure of everyman "after Auschwitz." In the process, Agamben, I think, tropes away from historical and sociopolitical specificity into an insufficiently qualified postapocalyptic vision of the postmodern. Or to put it somewhat differently, what is indeed disconcerting and provocative in the work of a Samuel Beckett becomes in Agamben the dubious basis of a theoreticist philosophy of history.

The final chapter, which focuses on issues raised or prompted by a critical reading of Bill Readings's *University in Ruins*, turns directly to institutional and normative problems. Readings, like Agamben, makes little of his own experience in a university setting, though there are scattered references to it. In a sense Syracuse University, where Readings taught before moving to the University of Montreal, might be seen as a paradigmatic university for Readings's account. But there is no analysis of Readings's own daily life there or in Canada. At points I intimate how such an analysis might have given another dimension to his account and even more force to his critique. I think Readings's experience of the North American university was important in his theorization of the modern university and its essential features. He may well take the North American university in too undifferentiated a sense—there are, after all, almost four thousand universities and colleges in the United States alone, and they are of very different types. And he may generalize from it at times in an implicit and unargued manner. Moreover, his theoretical position and postapocalyptic sensibility are in certain important ways close to Agamben's, as are his intellectual reference points and his manner of construing them. For Readings, Lyotard and Gilles Deleuze are probably more significant than Heidegger, but there is in his approach, as in Agamben's, the inclination toward an ecstatic, anarchistic utopianism as the complement or supplement to a searingly radical critique that not only leaves little of its object standing but also suggests alternatives in at best a vague or spectral form.

In *Readings* the object of immediate concern is not all of post-Auschwitz society, as it is in Agamben, but the modern university analyzed and indicted in what is seen as its larger capitalistic, globalizing context. In fact the "after Auschwitz" sensibility, which is so pronounced in Agamben that it goes to the extreme of an "Auschwitz-now-everywhere" hyperbole, has no explicit role in *Readings*. Conversely and perhaps more surprisingly, capitalism is not an object of analysis in Agamben, and *Readings's* stress on it, despite his very general notion of it, is a useful supplement to Agamben.

One may ask why Agamben and Readings have recently risen to prominence and have even emerged as standard references in works addressing problems they have discussed. I think their texts bring out in stark relief problematic tendencies that are more modulated, complex, and internally contested in their own theoretical reference points, such as Jacques Derrida, Michel Foucault, Heidegger, and Lyotard. Indeed one reason Agamben and Readings have occupied such a prominent place in recent work may be the perceived deficit or vacuum of compelling theoretical reflection, at least in comparison to the "golden age" of critical theory, typified by the role of post-structuralism and its encounter with both psychoanalysis and critical theory in the tradition of the Frankfurt school. These theorists may be more remarkable today than they would have been in the heyday of the great theory wars of ten or twenty years ago. Still, such a formulation may concede too much to misplaced nostalgia and a sense of *Epigonentum*, or late-comer "blues." Agamben and Readings are certainly important in their own right, and the aspects of their work on which I focus are hyperbolic variants of influential tendencies of the giants on whose shoulders they, along with many others (myself included), stand. And they provide a welcome occasion for reassessing those earlier theoretical tendencies that still play an important role in contemporary thought, even in those who would resist, denounce, or evacuate them.

Particularly open to question in both Agamben and Readings is what I see as a prevalent all-or-nothing orientation that is not sufficiently counteracted by a more complex, less sweeping, less rashly generalizing response. Or, to put it another way, the undeniable appeal of an all-or-nothing response, in a situation in which there is indeed much to criticize, should be set in greater dialogical tension with a perspective that is more attentive to unrealized possibilities in the past and productive countertendencies in existing society and culture. In a broader sense, the latter perspective would be oriented to the crucial issue of the actual and desirable interaction of legitimate normative (including institutional) limits and challenges to them, including more or less transgressive modes of excess. I find in Agamben and Readings an antipathy to the institution in the sense of collective practice articulated by norms that are limiting but also enabling and subject to challenge. Since working-through is itself an articulatory practice that counteracts the compulsive effects of post-traumatic symptoms without pretending to achieve full mastery or total conscious dissolution of past traumas, it is vitally bound up with social and political action in the present, including the attempt to create institutional conditions and norms that further desirable forms of social bonding, the viable binding of anxiety, and the integration of affect and knowledge, including empathic or compassionate relations to others. No doubt a stress on a certain understanding of how to work through problems is less "exciting" and apparently less sublime than an all-or-nothing critique with postapocalyptic, utopian overtones, but it may be defended as a desirable critical counterforce to more unlimited, elated initiatives. It may also have implications for an ethics and politics of everyday life that is not simply subordinated to sublime, ecstatic, or peak experiences.

To a significant extent I share the intellectual reference points and theoretical concerns of Agamben and Readings. I am also very much interested in the problems they attempt to analyze critically. But I obviously move in significantly different directions. I am occupied by issues that do not play a prominent role in their work. One is the relation between the critique of institutions and the building and functioning of more desirable institutions, including the university, that are crucial in the collective articulation of everyday life. This concern places in question an excessively nihilating or unqualified utopian notion of ethics and politics that amounts to a sweeping critique of what exists and a blind hope for an apocalyptic change in the direction of incalculable risk and complete openness to the radically other. I see the appeal of anarchism in the critique of sovereignty and in the deconstruction of essential foundations or "arches." But I would not carry such critique to the point of delegitmating all institutions or limiting norms and uncritically placing hope in a blank utopianism or confiding in the postapocalyptic upsurge of an unqualifiedly risk-laden, ecstatic openness to the radically other. Still, I think basic structural change is necessary, especially given a rampant, invasive, capitalistic economy that breeds severe inequality both within and between countries. Hyperbolic overtures may also be necessary to signal the importance of a problem that is underemphasized or ignored in dominant approaches. But hyperbole itself tends to become banalized when it is rashly generalized and its exclamatory force sweeps so broadly as to efface distinctions indiscriminately. Moreover, it is important to articulate critical-theoretical and historical concerns in a manner that, while having a "utopian" dimension in that it strives for significantly different and more desirable institutions and practices, is informed and specific in its critiques and as substantive as possible in its proposed alternatives.

No doubt there is a significant dialogic or openly dialectical relation between my theoretical views and my experience and subject position in the university. I have been a member of departments and graduate fields of history and comparative literature as well as of graduate fields in French and German studies. In these capacities, I have worked with many graduate students and been the primary director of the work of quite a few of them. Hence I have lived (I hope empathically) through the difficult, sometimes frustrating, sometimes rewarding attempts of young scholars to find suitable work in a limited job market shaped in good part by the questionable priorities of a capitalistic system in which the recent trends are downsizing, absurdly skewed distribution of resources, and centralized corporate power. Also quite important for perspective on my views is the fact that I directed for over ten years a humanities center and have been involved, first as associate director and then as director, in the School of Criticism and Theory. In these respects I have interacted with many scholars—notably younger scholars—in diverse humanistic and social-scientific fields, have offered and taken advice about research, and have organized events such as conferences, colloquia, lectures, and seminars. These activities, which closely combine the intellectual and the administrative, have made me less of a free-lance or free-floating academic and have brought home to me the importance of what I term critical intellectual citizenship in the public sphere of the university. They have also impressed on me the importance of committed work within a cooperative, collective setting that nonetheless is open to vigorous criticism and argument as well as to jokes and laughter. And they have made me sensitive to the effect in people's lives of initiatives, improvements, and modes of relating that create opportunities short of apocalyptic change but nonetheless of a nature that is both experientially and institutionally worthwhile.

One issue with a significant bearing on subject positions is the relation between professional history and varieties of critical theory. Both Agamben and Readings are in fields—Continental philosophy and literary criticism or cultural studies—that are less concerned with disciplinary identity than is history. And Agamben and Readings join others in these fields who try to thematize the problem of cross- or transdisciplinarity to the point of affirming an utterly divided, disseminated identity or nonidentity, which in Readings takes the form of advocating the devolution of the university into evanescent work groups or task forces. In a sense the groupuscules in 1968 metamorphose to become study and work groups in the university in ruins. As is evident especially in the first chapter of this book, I am concerned with questions of identity but try to provide what I think are more nuanced answers than those found in Agamben or Readings.

As an intellectual and cultural historian who believes one should engage varieties of critical theory (hence read and reflect critically on such work as Agamben's or Readings's), my experience and orientation are significantly different from those of many historians. One of my principal concerns is to focus on the relation of texts to contexts in a way that raises the problem of reading thought-provoking texts and investigating their interaction with—not only their symptomatic replication or reinforcement of, but also their critical challenges to—multiple contexts. By the same token, I am deeply concerned with the bearing of a past, which has not passed away, on the present and future. Contextualization is necessary for historical understanding. But as an exclusive mode of explanation or when taken to the extreme of overcontextualization that excludes responsive understanding, it becomes dubious. Indeed its manner of objectifying or even fixating the past is in important ways challenged by texts and other phenomena to the extent that the latter explicitly or implicitly place in question their contexts of production and reception, indicate possibilities of transformation, and may provide leads in or pose problems for our attempt to come to terms with our own contexts. Texts may rethink contexts as well as disorient them in ways that demand responsive understanding and may even have political and social implications.

Texts may also have a transhistorical dimension—including the ability to pose problems that call for renewed thought in different contexts over time—that cannot be explained in narrowly circumstantial or immediate contextual terms but should not be confused with intemporality or a *philosophia perennis*. The transhistorical dimension of texts relates to the way they can still challenge contemporary readers and present problems that both "transferentially" implicate us and call for a response not limited to contextualizing objectification. Hence I think contextualization is an altogether necessary but problematic condition of historical understanding, especially understanding that is related to critical-theoretical reflection and practice; it appears sufficient only in a reductive frame of reference.[8] Moreover, one's response to a past text or problem may involve the explicit attempt to rethink or think further the issues it raises, especially in working out assumptions and drawing implications for contemporary thought and practice—a dimension of response eliminated by a restrictive historicism. The critique of contextual reductionism is, however, the counterpart of a critique of quasi-transcendental theoreticism or the derivation, subordination, or even utter marginalization of the historical with respect to the transhistorical in a manner that excludes or downplays the specificity of different historical events and contexts. I see such theoreticism as rampant in Agamben and as playing a significant role in Readings.

[8] One may argue that the early work of Derrida has a symptomatic dimension in that it often reads like a posttraumatic response to an unnamed trauma. In this way it resembles a survivor's discourse that has not sufficiently worked through problems. But this does not imply that Derrida's notions of displacement, *différance*, and trace can be reduced to symptomatic responses to the Holocaust as the unnamed event that Derrida in his later writings attempts to address in more explicit if still contestable ways. Hence I think James Berger, in his excellent book *After the End: Representations of Post-apocalypse* (Minneapolis: University of Minnesota Press, 1999), may go too far in a contextually reductionist direction when he writes: "we can recontextualize the structural post-apocalypse of early deconstruction into a response to the Shoah, seen as an apocalypse within history. The nameless apocalypse that, in Derrida's early work, was never not and always-already occurring can now be recognized as the Holocaust" (119). Still, Berger's analyses are consistently insightful and thought-provoking, and he critically explores the role of postapocalyptic dimensions in recent thought and culture. For an attempt to articulate the problem of relating structural or transhistorical and historical trauma, see my *Writing History, Writing Trauma*, chap. 2. I would agree with Berger's argument that Derrida himself, even in his later work that addresses the Holocaust, at times tends to go in a theoreticist direction that does not do justice to the specificity of historical events.

An opposition I try to explore critically (or even deconstruct) continues to play an important role in modern thought and culture, and it cuts across many of the problems I address: the opposition between immanence and transcendence. The immanent is within the world, hence amenable to both experience and representation. But the utterly or absolutely immanent ("thinking" with the blood or even eyes "glued" to the screen) may undercut the critical distance and mediation necessary for experience or representation and may thus be, paradoxically, akin to the radically transcendent or totally other. Immanence and transcendence would seem to function at least at times as secular displacements of religious concepts, and the question of the immanence or transcendence of the sacred or the divine has been vexed in the history of religion and theology. One crucial issue is whether the two form a binary opposition between incommensurables or whether they form a compromise formation allowing for at least limited mediation and interaction, even if one questions the process of totalization or dialectical *Aufhebung* leading to ever higher syntheses. I address the opposition between immanence and transcendence with respect to the sublime, which I suggest may itself be seen as a kind of displaced secular sacred (just as the sacred might be seen as a religious displacement of the sublime). I also suggest that the sacred may itself be immanent, may somehow appear in the world, even as it ecstatically or diremptively escapes it (notably in sacrificial processes); it may also be figured as radically transcendent or totally other in a way that may bar sacrifice as well as representation and experience (other than the aporetic attempt at continually failed representation and the anguished experience of absence—or a void—often perceived as loss).

I would note that the immanent/transcendent opposition has had a role in the figuration of activities, faculties (such as the imagination), and disciplines. History, including empirical research and contextualization, has typically been understood in terms of, or as addressing, immanence; at the extreme, it becomes reductive and denies all transcendence, including nontotal forms of situational transcendence. (As intimated earlier, situational transcendence refers to the way an act or artifact, while being situated or subject to contextual constraints and limited understanding, may also get beyond, or work through, its initial situation critically and transformatively, thereby giving rise to newer, more or less unpredictable, at times uncanny situations.) The archive itself, often privileged in historiography, may be seen, ideally, as the repository of unknown facts that furnish an ultimate way to bring things down to earth by revealing their hidden or secret involvements in the world, at times their shadier or dark sides. (This conception of the archive is similar to certain truncated understandings of the unconscious.) Indeed the renowned *Sitzfleisch* of historians acquires its imposing mass from research, particularly archival research that divulges countless nourishing, yet sometimes indigestible facts. I have already indicated that a certain conception of psychology or psychoanalysis may also be reductively "immanentist" in that it provides purely symptomatic readings of acts and artifacts. By contrast, theory, philosophy, and art (including literature) are construed as radically transcendent when one sees the concept or the imagination as disimplicating its processes and products from the world (or contexts), which it disarticulates, disseminates, or even nihilates while giving rise to utter risk, incalculability, and contingency (including the risk of madness). Radical transcendence and immanence, along with the absolute opposition between them, are particularly alluring for an apocalyptic or postapocalyptic orientation, which itself is prone to an all-or-nothing "rigor" or intransigence. But even short of this extreme, the opposition between immanence and transcendence is often at play as an unquestioned assumption, as in the following quotation from a review of a biography of Herman Melville, where historical contextualization becomes the paradigm of immanence (indeed incarnation), which the literary imagination in its radical freedom negates and transcends:

> The significance of a writer's background, his context, is that of a point of departure: art is an escape, a flight of speech to the printed page, where the reader's imagination is free to encounter the writer's; biography moves in the opposite direction, dissolving the text back into conversation, returning the writer to his "household," reincarnating his family, bringing him back to earth. The better the biography, the worse: the great smooth luxurious Rolls [Royce] reconverts the energy of the writer's ascent into mere horizontal force.[9]

[9] Danny Karlin, review of Hershel Parker, *Herman Melville: A Biography*, vol. 2, *1851–91* (Baltimore: Johns Hopkins University Press, 2002), in the *London Review of Books* 25 (May 8, 2003), 11. Karlin's review contains many fine insights that could also

Here historiography in the form of biography is compared to a luxu-rious, smoothly running, but utterly *terre-à-terre* automobile in rela-tion to which the literary imagination is a spectral airship that takes one somewhere out of this world. The obvious question is whether these analogies, along with the binary opposition between imma-nence and transcendence on which they implicitly rely, are suitable for attempting to explore the more enigmatic, tangled, and discon-certing dimensions of art as well as the complex interactions between texts and contexts or the specific distinctions between various fields of activity, including disciplines.

Even if intellectual and cultural historians question the positioning of theory, philosophy, or art in terms of the dichotomy between imma-nence and transcendence, their professional experience is in certain significant ways often, if not typically, closer to that of philosophers, literary critics, and critical theorists than it is to that of archival his-torians. Intellectual and cultural historians certainly may and indeed should turn to archives to investigate certain issues, but they also spend a great deal of time reading and thinking critically about pub-lished texts and documents and their intricate relations to contexts. In addition they are attuned to the complex relations between history and critical theory. Still, intellectual and cultural historians may undervalue these activities insofar as they accept both the emphasis on archival research and the equation of historical understanding to objectifying contextualization, which are at times pronounced in the work of other historians. Historical understanding involves research in the broad sense (including work in the archives) but is not restricted to it. Such understanding is necessarily self-reflexive in that it criti-cally raises the issue of the interaction between history, which is focused on the reconstruction of objects (events, experience, struc-tures) in the past, and more theoretically oriented metahistory, which

---

have been accommodated in a critique of overcontextualization that did not rest on the immanence/transcendence binary. Perhaps the strongest assertion of this binary whereby the imagination negates or nihilates and transcends reality is Jean-Paul Sartre's early *L'Imaginaire* (1940), translated as *The Psychology of the Imagination* by Bernard Frechtman (New York: Washington Square Press, 1966). One of the best attempts to question this frame of reference in terms of an open dialectic or dialogic relation between immanence and transcendence, including historical contexts and artistic or philosophical texts, is the work of M. M. Bakhtin. See especially "Discourse in the Novel" (1934–35), in *The Dialogic Imagination*, ed. Michael Holquist, trans. Caryl Emerson and Michael Holquist (Austin: University of Texas Press, 1981).

analyzes processes of historical inquiry. Prominent among these processes is the conceptualization of problems bearing on the present and future, including the relation of historians to their objects of study (hence the problem of the construction and use of archives). In any event intellectual and cultural historians, even when their work takes them to the archives, may not find the archival experience to be as initiatory or defining as it is for, say, social historians. But this distinction should in no sense be understood as a dichotomy, and it may be more applicable to older historians for whom it was difficult if not impossible to manage the serious demand on time and energy required both by extensive archival work and by the often autodidactic effort to come critically to terms with, and figure out the implications for history of, various difficult critical theories that had many prerequisites in previous work. (Hence one cannot competently read Derrida without having read Freud, Heidegger, Hegel, Husserl, Plato, Aristotle, and quite a few others.) Given the preparatory work relating history and theory that is now available, it is feasible for younger scholars in history and related areas critically and judiciously to combine the sophisticated theoretical reflection crucial for concept formation and sustained work in the archives. For example, one cannot do a comparative study of fascism without some working concept of fascism involving the relative significance of ideology in relation to movements and regimes, the nature and very understanding (or "experience") of violence, the search for a third way beyond both "materialistic" capitalism and communism, the role of anti-semitism and scapegoating in general as well as of charismatic leaders, the media, advanced technology, and so forth. Such a concept may well be changed or refined in the course of research, but it is also necessary so that research not be an aimless, neopositivistic accumulation of information.

The distinction between intellectual and cultural historians and more insistently archival historians has not entirely disappeared. Nor have professional historians sufficiently achieved the possible and altogether desirable interaction and articulation of archival research and critical theory, which involves the reading of often difficult texts whose relevance to historiography is not immediately apparent. As I have intimated, at times the tendency among historians is to learn enough about a theoretical approach (deconstruction, psychoanalysis, phenomenology, and so forth) to be able to fend it off in a more or less literate manner (but often in a fashion that allows uncritical entry through the back door of concepts and concerns that are ostentatiously ushered out through the front). As will be evident in the concluding chapters of this book, I think that certain theoretical or theoreticist tendencies should indeed be criticized, but I also think that the criticism, however strong or even impassioned, should be informed, open to counterargument, and itself shaped by significant theoretical concerns, especially as they bear on the problem of historical understanding and the interaction between past, present, and future. And, if only to recognize the difficulties still to be surmounted, one must acknowledge that the difference, at times the mutual uneasiness if not tension, between archival and textually oriented historians has not been entirely overcome. While the dubious tendency of some textually based, theory-oriented historians may be to consider aspects of research a form of hunting and gathering if not painting by number, the equally dubious inclination of historians for whom the archival experience is normative or even foundational may at times be to exclude or at best marginalize the type of intellectual and cultural history for which theoretical or metahistorical reflection and work on published texts are essential.

Indeed *Archive* could have been a heading of one of the sections of the first chapter, in which I raise the question: what is not experience or at least not encompassed by a certain conception of experience? The relation of the archive to experience is dual. As archive it is the paradigm of nonexperience—the repository of what is not, or at least no longer, experience or even the memory of experience. The archive is in this sense a supplement to or prosthetic device for experience and memory. One reason for archiving something is that it guards against forgetting or misremembering it and allows one to check what memory recalls—to preserve it in a form that is as close as one can get to its real, undistorted, "original" form.[10] The archive becomes a source of documented evidence in the form of presumably factual information, and references to it in footnotes are the infrastructure or at least the ballast of a historical account. But the archive, while the

---

[10] Of course the form and the very retention or nonretention of something may be heavily influenced by political motives and other considerations that complicate the issue of why one archives something. One particularly questionable form of archival document records the memory of one party in an exchange that includes assertions about what other parties did or did not say or do.

repository of what is not or is no longer experience, is also the often privileged object of the experience of the archival historian as well as the source of phantasmatic investments. Some of these have been explored by Bonnie G. Smith and others evoked (recounted and at times enacted) in an intriguing recent article by Carolyn Steedman, to which I shall return.[11] For Jules Michelet, the historian breathed life into the dead scrolls and the dusty parchment, indeed into the haunting, mummified inhabitants, of the archives, while for Steedman the historian also runs the risk of inhaling the remnants of the dead, which may produce a literal as well as a figural illness—the kind of "archive fever" that gets under the skin of the historian but that, Steedman claims, Jacques Derrida never experienced, knew about, or even conjured up.

The image of the archive as the supplement to experience and memory may of course be reversed, with the archive positioned as the most direct form of contact with reality or at least its traces and material residues. It has thus been tempting to envision the archive, at times in oneiric form, as the navel of historiography, the point at which it reaches down into the unknown (to paraphrase Freud's designation of the most uncanny moment in a dream). Along with a quest for origins, this temptation has been deconstructed and in certain ways criticized (not simply dismissed) by Derrida and given a more sociohistorical significance by Foucault.[12] The archive has of course been of crucial importance to modern historiography, and many within the Annales school during the "serial" phase of its own history based historiography on the correlation between the mass of information contained in the archive and its processing by computer. This orientation implicitly relied on the link between the archive as a facility for storing or stocking information and the computer itself as an archiving and processing machine. The archive came almost to seem like a *hylē*, or content, awaiting the *morphē*, or form, provided by com-

[11] Bonnie G. Smith, *The Gender of History: Men, Women, and Historical Practice* (Cambridge: Harvard University Press, 1998); Carolyn Steedman, "Something She Called a Fever: Michelet, Derrida, and Dust," *American Historical Review* 106 (2001): 1159–80. A version of Steedman's article has been included in her book *Dust: The Archive and Cultural History* (New Brunswick: Rutgers University Press, 2001).

[12] See Jacques Derrida, *Of Grammatology*, trans. Gayatri Chakravorty Spivak (1967; Baltimore: Johns Hopkins University Press, 1974) as well as Derrida's *Archive Fever: A Freudian Impression*, trans. Eric Prenowitz (1995; Chicago: University of Chicago Press, 1996). For Foucault's analysis, see the appendix to *Folie et déraison: Histoire de la folie à l'âge classique* (1961; Paris: Gallimard, 1972).

puterized processing. And as archives have become "digitized," one of course has witnessed a convergence between the archival source and the computerized memory bank. Indeed the archive in its permutations over time as a technique of information storage could serve as a metaphor for Heidegger's notion of the modern *Gestell*, or framework, as a technological principle and the reduction of the world to raw material, information bits, or data that may be housed in stockpiles or storage tanks and reprocessed to serve anthropocentric ends. The archive would even be subject to "meltdown" whether through a virus leading the computer to crash or as the contents of older archives, especially material printed on brittle paper, disintegrate, emitting dust and spores that would be inhaled by those working in its enclosures.

As the stockpile or dustbin of historical information, the archive would also be open to interrogation about the manner and motivations according to which it was put together and used or abused over time; and it would be subject to the shaping forces of the historian who posed different questions or employed various narrative devices in "emplotting" or, more generally, processing its contents (for example, through the formulation and testing of hypotheses). This is of course the scenario made famous by Hayden White. But White at times put forth this scenario in an unguarded manner that enacted or replicated prominent if not dominant tendencies in modernity without taking sufficient account of critiques of, and forces that resisted or countered, radical constructivism and the reduction of the object to nonresponsive raw material or unprocessed data. One such force is the prior "constructions" of the archive itself, which render it something other than a stock of raw material or a series of mere facts, in that the material it contains is preselected and configured in certain ways, for example, in terms of state interests or the interests of other institutions (such as religious institutions) that create and manage archives, often suppressing or getting rid of embarrassing material. Another force is the often subordinate role of currents or voices, including those of the oppressed or repressed, that may be elicited by nonobjectifying inquiry (comparable perhaps to Freud's *freischwebende Aufmerksamkeit*, or free-floating attentiveness) and a certain openness to what one may not explicitly be looking for or trying to prove, including material both in literal archives and in oral accounts as well as media or digital events that are part of the archive in a more comprehensive sense. One may also note the role of various representations, including phantasms, of the archive that may themselves have an impact on the way the archive is constituted and on how one conducts work or research in it.

Steedman's article gives a few intriguing twists to the above considerations. And it is fitting that I end this introduction with a commentary on a text that itself addresses the archive, textuality, psychoanalysis, and historical understanding. Steedman begins and ends her reflection with a discussion of Derrida's *Archive Fever*. In good part her discussion of Derrida consists of discursive ships passing in the night with occasional close, at times uncanny, encounters of a more engaging sort. Steedman writes:

> For those historians who have heard or read "Archive Fever," it raised the puzzling question of what on earth an archive was doing there in the first place, at the beginning of a long description of another text (someone else's text, not Derrida's), which dealt, as he himself would go on to do at length, with Sigmund Freud and the topic of psychoanalysis. For the main part, "Archive Fever" is a sustained contemplation of Yosef Yerushalmi's *Freud's Moses: Judaism Terminable and Interminable* (1991). . . .
>
> Derrida had long seen in Freudian psychoanalysis the desire to recover moments of inception, beginnings and origins, that he has spent nearly half a century writing against. In "Archive Fever," desire for the archive is presented as part of the desire to find, or locate, or to possess that moment, as a way of possessing the beginning of things. (1161)

If one can extract a main point from an essay that, in its wit and subtle humor (whether intentionally or not), owes more to Derrida's style than might initially be apparent or that Steedman might be inclined to allow, it is that Derrida quite simply did not get the point of the historian's interest and involvement in the archive. The historian is not engaged in a metaphysical search for origins, and one should disengage this supernal quest from the more everyday, humble, and often grubby activity of the historian. How, from Ranke to Braudel and beyond, the grandeur of the metaphysical quest may at times motivate, or adorn with figurative blazons, the grubbiness of more everyday archival activity is not investigated in Steedman's essay, nor is the way the ability and the inclination to distinguish between the two may owe much to Derrida's work and to attempts to show its possible relevance for historical understanding. Nor does she pay more than scant attention to the question of the archive in a larger sense as it relates to the problem of inscription in general, including both intertextuality (explicitly explored by Derrida with respect to Yerushalmi among others) and the psyche as a mode of inscription involving an unconscious "archive" and conscious experiences and memories—the Freudian dimension of the archive that most interests Derrida and that is not simply reducible to the metaphysical quest for origins. Instead Steedman limits herself to rather easy targets, including Hayden White's *Metahistory*, which, as she puts it, is "now nearly thirty years old" (1178). She does not observe that the book owed little if anything to Derrida or deconstruction (or psychoanalysis for that matter) and might even be criticized in part on deconstructive and Derridean grounds.[13] Instead she draws a divide between deconstruction and history by appealing to Christopher Norris: "On several occasions during the 1980s and 1990s, it was very sensibly suggested by Christopher Norris that it was best for historians not to mess with deconstruction, that as a method of reading devised for the interrogation of philosophical texts, its power lies solely in the particular terrain of philosophy (and possibly of literature). One might with some profit treat a work of history *as* a literary text and make deconstructive approaches to it as a form of writing, but those approaches could do nothing to, or for, the reading matter found in the archives, out of which the historical work is (partly) constructed" (ibid.).

This "sensible" conclusion is open to question. It fetishizes the archive and turns it into a sanctuary somehow impermeable to deconstructive and perhaps all critical-theoretical approaches. In so doing, it puts forth an undefended and altogether dubious opposition between history as written text and "reading matter found in the

---

[13] See the discussion, itself almost twenty years old, in my *Rethinking Intellectual History: Texts, Contexts, Language*, chap. 2. In that book and elsewhere, I try to indicate ways deconstruction may indeed be relevant for historiography, especially but not exclusively intellectual history. Subsequently I have also tried to formulate nuanced but at times forceful criticisms of certain tendencies in the work of Derrida and others affiliated with deconstruction. Of course deconstruction as a critical tendency is by now far-ranging and intricate, and it is important to formulate critiques that are informed and not oversimplifying or sweepingly general.

archive," as if the way archival material is itself put together by those who create the archive, and actively read and made into the historical work by the historian, were not itself a problematic issue for critical reflection. (In Steedman's formulation there seems to be no significant reading and interpretive process through which reading matter "found" in the archives is transformed into the "constructed" historical work.)[14] Steedman drives an impenetrable wedge between historical research and metahistorical or critical-theoretical analysis. And she seems to ignore intellectual history, which is very much concerned with philosophical and literary texts and their contexts, hence implicitly marginalizing if not excluding it from "proper" history (which here appears to be identified primarily as a certain kind of social or sociocultural history). Moreover, does the deconstructive archive itself house only intellectually radioactive material to be strictly cordoned off, forbidden to the historian, and beckoning at best to philosophers, literary critics, and other outsiders who glow in the dark? Is there nothing the historian, including the archival historian, can learn from varieties of deconstruction concerning historical processes, the problem of temporality, and ways of accounting for them? Has not much recent critical thought (including Derrida's) placed in question the assumption that one may understand philosophy or literature as a delimited terrain neatly separated from other terrains? After such critiques is it not necessary to attempt to elaborate more subtle, differentiated, argumentatively defended distinctions among disciplines or fields?

Closer attention to the "deconstructive" problem of internal differences and self-questioning in a text might have provided Steedman with a better vantage point to elaborate and explore tensions in her own text and possibly prevent them from becoming disabling. For, on the very page following the above comments, she does a remarkable turnabout into the kind of radical constructivism and anything-goes subjectivism against which she seems to have been defending history. The historian becomes a neo-idealist "maker" with quasi-divine powers of creation ex nihilo (which of course presuppose an unexamined prior process of reducing the nonresistant other or object to objectified raw material—"stuff"—or even annihilating it): "It is, in

---

[14] On this problem, see my "History, Language, and Reading: Waiting for Crillon," *American Historical Review* 100 (1995): 799–828 (a version of which is republished as chap. 1 of my *History and Reading: Tocqueville, Foucault, French Studies* (Toronto: University of Toronto Press, 2000).

fact, the historian who makes the stuff of the past into a structure or event, a happening or a thing, through the activities of thought and writing: . . . they were never actually there, once, in the first place, or at least not in the same way that a nutmeg grater actually once was, and certainly not as the many ways in which they 'have been told.' There is a double nothingness in the writing of history and in the analysis of it: it is about something that never did happen in the way it comes to be represented (the happening exists in the telling or the text), and it is made out of materials that are not there, in an archive or anywhere else" (1179). This kind of loose formulation does not articulate cogently the relation between the referential dimension of historiography related to truth claims about both events and structures, on which Steedman herself convincingly insists, and the role of "construction" in the making of the historical text.

Deferring a more extensive discussion to chapter 2, I would simply note that the historian does not simply "make the stuff of the past into a structure or event." The idea that he or she does is reminiscent of Hayden White's most unguardedly constructivist views. The "happening" of the past does not exist only in the telling or the (historian's) text. If it did, there would be no referential dimension to historiography. It would be self-referential, formalistic fiction. Moreover, the past is never simply (or doubly) absence or nothingness, for one "thing" because it was never fully present or "being." It was marked by its pasts and more or less misguided anticipations of its futures, as we are by ours. Even the nutmeg grater was there the way other "things" were there in the past—as objects having a more or less intricate history and an uneven, in part unpredictable, future that bring them into the (sedimented, divided) present and its possible future(s).[15] This (re)marking of the present is a crucial dimension of Derrida's

[15] Not having Steedman's enviable familiarity with the nutmeg grater, I turn to the Oxford English Dictionary and find these entries under "nutmeg"—entries that place the nutmeg grater in the complex history of colonialism, diaspora, imperial expansion, regional difference, and even fraud: "1. A hard aromatic seed, of spheroidal form and about an inch in length, obtained from the fruit of an evergreen tree (*Myristica fragrans* or *officinalis*) indigenous to Molucca and other east Indian Islands, and largely used as a spice and in medicine. Inferior kinds are also obtained from other species of *Myristicaceae* in various parts of the world; and with distinguishing epithets, as *American, Brazilian, Peruvian,* the name is occasionally applied to the produce of trees belonging to other genera. b. *Wooden nutmeg,* anything false or fraudulent; a fraud, cheat, deception. *U.S.*" The OED also includes these captivating quotations: "About a little nutmeg-grater, which she had forgot in the caudlecup" (Congreve) and "Just as if you were swallowing a nutmeg-grater three and a half yards long" (Beresford). One wonders just how "a nutmeg grater actually once was."

notion of a trace-structure (as well as the related notion of intertextuality), which revises Husserl's idea that temporality involves protention and retention. These "deconstructive" thoughts are not purely "philosophical." They have a bearing on one's understanding of historicity or temporality in terms of the role of displacement as a complex, variable, internally divided process of repetition with more or less drastic and traumatic change.[16]

The point I would stress is that Steedman's own essay is itself an exercise in disciplinary identity politics, something signaled by the reference to clear-cut "terrains" with seemingly unproblematic boundaries that do not call for careful, discriminating treatment. It is also an exercise in implicitly marginalizing or even silencing historians who do not accord with her understanding of history and its protocols, notably historians with a significantly different response to the relations between history and various critical theories, including deconstruction. In these respects, it is an exploration and enactment of the experience, notably the archival experience—including the haunting phantasms or what might be termed the professional imaginary—providing identity and shared subjectivity for certain historians, and Steedman is explicit in indicating how this is the case:

> The historian's massive authority as a writer derives from two factors: the ways archives are, and the conventional rhetoric of history writing, which always asserts (through footnotes, through the casual reference to PT S2/1/1) that you *know* because you have been there. The fiction is that the authority comes from the documents themselves, as well as the historian's obeisance to the limits they impose on any account that employs them. But really it comes from having been there (the train to the distant city, the call number, the bundle opened, the dust), so that then, and only then, you can present yourself as moved and dictated to by those sources, telling a story the way it has to be told. (1176)

One might of course object that the historian can claim a certain authority with respect to the archives on the basis of a professional practice which, through training, provides a familiarity with archival research, and in particular with certain sets of archives, that allows

---

[16] I address these questions at greater length in *Writing History, Writing Trauma*, chap. 1.

him or her to derive from them what someone without comparable training would not derive. (One's untutored initial experience in the archives is probably extreme disorientation.) But Steedman's assertion is important, and it is implicated both in a contestable assumption concerning authentic historiography (it must be based on the archival experience as the archive is understood by Steedman) and in certain everyday "metaphysical" assumptions about the nature of experience. There are excellent reasons for doing archival research to address questions that require it. And many, but not all, historical questions and questions relevant to historical understanding do indeed require such research. As I shall intimate in the first chapter, one might even want to give a certain credibility to everyday "metaphysical" assumptions on a prima facie level. In other words, having a certain experience, say as an African American or a German Jew, might give epistemological authority to assertions concerning that experience. But such a presumptive authority would not be absolute, nor would it extend beyond the range of one's experience to validate without further ado statements of fact, judgments, or arguments. And it would have to be legitimated with respect to claims that are actually made—claims that are subject to discussion and debate.

The historian for Steedman is not making claims only about the archival experience (for example, the effects of dust on body and psyche) but about the past based on research involving archival material. In the latter case, actually having been in the archives is a problematic if not dubious basis for legitimating claims. In other words, the claim that the historian knows about what happened in the past because he or she has "experienced" the archives is as "fictitious" as the idea that the claims simply come from the documents themselves (or from "the way the archives are"). If it is not restricted to the tautological assertion that only one who has access to certain archived items can, before their publication, justifiably make claims about them, it is analogous to the idea that one is in a more "authoritative" position to analyze water because one has drunk from the well. But the fact that the claim may be put forward and taken seriously is itself of great interest. Moreover, the archival experience as discussed by Steedman is compared to the experience of workers in areas such as the leather industry, thus almost making the historian a working-class figure if not a certain kind of manual laborer. In addition, the archival historian's experience is presented as potentially life-threatening or at least as dangerous to your health, for in its relation to the archive historiography is in its own way a hazardous industry. Some of the passages in which Steedman describes the archival experience and the way it places historians at risk are reminiscent of nineteenth-century realism or even naturalism, which occasionally takes a turn toward sensationalism or camp. Indeed the archive seems to be figured on the model of the prostitute, and the historian's anxiety makes the polluting, necrophiliac power of archive fever seem bizarrely venereal.

> Actually, archive fever comes on at night, long after the archive has shut for the day. Typically, the fever—more accurately, the precursor fever, the feverlet—starts in the early hours of the morning, in the bed of a cheap hotel, where you cannot get to sleep. You cannot get to sleep because you lie so narrowly, in an attempt to avoid contact with anything that isn't shielded by sheets and pillowcase. The first sign, then, is an excessive attention to the bed, an irresistible anxiety about the hundreds who have slept there before you, leaving their dust and debris in the fibers of the blankets, greasing the surface of the heavy, slippery coverlet. The dust of others, and of other times, fills the room, settles on the carpet, marks out the sticky passage from bed to bathroom. (1164)

The pathos of this scene, worthy of *Hard Times* or *Germinal*, intensifies when Steedman actually enters the archive, there to discover even more insidious, health-threatening phenomena and phantoms, most prominent among which is the ubiquitous dust.[17] The dust of crumbling leather bindings, made more noxious by "stinking glue" (1169), poses a hazard of a special order: "That stinking glue was probably also one among several of the actual transmitters of the Archive Fever that is discussed here. The bacillus of anthrax was the first specific microorganism discovered," and anthrax is among the threats posed by the archive fever that Steedman offers as a possible diagnostic category.[18] In light of this fever, the type of fever discussed by Derrida must seem particularly ethereal and elitist, a mere

[17] One may ask how the experience of historians who agree with Steedman, as well as their phenomenology of disciplinary practice, will be transformed by the development of antiseptic, notably digitized, archives where viruses take electronic form. Steedman's article may in the future seem uncannily nostalgic.

[18] It would seem that Steedman wrote her article with its unanticipated link to the transmission of anthrax spores in the mail before this phenomenon became a preoc-

figment of the philosopher's or the *littérateur*'s unhistorical imagination. And no "sensible" historian, apparently ready to sacrifice the body but not the spirit, would be inclined to add to "material" archive fever the intellectual hazards of deconstruction as an overheated mode of reading or analysis.

The archival experiences discussed by Bonnie G. Smith are both more various and at times more intoxicating than those rehearsed by Steedman. They even include "narcohistory" written under the influence of drugs that induce both delirium and wildly lyrical prose. But the very interest in the experience of the archive is itself further testimony of the turn to experience and the role of self-implication in the object of research, and the latter's relation to transference and disciplinary formation on an affective and evaluative level might provide a more than narrowly autobiographical dimension to discussions. It is interesting that experimental physicists, at least to my knowledge, do not refer to the experience of the laboratory as a way of delegitimating the work of theorists. Rather the two forms of activity complement, supplement, and test each other. Historians are tempted to use the archival experience, as anthropologists have used the field experience, as normative in authenticating their own work and delegitimating the work of others (the notorious "armchair" theorist in anthropology who inter alia is someone who spends much time reading texts and thinking intently about them—for example, Durkheim in composing *The Elementary Forms of the Religious Life*). Yet in any field that is intellectually diversified, with different types of people able to make different types of contribution, different experiences might well be legitimate. Take, for example, the experience of reading one of those philosophical or literary texts to which Steedman alludes, say, Heidegger's *Being and Time*, Thomas Mann's *Doctor Faustus*, or Art Spiegelman's *Maus*—indeed a text by Derrida that combines philosophy with experimental "literary" writing, say *Glas*, and consider the "experience" of reading it and trying to decide what is or is not pertinent to historical understanding or allowable in a historical treatment of problems that is critically open to inter- and cross-

---

cupation in the wake of the suicide bombings of the World Trade Center and the Pentagon. Retrospectively, in light of her discussion, the archive as the repository of dead letters comes to have an uncanny affinity with the contemporary letter, which may have deadly effects whether or not it reaches its intended destination.

disciplinary currents. The answer is not obvious or easy, and it does not admit of clear-cut "terrains" (or modes of professional "illness") as a decisive criterion of judgment. Such experiences of reading and writing are as "authentic" or valid as any other, such as the archival experience(s), and it is conceivable that history is a more engaging and enlightening field to the extent that both experiences are not only admitted but allowed to interrogate and to respond to each other in ways that could not be predetermined by professional boundaries, rigidly delimited terrains, or disciplinary identity politics. The results might themselves be "ecstatic" in the sense of taking or even jolting one out of the (subject) positions or discursive postures in which one usually finds oneself. And the outcome might be a perspective that would still engage in a critical and self-critical interaction with various historical or theoretical initiatives, but an interaction that could conceivably engender more cogent if contestable distinctions between approaches or fields and more viable articulations of them as well as of their actual and desirable relations.

CHAPTER ONE

Experience and Identity

Contributors to the important recent volume *Reclaiming Identity: Realist Theory and the Predicament of Postmodernism* join in a postpositivist, realist project and argue that the key concepts of experience and identity need not be essentialized and that the critique or deconstruction of these concepts went too far, often having counterproductive effects both intellectually and politically.[1] Hence the time has come for a cogent recuperation of these and related concepts (such as objectivity and realism) in a concerted effort of epistemological and sociopolitical reconstruction. Contributors have also objected to extreme forms of radical constructivism as the dubious opposite of essentialism, especially in certain versions of the so-called linguistic turn in which experience and identity become discursive constructs

[1] *Reclaiming Identity: Realist Theory and the Predicament of Postmodernism,* ed. Paula M. L. Moya and Michael R. Hames-Garcia (Berkeley: University of California Press, 2000). I am especially concerned with the articles of John H. Zammito, "Reading 'Experience': The Debate in Intellectual History among Scott, Toews, and LaCapra"; and Linda Martin Alcoff, "Who's Afraid of Identity Politics?" As intimated by her title, Alcoff provides an extended defense of identity politics that is informed by concepts of experience, objectivity, and realism. Zammito finds that much in my own work is compatible with postpositivist realism but thinks that I err in the direction of hyperbole. Joan Scott is for him even more hyperbolic. By contrast John Toews strikes the right dialectical balance in his neo-Hegelian project of triangulating experience, meaning, and language. The relevant articles to which Zammito refers are Joan Scott, "The Evidence of Experience," *Critical Inquiry* 17 (summer 1991): 773–97, and, in a more widely circulated shorter version to which I shall make reference, "Experience," in *Feminists Theorize the Political,* ed. Judith Butler and Joan Scott (New York: Routledge, 1992), 22–40; John Toews, "Intellectual History after the Linguistic Turn: The

and objectivity is evacuated in favor of exaggerated notions of performativity, fictionality, relativism, and incommensurability.[2]

There are significant ways in which I am in general agreement with more qualified approaches to performativity and incommensurability and with caveats or even objections concerning radical constructivism and deconstruction. I would, however, like to examine the concept of experience and, to some extent, that of identity in a manner that may allow for an acknowledgment of aspects of constructivism and deconstruction that, if not unguardedly taken to extremes, com-

---

Autonomy of Meaning and the Irreducibility of Experience," *American Historical Review* 92 (1987): 879–907. My own works to which Zammito refers are *History and Criticism* (Ithaca: Cornell University Press, 1985); "History, Language and Reading: Waiting for Crillon," *American Historical Review* 100 (June 1995): 799–828; *Representing the Holocaust: History, Theory, Trauma* (Ithaca: Cornell University Press, 1994); *Rethinking Intellectual History: Texts, Contexts, Language* (Ithaca: Cornell University Press, 1983); and *Soundings in Critical Theory* (Ithaca: Cornell University Press, 1987). I would note that three of my later books are also relevant to the topics discussed by Zammito and in the present essay: *History and Memory after Auschwitz* (Ithaca: Cornell University Press, 1998); *History and Reading: Tocqueville, Foucault, French Studies* (Toronto: University of Toronto Press, 2000); and *Writing History, Writing Trauma* (Baltimore: Johns Hopkins University Press, 2001). See also the exchange between Laura Lee Downs and Joan Scott in *Comparative Studies in Society and History* 35 (April 1993), which includes Downs, "If 'Woman' is Just an Empty Category, Then Why Am I Afraid to Walk Alone at Night? Identity Politics Meets the Postmodern Subject," 414–37; Scott, "The Tip of the Volcano," 438–43, and Downs, "Reply to Joan Scott," 444–51. Downs's conception of the results of the exchange is optimistic, but Scott, after treating what she considers to be Downs's combination of "ignorance and misrepresentation" (438) in discussing her work, concludes: "For me writing this response has been an exercise in frustration, not a meaningful exchange" (443). On the question of experience, see as well the essays in *Rediscovering History: Culture, Politics, and the Psyche*, ed. Michael S. Roth (Stanford: Stanford University Press, 1994), especially Martin Jay, "Experience without a Subject: Walter Benjamin and the Novel," 121–33.

[2] I would note that I have never defended a linguistic turn in a radically constructivist sense or in the sense deriving from the work of Ferdinand de Saussure. Instead I have stressed the importance of the concept of signifying practice of which language is one crucial or even paradigmatic—but not privileged—instance, and I have insisted on a notion of language in historical use owing more to Mikhail Bakhtin than to Saussure. Bakhtin's understanding of language does not conform to the binary opposition between *langue* (formal linguistic system or code) and *parole* (individual usage that presumably instantiates codes with the possibility of error or variation related to change). Bakhtin does not see usage only as individual or change as always a matter of deviation or error with respect to codes. His notion of language (or the word in use) focuses on the role of language and other signifying practices in history and society, including the problems of ideology and social conflict. This notion mediates the abstract, analytic categories of *langue* and *parole* and is not beholden to the quasi-transcendental idea of the arbitrariness of the signifier.

pulsively fixated on, or inserted into an all-or-nothing response to problems, are instructive.[3] I shall especially insist on the importance of more or less performative processes, including elaboration, construction, work, and play, with respect to experience and identity. Hence I shall stress experiential processes and processes of identity formation (not reducible to fixated postulations of identity). Identity should be neither idealized as always beneficent nor demonized and seen as a (if not the) source of the political ills of the modern world. Nor should it be conflated with identification in the sense of total fusion with others wherein difference is obliterated and criticism is tantamount to betrayal. But identity does involve modes of being with others that range from the actual to the imagined, virtual, sought-after, normatively affirmed, or utopian. Moreover, it is important to explore the relations and articulations among various qualifiers of identity, especially group identity, which may be ascribed by others, taken up or confronted by the self or by members of the group, deconstructed, refunctioned, affirmed or acknowledged in more or less revised fashion, earned though collective activity, and recognized, validated, or invalidated by others. One issue here is the extent to which a group is what may be termed an existential group eliciting and demanding commitment, in contrast to a statistical category that "groups" together those sharing some objective characteristic such as height or weight. (For the latter characteristics to be relevant to an

---

[3] An especially dubious gesture is arresting deconstruction at the stage or moment of reversal whereby a rejection of essentialism or foundationalism seems to leave only its binary opposite: the idea that experience or identity is a mere construct or even an invariably unreliable product of ideology. One may note that the most cogent aspect of the critique of foundationalism is directed at absolute foundations or an uncontested, sovereign principle or criterion from which particular positions, decisions, or judgments are presumably derived or even deduced. The alternative is not the total absence of grounds but the need to elaborate good or cogent grounds for a nonabsolute position, decision, or judgment, for example, discursively, argumentatively, and even through an appeal to narrative. In general, absolutism and varieties of relativism have always been mutually reinforcing complements, not viable alternatives. For a thought-provoking discussion of related issues, see Diana Fuss, *Essentially Speaking: Feminism, Nature and Difference* (New York: Routledge, 1989) and *Identity Papers* (New York: Routledge, 1995) as well as the discussion of the earlier book, in *Reclaiming Identity*, in the chapters by Satya Mohanty ("The Epistemic Status of Cultural Identity: On *Beloved* and the Postcolonial Condition"), Paula Moya ("Postmodernism, 'Realism,' and the Politics of Cultural Identity: Cherrie Moraga and Chicana Feminism"), and William S. Wilkerson ("Is There Something You Need to Tell Me?: Coming Out and the Ambiguity of Experience"), esp. 57–58n., 8on., and 270–75. (Wilkerson combines a discussion of Fuss and Joan Scott.)

existential group, such a group would have to be formed at least in part on the basis of them.) In addition, experiential processes, including processes of identity formation, may and ideally should involve reality-testing and its relation to what in psychoanalytic terms may be termed working over and through problems (an often intricate process that does not entail definitive closure or obviate the role of play and laughter, including gallows humor in responding to traumatizing events).

Hence a complex, process-oriented notion of identity formation does not exclude the importance of difference and differentiation with respect to experience, the experience of both self and other, or of analyst (historian, critic, theorist) and object of study—an issue that is especially important in the study of the past or of other cultures and that may be obscured when the subject and object of research are presumed to be identical (a presumption active in much research related to identity politics).[4] Joan Scott may have gone too far in stressing the construction, especially the discursive construction, of experience and in seeing the role of experience as foundational in those she criticized (notably John Toews). But one may recognize the value of her insistence on the importance of processes of construction, at least insofar as constructivism does not become an all-encompassing secular creationism in which the human being is assumed to be, or is postulated as, the source of all meaning and value in the world, often with the nonhuman, including other animals, as the ignored, excluded, or scapegoated other (a tendency that may also exist in humanistic forms of realism).

Experience. In ordinary and even some scholarly usage, the notion of experience often remains a black box or an extremely loose and encompassing concept that is not defined because one has had an experience and presumes to know what is meant by the term. It is used to discuss or define other problems while itself remaining impervious to definition or perhaps strategically vague. In John Toews's important essay, "Intellectual History after the Linguistic Turn," despite the admirable care and complexity of the argument, there is

---

[4] For a subtle exploration of important dimensions of difference involving multicultural contestations of monocultures, see Doris Sommer, *Proceed with Caution, When Engaged by Minority Writing in the Americas* (Cambridge: Harvard University Press, 1999).

never an attempt to define the key concept of experience or even to differentiate among types and subjects of experience (for example, historians and their objects of study).[5] Experience seems even to function as a residual concept—what remains or is left over when meaning and language do not exhaust their objects. The notion of experience as undefined residue might be argued to hold a position analogous to that of divinity or the sacred in negative theology, to wit, "something" that may only be defined by what it is not. The seeming paradox is of course that experience is in phenomenology and neo-Hegelian dialectics the mainstay of a secular mode of thought that is often sharply separated from religion but may in important respects be its displacement. In any event, it may be useful in discussing "experience" to resort to what has almost become a classical gesture: listing the meanings of a term from the Oxford English Dictionary.[6]

The OED, a traditional if not venerable source, is of special interest in that it often does not smooth over difficulties in a concept, or meld different meanings into a unified narrative, but instead enunciates tensely related or even conflicting meanings that at times almost seem to deconstruct, or raise questions for, one another. It is thus of special interest for an open, internally dialogized, essayistic approach to problems such as the one I am trying to take. Let us then look to the OED's definitions of "experience."

OED: "1. The action of putting to the test; trial."

2. "Proof by actual trial; practical demonstration." I would simply point out, in the first two definitions of experience, the role of process, specifically the process of testing—or putting to the test—self or other. I would also note the juridical dimension of the concept, arguably related to judgment, and even the proximity of experience to the ordeal. With the notion of "practical demonstration" there is a movement or even slippage toward a meaning obsolete in English but not in French: experience as experiment, which suggests an active, indeed performative, implication or even intervention of the observer in the

---

[5] One may distinguish between history (or historiography) and metahistory on the basis of the former's focus on events and developments (including experience) in the past and the latter's focus on investigative processes and problems (including transference) undertaken (or undergone) by historians and other analysts in the present. Both activities are important, and a crucial, contested issue is posed by the different ways in which they interact and have implications for the future.

[6] *The Compact Edition of the Oxford English Dictionary*, vol. I (New York: Oxford University Press, 1971). All references are to p. 430.

observed—an implication that cannot be reduced to observation alone since it also changes what is investigated.

3. "The actual observation of facts or events, considered as a source of knowledge." Here I am reminded of Satya Mohanty's oft-quoted definition of experience: "'Experience' refers very simply to the variety of ways humans process information."[7] I would note that this is a definition, apparently restricted to humans, that may refer to a necessary dimension of certain forms of experience, but it does not seem to get at either additional senses in the OED or still others one might offer. Thus it may have to be supplemented by other considerations before it can qualify more comprehensively as one definition of experience. Would the way a computer processes information count as experience? If one answers in the negative, is it because for something to qualify as experience (say, what occurs in a cyborg), it would have to be related to affect and perhaps to at least the possibility of understanding, including mutual understanding? (Recall the significance of the ability of the replicant to cry in *Blade Runner* and its relation to the rapport—in certain ways the undecidable rapport—between human and other-than-human.) Is processing information, even when construed as or complemented by knowledge, too narrow and epistemocentric as a criterion of experience?[8] Can nonhuman animals be said to be devoid of experience or would such an anthropocentric idea of experience be too restrictive, based on too narrow a conception of affect and mutual understanding, and even too related to the primacy of science in however postpositivistic a form?[9]

[7] *Literary Theory and the Claims of History* (Ithaca: Cornell University Press, 1997), 204–5. Quoted by Zammito, 305. Mohanty does examine the role of affect or emotion within a broad conception of the epistemic. See his "The Epistemic Status of Cultural Identity: On *Beloved* and the Postcolonial Condition," in *Reclaiming Identity*, esp. 33–38. There are of course cases more ambiguous than the one Mohanty focuses on—that of a woman who through consciousness-raising comes to convert her depression into (or see it as "really" being) anger, which provides greater insight into her objective situation. It is also conceivable that a thicker account of the case he discusses would reveal complexities (including affective and epistemic complexities).

[8] I would nonetheless note that the emphasis on knowledge may be justified in cases where one is contesting the delegitimation as sources of knowledge of groups or individuals who are seen at most as witnesses or "native informants" providing something analogous to raw material that experts or scientists must process into "real" knowledge.

[9] Is John Zammito close to this restricted definition in the OED when he tends to conflate experience with evidence? I would note that the conflation is questionable in that evidence may contradict experience, for example, the remembered experience of eyewitnesses or survivors of an event.

4. "The fact of being consciously the subject of a state or condition, or of being consciously affected by an event. Also an instance of this; a state or condition viewed subjectively; an event by which one is affected." Here the OED explicitly links experience to consciousness as well as to subjectivity. The linkage with subjectivity sits somewhat uneasily with the stress on "the actual observation of facts or events," which would seem aligned with objectivity. In addition, one may note the typical linkage of experience with the subject and subjectivity as well as its extremely problematic nature, indicated by the appearance of objectivity with the attendant double binds of the subject-object aporia. But one may also argue that one should not oppose subjectivity and objectivity, notably when one introduces the question of subject positions, which are crucial in identity formation and mediate the relation between the self and society, as I shall later suggest. The OED's stress on consciousness would seem to exclude unconscious processes from experience. One may find this exclusion, frequent in phenomenology, to define a certain conception of experience. But one is then left with a limited concept of experience that ignores the problem of the unconscious and of that which impinges on, indeed internally differentiates or even splits, yet is not encompassed by the conscious control of, the presumably unified subject—a problem I shall address when I ask the question: What is not experience or at least not entirely derivable from, or reducible to, experience (or at least a certain conception of experience)?

5. "In senses 3, 4 often personified; esp. in various proverbial phrases." The wonderful example given of personification or prosopopoeia might lead one to believe that the authors of the OED entry had read Paul de Man:[10] "If experience be the mistress of fools, I am sure it is the mother of wisdome." Is one supposed to infer from this puzzling if not mystifying statement that the mother of wisdom, prone to fooling around with fools, is identical with the mistress of fools—a promiscuous identity that might provoke an identity crisis in proponents of reason as the sober-sided father of wisdom? Or is there some intimation of the relation between reason or serious understanding, indeed wisdom, and the carnivalesque role of the fool and the jester—or, more broadly, between work and play? Might this inti-

[10] It would be interesting to explore the relations between analyses of prosopopoeia in de Man and of projective identification in psychoanalysis.

mation be of interest to a defensible form of identity politics in which the concept of identity remained problematic, and the identification between self and other was countered by the recognition of alterity related both to internal self-questioning and to empathy or compassion attentive to difference and to the requirements of respect for the other as other?[11]

6. "What has been experienced; the events that have taken place within the knowledge of an individual, a community, mankind at large, either during a particular period or generally." This is a very expansive definition of experience, but it at least serves to bring up the question of the relation between those who have directly experienced a series of events (for example, slavery, apartheid, or the Holocaust) and those who are related to them through memory or a shared heritage or subject position (say as African American, black South African, or Jew, or as non–African American, white South African, or "Aryan").[12] I doubt whether knowledge in a delimited sense would be enough of a basis for arguing that a later generation's relation to the past is in some significant sense experiential or related to complex processes of identity formation. At least there would have to be memory not reducible to (but also not excluding) objective knowledge claims, and perhaps one might also require affective response—a feeling for the history of a group and one's inherited, acquired, or earned involvement in it. Another experiential and existential dimension not reducible to knowledge would be bearing witness in a secondary, nonidentitarian way to that past and its primary witnesses while recognizing and respecting their difference from oneself. By circumscribing a relation to the past within delimited forms of knowledge and representation, commentators such as Peter Novick and Walter Benn Michaels have (I think mistakenly) argued that there is nothing experiential in any relevant sense about "memory" of a past

[11] Contributors to *Reclaiming Identity*, particularly Linda Alcoff, are justifiably concerned with knee-jerk appeals to internal difference or alterity whenever identity is at issue. One might formulate this dubious kind of reaction thus: whenever I hear "identity," I reach for my internal alterity. The problem is rather to articulate alterity with a nondogmatic notion of identity in a manner that does not obscure tensions between the two.

[12] One may add the complex case of those who have earned an identity or partial identity by engaging in activities (from shared social life or political action to research) that are recognized by members of a group as constituting bases of an identity claim. Hence a non–African American, non-Jew, and so forth may, on "achieved" rather than "ascribed" grounds, come to have and to claim a problematic identity that is accepted

one did not personally and directly live. Indeed, for them, what is at issue in movements beyond delimited claims to knowledge is only a misguided identity or memory politics. The latter misappropriates past experience as symbolic capital in the service of current political and social self-interest.[13] Benn Michaels sees such identity politics at play even—indeed paradigmatically—in Toni Morrison's *Beloved*, a novel that might be read instead as a significant, critical staging of the relation of a community to its past in terms of shared traumatic memory and the inevitable acting-out of collective and individual trauma, with the possibility that art, in its specific (often highly mediated, indirect, darkly playful, powerful but other than narrowly documentary or informational) forms of bearing witness or testifying to that past, might assist in partially working that past over and through, thereby making more available other possibilities in the present and future.[14] Morrison's novel also features what Novick and Benn Michaels ignore or deny: the intergenerational transmission of trauma whereby, through often unconscious processes of identification particularly with intimates, one may be possessed by the past and relive the hauntingly posttraumatic symptoms of events and experiences one may not have directly lived through.

7. "Knowledge resulting from actual observation or from what one has undergone." The OED combines two quite different definitions here. Actual observation may be that of an eyewitness who remains a bystander distanced from events. Undergoing something characterizes a person having the experience as well as those (perhaps unconsciously) identifying with (even being haunted or possessed by) him or her or, in distinguishable ways, those empathizing with him or her while recognizing and respecting alterity and even resisting identification. I think it is crucial to take into account the process of undergoing or "going through" in any acceptable definition of expe-

---

by members of the relevant group, who may of course be divided both factionally and internally over the question of acceptance of the other as one of "one's own."

[13] Peter Novick, *The Holocaust in American Life* (Boston: Houghton Mifflin, 1999); Walter Benn Michaels, "'You Who Never Was There': Slavery and the New Historicism—Deconstruction and the Holocaust," *The Americanization of the Holocaust*, ed. Hilene Flanzbaum (Baltimore: Johns Hopkins University Press, 1999), 181–97.

[14] Such a reading is elaborated in Satya Mohanty, *Literary Theory and the Claims of History*. See also the convergent reading of *Beloved* in James Berger, *After the End: Representations of Post-apocalypse* (Minneapolis: University of Minnesota Press, 1999), chap. 6.

rience, and that process would involve an affective, not only a narrowly cognitive, response, with affectivity having a significant relation to an attempt (however cautious, constitutively limited, nonleveling, imperfect, and at times failed) at understanding the other (who may sometimes be, in the most significant respects, opaque or standoffish). That process is also crucial in giving an account of the relation between one directly having the experience, belated effects of certain experiences in later life (notably traumatic experiences), and the response to the experience of various third parties, including those born later—an issue that involves the question of subject positions vis-à-vis identities.

8. "The state of having been occupied in any department of study or practice, in affairs generally, or in the intercourse of life; the extent to which, or the length of time during which, one has been so occupied; the aptitudes, skill, judgment, etc. thereby acquired." We here, perhaps inevitably, veer once again toward the extremely general and "spongiform." But one can give many ordinary examples of what seems to be suggested in this definition: the experience of a doctor or businessman, the experience of childbirth, the experience of a graduate student, and so forth. It is also common to refer to someone with much or little experience in a given activity. Fortunately, the OED ends with this definition, about which there seems relatively little of interest to say that has not already been said about the other definitions.

In his important article, John Zammito adds elements to the OED's definitions of experience that introduce important considerations but also tend to idealize the concept and to obscure other possibilities: "The appeal to agency and to the materiality of context both stand, in my view, indispensably at the center of the historian's task, and 'experience' is the theoretical term Toews invokes to identify them. . . . It is essential to recognize learning, acknowledgment of error, changing one's mind, as elements of experience" (291, 295). Agency, context, learning, acknowledgment of error, changing one's mind, and fallibility in general are indeed important considerations—and not only for historians. What do they ignore or obscure, and what do they have to engage to be effective? I would mention: disempowerment, decontextualization or disorientation, meaninglessness, and impermeability to learning because of dogmatic belief, fixation, and even fanaticism. These too are important experiences. Disempowerment that may return one to the helplessness of a child is particularly important with respect to those traumatized by certain experiences, but it may also in other respects (for example, economically or politically) characterize people in oppressed positions. The actuality and possibilities of agency are key issues in understanding behavior and enabling action, and one should neither hypostatize the victim nor simply impute agency (typically along with responsibility and blame) when agency is unavailable or at least severely limited.

Along with disempowerment, trauma may bring radical disorientation, confusion, a fixation on the past, and out-of-context experiences (such as flashbacks, startle reactions, or other forms of intrusive behavior). A disorienting or diremptive feature of trauma and the posttraumatic symptom is that they are out-of-context experiences.[15] Working through trauma involves gaining critical distance on those experiences and recontextualizing them in ways that permit a reengagement with ongoing concerns and future possibilities. But I shall have more to say about trauma in a moment. I would simply note here the ways in which agency is placed in question, and reason along with it, notably with respect to unconscious processes and uncontrolled, even delirious, aspects of thought and action. The latter literally take one out of the furrow of ordinary and idealized expectations yet in certain respects may not be altogether avoidable or even undesirable as experiences. In fact there may be a problem with an overly circumscribed conception of reason that is too readily conflated with reasonableness, including a stylistic reasonableness or equanimity, that does not somehow engage affect in general and more extreme, disorienting, or ecstatic possibilities in particular.

I would also note that the meaningless experience is very significant. It may help to delegitimate a status quo and prompt a search for alternatives in which reason and reasoning have a role to play. It may also be put to work and play in forms of art and political contestation that stress or introduce anxiety or doubt about the familiar in ways

[15] What is experienced as traumatic is perhaps typically unanticipated in that it does not fit a real or imagined context, for example, what one would expect or believe an authority figure would do to one. Freud referred here to the absence of *Angstbereitschaft*—the readiness to feel anxiety. Certain ideologies or forms of training may attempt to avert traumatization of the self by making one ready to perpetrate or undergo the unexpected or the extreme. And the symptom is "inappropriate" or incommensurate with a present context, which it disrupts through the intrusion of something returning from the past.

that enable one to take critical distance on standard practices or see them in a different light.

Here I would like to explore the question I brought up earlier: what is not, or not entirely, derivable from, or reducible to (a certain conception of) experience?

Commodified Experience. Does commodified experience, so important in modern and postmodern society, count as experience? If one answers in the negative, is one necessarily indentured to an essentialized or exclusionary concept of "authentic" experience? I think one can take a critical approach to the commodification of experience without holding up, or at least assuming, some idea of truly authentic experience. (I prefer the notion of desirable experience, which requires one to make norms or values, especially as they bear on public life, as explicit as possible yet does not imply the utter transparency of intimate relations or rely on any ontology, however weak or commonsensical.) But the critique of commodified experience would have to be part of a general critique of commodification rather than a general critique of experience or the concept thereof. In other words, one would see the commodification of experience as a stage or aspect of commodification, along with the commodification of goods and services. And one's critique would be economic, social, and political—not simply experiential.

I initially intended to entitle this chapter "Experience: You've Lived the Book—Now See the Movie!" That title seemed to get at the problem of the commodification of experience. I am referring to such experiences as being a Club Med South Sea Islander for a week, getting an identity card for (and presumably identifying with) a survivor at the Holocaust Museum in Washington, or even watching *Schindler's List* as a nonsurvivor who is moved by the experience. (Apparently many survivors have also been moved by the experience and liked the film, but here the question arises of the status of the survivor with regard to the experience of different events—events such as the Shoah or events such as representations of it that may, for example, be therapeutically uplifting—in contradistinction to his or her role as viewer and critic of certain representations. One may respect or even honor the survivor when addressing the former experiences but may take issue with him or her as viewer and critic of certain representations of those experiences and related events.) Commodified experience poses many issues that are difficult to address in a critically informed manner, but these issues should be brought up and considered in any discussion of experience, notably the so-called meaningful experience.[16]

Virtual Experience. In the present context there often seems to be in practice an identity between commodified and virtual experience, but it is nonetheless possible to distinguish between the two analytically. There are many varieties of virtual experience, of which I shall mention a few. One is utopian experience, which always goes beyond actual experience or realism in the representation of experience. Indeed the more utopian the experience, the more distant it would seem to be from the actual or the realistic. At the limit the utopian may be empty, vacuous, or totally open-ended and even defended as such insofar as one desires a complete rupture with existing conditions and a radically different form of life or civilization. Here the utopian may be close to the transcendental or quasi-transcendental, which I shall discuss in its own right in a short while. And one may argue that without reality-testing, which requires a certain realism, the utopian amounts to wishful thinking or at least to a secular analogue of creation ex nihilo or even the otherworldly.

The recent work of Derrida often alludes to the *à-venir*, a beyond that is always to come, the seemingly pure virtuality or messianic *attente sans attente* (waiting without expectation, including expectation of the actual coming of the Messiah). (Derrida disarticulates the noun *avenir*—future—reconfigures it as a verbal form, and defamiliarizes its meaning.) Derrida refuses to see this messianism without a Messiah as utopian because he believes it is a universal structure of ... experience. Another variant of the utopian might be related to immanent or situational, in contrast to radical or forever deferred (if

[16] Benjamin Wilkomirski's *Fragments: Memories of a Wartime Childhood*, trans. Carol Brown Janeway, 1995 (New York: Schocken Books, 1996) purports to be an "authentic" memoir. The blurb on the back cover asserts: "An extraordinary memoir of a small boy who spent his childhood in the Nazi death camps. Beautifully written, with an indelible impact that makes this a book that is not read but experienced." Here the commodified appeal to experience is opposed to reading and thereby seems to suspend even the possibility of critical analysis and judgment. This appeal becomes particularly dubious in light of subsequent findings that the book is in all probability a fabulation. It is possible that the fabulated "experience" (or recovered memory) was based on confused, phantasmatic processes of identification with Holocaust victims. See the discussion in my *Writing History, Writing Trauma*.

not otherworldly), transcendence—that is, what goes beyond existing circumstances or the status quo but may be realized in a future that is in some sense possible as a here and now (without being identified with parousia, full presence or beatitude). Georg Lukács had in mind a version of this form of immanent transcendence when he contrasted revolutionary romanticism to critical realism, which postulated realizable goals related cogently to objective historical possibilities. While stressing more than Lukács the desirable role of a grotesque realism, Bakhtin proposed the carnivalesque as something of a historical utopia in that it would be possible as an institutionalized dimension of social life that approximates utopia but alternates with more everyday, constraining realities of life, such as economic activity. (Durkheim saw a comparable role for feasts as historical utopias that celebrated social values that were necessarily realized at best in compromise formations in everyday life.) In any event one has here the entire problem of the utopian and its relation to experience as well as to various realisms.

Objectified, Structural Processes. I shall simply mention these processes, which include such phenomena as price fluctuations, demographic movements, climatic changes, and the long-term process of commodification. These processes, quite important in history, have experiential effects but are not directly objects of experience. Hence one may experience the effects of commodification in the commodity as fetish, but there is an important sense in which one does not experience the long-term structural process of commodification in the transformation and functioning of an economy and a society (for example, as analyzed by Marx in *Capital*). One might also include among objectified processes certain linguistic developments such as transformations on the phonemic level or even in grammar, syntax, and perhaps semantics. One may in some sense experience the obsolescence of a word but does one experience, other than in retrospect, its becoming obsolete? How to articulate cogently the analysis of structural processes with that of experience is a crucial problem in that one without the other is necessarily one-sided and often misleading.

Transcendence. The transcendental is not a possible object of experience, although it may be taken as a condition of possibility of experience, as it was by Immanuel Kant.[17] Radical transcendence is totally other. This is the status or a-positional "position" of the Hidden God. The affective state of the believer toward such a divinity or sacred being is anxiety—unrelieved anxiety that may not be subject to mitigation, for example, through sacraments or rituals as processes of mediation that provide access to the sacred or divinity.

The desire for, or affirmation of, radical transcendence in one form or another, whether manifestly religious (as in Saint Augustine, Blaise Pascal, or Søren Kierkegaard) or displaced in the secular, indeed at times in a paradoxically religious atheism (as in certain ways in Kant, Derrida, or Lyotard), is a very powerful force in the Western tradition. It may be accompanied (as in de Man) by a theoretical insistence on rigor whereby compromise formations seem unacceptable, and all dialectical or hermeneutic mediation, including that provided by experience and identity, is seen as a dubious if inevitable fall. The body itself may be experienced or figured as the source of suspect "phenomenalist" experience, a fallen object and the literal occasion of falls. There is a sense in which radical transcendence requires absolute purification—getting beyond or out of the body, perhaps through its

---

[17] The quasi-transcendental grounds of morality in Kant prevented him from deriving it from experience, and the role of experience in moral reasoning was at best problematic: "Hence everything that is empirical is, as a contribution to the principle of morality, not only wholly unsuitable for the purpose but is even highly injurious to the purity of morals; for in morals the proper worth of an absolutely good will, a worth elevated above all price, lies precisely in this—that the principle of action is free from all influence by contingent grounds, the only kind that experience can supply. Against the slack, or indeed ignoble, attitude which seeks for the moral principle among empirical motives and laws we cannot give a warning too strongly or too often; for human reason in its weariness is fain to rest upon this pillow and in a dream of sweet illusions (which lead it to embrace a cloud in mistake for Juno) to foist into place some misbegotten mongrel patched up from limbs of varied ancestry and looking like anything you please only not like virtue, to him who has once beheld her in her true shape." Immanuel Kant, *Groundwork of the Metaphysic of Morals*, trans. H. J. Paton (New York: Harper and Row, 1956), 93–94. The way Kant is carried away in this passage in a rather atypical recourse to confusingly mixed, hyperbolic figural language might be read as a sign of his affective investment in the problems at issue, which even induces him to repeat linguistically the "misbegotten" mongrelization to which he objects. In his significant modification of Kantian morality, Emile Durkheim also saw the inadequacy of utilitarianism and pragmatism as bases for ethics, but he argued for the relevance of social and historical experience in moral reasoning. He also sought a compromise formation that explicitly rendered morality an "impure" hybrid between the quasi-transcendental and the worldly or experiential, including the role of socially structured affect whereby desirability complemented and supplemented duty and obligation. On Durkheim see my *Emile Durkheim: Sociologist and*

extreme (orgiastic or ascetic) exhaustion in sex, exercise, or mind-bending, body-disdaining, often insomniac mental activity. Hence there is also a possible relation to death, perhaps a death drive, including the compulsive repetition of traumatic-sublime scenes, or, in Heidegger's phrase, a being-toward-death. Any other, at least the (big) Other, may be foreclosed, barred, or situated beyond any possible experience, and ecstatic or sublime experience itself may be the paradoxical, riven experience of this impossibility. Perhaps especially in a secularized context, radical transgression of norms may become the displacement of transcendence in which at least a momentary release from reason and ordinary reality, including institutions, may seem to be in the offing (however illusory that seeming may be). When every other is situated as radically other (as the other has recently been situated in one dimension of Derrida's thought), then every other is in the (non)position of the radically transcendent, uncanny, utterly opaque, strangely disconcerting, now perhaps absent, divinity who is inaccessible to mediation, ordinary social relations, dialogue, and mutual expectation. In this (non)position every other is indeed Other.

I indicated the force of the radically transcendent in the Western tradition and the problem it poses for a concept of experience as well as for identity, realism, reason, and the significance of the social or even the political. (In a certain current of Christian thought and practice, identity is irremediably sundered, anxiety is all-consuming, reason is a "whore" or "slut," ordinary reality is illusory or relatively inconsequential, society is the scene of *divertissement*, and the basic problem is the leap of faith toward the impossible or the rationally scandalous.) But the force of (the desire for) radical transcendence, while not subject to mediation, may nonetheless be countered by an insistence on the importance of reality-testing, institutions, social interaction, justice, and seemingly impossible compromise formations.

I think that the relation between the transcendent and the immanent is a crucial, if not the crucial, instance of incommensurability in the West. I also think that it is displaced onto such seemingly diverse questions as the relation between individual (or self) and society, sign

Philosopher (Ithaca: Cornell University Press, 1972; repub. Chicago: University of Chicago Press, 1985 and, in a revised edition, Aurora, Colorado: The Davies Group, 2001).

(or signifier) and meaning, or sublimity and beauty.[18] One can ignore, bracket, or deny the force of radical transcendence through a seemingly consistent realism, materialism, or pragmatism. But such a gesture will never convince those affirming, or consumed by, this force, not least those for whom universalizing theory is itself a "sublime" or extremely sublimating force that seems (almost ritually) to purify the self, constitute an ascetic or ecstatic practice, and promise disengagement from contingent (including bodily) constraints or entanglements. Hence there may well be generated a social incommensurability between opposed groups with fundamentally incompatible convictions and nonnegotiable demands. The alternative may be a recognition of the force of (the desire for) radical transcendence and of the paradoxes with which it is accompanied, with at the same time an insistence on the translatability or at least the compatibility of seeming incommensurables—compatibility in the sense of the necessity of suffering, even of enjoying or being able noninvidiously to joke about, one another's "presence" and insistence. This would imply an ability to recognize the significance of institutions in the organization of social life and the importance of transforming institutions through political and social practice in the interest of greater social justice, solidarity, and nondiscriminatory interaction among various groups. It would also allow for a qualified realism that should, I would suggest, be strongly correlated with reality-testing in the psychoanalytic sense rather than remaining only an epistemological position defended on abstract philosophical grounds. Such moves would be mere beginnings, but I think they may be seen as necessary beginnings.

One aspect of the insistence on transcendence I would like to stress is the role of anxiety. Anxiety can become all-consuming and may be related to both social crisis and inconsolable melancholy, notably when the desired object (which may be the "dead" divinity or the barred big "Other") is seen not as absent but as a lost yet disorienting object of identification. It may also induce panic and either psy-

[18] Although the relation between transcendence and immanence is crucial, especially in Western religion and philosophy, the problem of incommensurability arises in politically forceful forms whenever there are claims to sovereignty or to an absolute, and such claims typically divide groups that may have no common ground to enable compromises. One issue with respect to incommensurability, at least on textual or conceptual levels, is whether one may, as in the case of natural languages, have the possibility of mutual translation, with a complex economy of gains and

chosis or the turn to charismatic, even extremely authoritarian or fascist, alternatives.[19] But, while affirming the necessity of counteracting anxiety through social processes, including institutions and even rituals (such as mourning), one may insist on the importance of anxiety in affectively inhibiting closure, complacency, or self-assurance, including disciplinary self-assurance.

I would also insist on the dubiousness of a certain disciplinary identity politics that marginalizes or excludes possibilities of inquiry, insists on strict boundary maintenance, and eliminates, as pertinent interlocutors, those in other disciplines, in variants of the same discipline, or in the general public. Here the affirmation of fallibilism, however desirable, is not enough, both because it may be associated with disciplinary exclusions or denigrations and because it often remains on an affectively neutral epistemological level that may not have an impact on motivation. By contrast, while there may be a need for agreement on certain basics within a discipline or approach, one should also validate anxiety that allows for the pursuit of a question or a problem wherever it leads, including in directions that may place certain basics in jeopardy or that may not be recognizable within existing disciplinary parameters. Such a validated anxiety is especially called for to the extent that institutional agencies (such as academic departments) stake a claim to disciplines or problems and become de facto regulators of what is privileged, allowable, marginalized, or excluded within a discipline.

Trauma. Anxiety is related to trauma and to the idea that at least humanistic and interpretive social-scientific disciplines should in certain significant ways always be in a state of crisis, including a kind of posttraumatic identity crisis wherein what is open for debate bears

---

losses, even if there is no metalanguage (or *Ursprache*) as a criterion for adjudicating claims. Such a question may be posed concerning the relation between sacred or master texts in a manner that may have political and social implications. It may also be posed concerning various subject positions and identities.
[19] This is in one sense the story of a crisis of investiture told by Eric Santner in *My Own Private Germany: Daniel Paul Schreber's Secret History of Modernity* (Princeton: Princeton University Press, 1996). Put in the simplest terms, Schreber took problems out on himself while the Nazi movement took them out on others and sought an illusory collective redemption from them.

on the identity or constitution of the discipline itself. Such a view is especially pertinent when the most important problems are themselves not simply interdisciplinary (in that they require the cooperation or combination of various existing disciplines to "solve" them) but cross-disciplinary in that they cut across existing disciplines and are owned by, or adequately addressed in the terms of, none of them. Trauma itself is one such problem.

I would note that John Toews does not treat the problem of trauma, and Joan Scott touches on it but does not thematize it. It arises with respect to her second interpretation or reading of Sam Delany's experience of "an undulating mass of naked male bodies" seen under a dim blue light in a bathhouse.[20] In contrast to her first interpretation, which relies on a rather pat experience of identity, Scott notes that Delany himself prompts a different reading: "Another kind of reading, closer to Delany's preoccupation with memory and the self in this autobiography, sees this event [in the bathhouse] not as the discovery of truth (conceived as the reflection of a prediscursive reality), but as the substitution of one interpretation for another. Delany presents this substitution as a conversion experience, a clarifying moment, after which he sees (that is, understands) differently" (34–35). It is not clear in Scott how a conversion experience, related to repetition with transformative change (here a second reading or substitution of interpretations) and bringing a possibly traumatic difference or disjunction in (self)understanding, bears on a theory of radical discursive constructivism, but the role of this shift in her account is noteworthy.

I would also mention here the at times traumatic role of the deconversion experience in modern life, which has its most obvious role in the loss of religion when religious language and ritual fail to cohere as meaningful and instead fall apart. One may have such an experience with secular orientations, theories, or ideologies, obviously in the case of Marxism, less obviously with respect to Derridean or de Manian deconstruction, Lacanianism, Foucauldianism, or other theoretical formations and methodological perspectives. Accepting one or another of them is a complex process with certain elements of conversion that may be related to the bonding and at times the dogmatism of initiates and the lack of interest, disparagement, or perhaps

[20] Quoted in Scott, "Experience," 34.

intolerance manifested toward any approach involving basic criticism of the theory or of the quasi-sacred texts of a master. Deconversion may be related in part to rational argument and the recognition of shortcomings of an orientation in addressing certain problems, but it also involves affective disengagement and the sense that a discursive formation no longer holds together in a way that elicits one's existential as well as intellectual investment. Deconversion in this sense has been justly compared to falling out of love which, like falling in love, is both performatively enacted and receptively undergone as an experience.

The shift in Scott's interpretation of Delany is not noted in John Zammito's spirited critique, and he tends to pass very lightly over trauma. Zammito writes: "Psychological 'opacities' are an important problem, but the very existence of such *categories* [underlined in the original] as 'trauma' suggests that we are not utterly without resources, and that to employ them we must use other 'experiences' to give us purchase on the repressed ones" (292–93). Here Zammito himself seems to take the linguistic turn or to be a pantextualist in a rather conventional sense. One could of course parody his statement by asserting: "The prevalence of undernourishment is an important problem, but the very existence of such *categories* as 'food supplies' suggests that we are not utterly without resources." The basic point is that the relation of experience to trauma poses problems that require much more serious and extended treatment than an affirmation that we can appeal to certain categories or even to other experiences in order to get beyond silence and approximate the experience of trauma. Indeed how to approach and study the traumas of others or of oneself in the past is a vexed issue that raises many problems, including the role of identification, compulsive acting-out, empathy, working over, and working-through. I doubt it would be desirable (although it may well be awe-inspiring) to actually relive or even approximate the experience of certain traumas (say, of victims of the Holocaust or of child abuse), but I would defend being unsettled by them and empathizing with their victims.

One may read Walter Benjamin as addressing some of these problems through the distinction between *Erlebnis* and *Erfahrung*. *Erlebnis* was unintegrated experience such as that of shock or trauma, for example, in the famous or infamous *Fronterlebnis*—the traumatic experience (often transvalued to become ecstatic or sublime) of soldiers on the front in the First World War.[21] *Erfahrung* was relatively integrated experience related to such procedures as storytelling or narration (although I would argue that narration need not reach closure in order to be related to *Erfahrung*). In the psychoanalytic vocabulary I have been employing in my recent work, *Erlebnis* might be related to acting-out and *Erfahrung* to processes of working-through, including not only narration but mourning and critical thought and practice. I also think that, with respect to severe trauma, the traumatized and, on a significantly different level, those empathically responding to them, may never fully overcome acting-out, or being compulsively possessed by the past and repeating it in some uncontrolled manner, but I also think that acting-out may be counteracted by processes of working through. In any case the problem of trauma and its relation to historiography and representation in general is a crucial problem that has to be addressed in a sustained fashion by anyone invoking the concept of experience.

Another distinction is pertinent with respect to trauma: that between the traumatic (or traumatizing) event (or events) and the traumatic experience. The event in historical trauma is punctual and datable. It is situated in the past. The experience is not punctual and has an elusive aspect insofar as it relates to a past that has not passed away—a past that intrusively invades the present and may block or obviate possibilities in the future. So-called traumatic memory carries

[21] I argue that there was an attempt to transvalue the traumatic into the sublime in Nazi ideology and practice. See my *Representing the Holocaust: History, Theory, Trauma* and *History and Memory after Auschwitz*. In addition, see the discussion of the *Fronterlebnis* and related "sublime" or ecstatic experiences in Klaus Theweleit, *Male Fantasies*, vol. 2, trans. Erica Carter and Chris Turner in collaboration with Stephen Conway (1978; Minneapolis: University of Minnesota Press, 1989). See also Georges Sorel's apologetic *Reflections on Violence*, trans. T. E. Hulme (1915; New York: Peter Smith, 1941), in which the "sublime," in its relation to redemptive proletarian violence, is a chord repeatedly struck. I would also note the interesting discussion and defense of certain forms of sublimity in Thomas Weiskel, *The Romantic Sublime: Studies in the Structure and Psychology of Transcendence* (1976; Baltimore: Johns Hopkins University Press, 1986). No doubt with reference to the questionable role of experience in *Lebensphilosophie*, Victor Klemperer, in his diary entry for April 25, 1937, makes this observation: "An always recurring word: 'Experience.' Whenever some Gauleiter or SS leader, one of the minor and most minor subordinate gods speaks, then one does not hear his speech, but 'experiences' it. Eva [Klemperer's non-Jewish wife] rightly says it was already there before National Socialism. Certainly, it is to be found in the currents that created it." *I Will Bear Witness: A Diary of the Nazi Years 1933–1941*, trans. Martin Chalmers (1995; New York: Random House, 1998), 216. Klemperer was a German Jew who converted to Protestantism and managed to live in Dresden while

the experience into the present and future in that the events are compulsively relived or reexperienced as if there were no distance or difference between past and present. In traumatic memory the past is not simply history as over and done with. It lives on experientially and haunts or possesses the self or the community (in the case of shared traumatic events) and must be worked through in order for it to be remembered with some degree of conscious control and critical perspective that enables survival and, in the best of circumstances, ethical and political agency in the present. How to work through the experience of these events in viable, ethically and politically desirable ways is one of the greatest challenges in coming to terms with personal or collective traumas for their survivors, intimates of survivors, and in certain respects all those living within a freighted heritage or responding empathically to a living past and those within it.[22]

With respect to identity formation, one should make special mention of the founding trauma in the life of individuals and groups. The founding trauma is the actual or imagined event (or series of extreme or limit events) that poses in accentuated fashion the very question of identity yet may paradoxically itself become the basis of an individual or collective identity. It may be undergone in the form of the deconversion or the conversion experience, even the sequence or coming together of the two, and it disorients and may reorient the course of a life. It may be related to—or more or less problematically converted into—a "mystical" experience of seemingly unmediated insight, witnessing, or revelation, and it may also become the basis of a new identity. One thinks, for example, of Paul on the road to Dam-

---

undergoing various forms of oppression throughout the Third Reich. He was a staunch supporter of Enlightenment values but also a German patriot who believed that the Nazis were "un-German."

[22] See the extended reflection on experience in Angelika Rauch, *The Hieroglyph of Tradition: Freud, Benjamin, Gadamer, Novalis, Kant* (Madison, N.J.: Associated University Presses, 2000). Although it does not emphasize the role of empathy in understanding and begins with a deceptive opposition between history and tradition, with memory and experience on the side of tradition, Rauch's analysis comes to develop more intricate relations between her key concepts and invokes psychoanalysis in the attempt to elicit the relation of affect and imagination to figurative language and allegory. Rauch valorizes melancholia, unmastered affect, and the "shock experience of trauma," and also compares "every experience" in the way it "affects the subject's mind" to the "belated effects of trauma" (80), thereby threatening to collapse transhistorical or structural trauma into historical trauma. But certain dimensions of her analysis are compatible with a nonstereotypical, critical understanding of working

ascus being interpellated by God and undergoing, as well as perfomatively enacting, transformation from persecutor of Christians to follower of Christ and institution builder of a church. One might also think of secular analogues of the deconversion/conversion experience, such as Sartre's original choice of being, its often opaque imbrication in *le vécu* (lived experience), and its implications for the rearticulation of a life's course. Some of the most extreme and dire experiences, including those involving radical loss, may be transfigured into founding traumas as the (variably earned or unearned) foundations for personal and collective life. Hence slavery and the Holocaust have become markers of group identity and, in contested ways, founding traumas for groups living with their fraught heritage. One may ask whether every group that is in some significant sense an existential group or locus of commitment whose members affirm (and may be pressured to affirm) a collective identity has in its past or in its mythology (often its mythologized past) a trauma that has become foundational and is a source of identity both for those who actually lived through it and in different ways for those born into its aftermath. In perhaps its most politically pointed dimension, the founding trauma may be a way for an oppressed group or an abused person to reclaim a history and to transform it into a more or less enabling basis of life in the present. But, insofar as it fixates one obsessively on old grievances or dubious dynamics and even induces a compulsive reenactment of them, it may also function to undermine the need to come to terms with the past in a manner that constructively engages existential, social, and political demands and possibilities of a current situation.

The Unconscious.   Another major set of problems not entirely encompassed by (a certain conception of) experience is the unconscious or, more precisely, unconscious processes such as displacement, condensation, repression, denial, disavowal, and compulsive repetition (related to the acting out of trauma). These processes, to which I can only allude, have experiential effects but, insofar as they are uncon-

---

through the past, notably her sensitivity to transferential dynamics, her defense of *Erfahrung*, her insistence both on the recognition of loss as loss and on the alterity of the other, and her critique of the denial of trauma in harmonizing narratives or interpretations.

scious, are in one sense not directly experienced. Especially interesting in this respect is the role of belatedness or what Freud termed
Nachträglichkeit. For Freud there was a period of latency between an
initial, potentially traumatizing event and a later event that in some
sense recalled it and triggered a traumatic response. The trauma
depended on the interval or period of latency between events—an
interval that was not itself experienced but was related to a very
intense form of experience in the acting out or compulsive repetition
of the past, itself experienced as if it were fully present. One may also
refer here to the role of belated recognitions following the passage of
time and a series of subsequent developments that enable one to see
something in the past that agents in the past (including oneself) could
not see in the same way. For example, one reads Heidegger differently
after the disclosure of aspects of his past that were either not known
or not deemed relevant in an earlier reading, and even if one returns
to previous readings one is constrained to provide different defenses
of them that come to terms with later disclosures, if only to deny their
relevance. One also sees certain movements or orientations of the
interwar period differently in the light of later happenings, such as
the events of the Nazi regime. These belated recognitions do not
imply a teleological vision of history, and it would be a misunderstanding to see them as mere anachronisms. But they do allow one to
ask questions of the past that its actors did not ask of themselves. But
neither they nor we necessarily experienced the intervening events or
variables that enable belated recognitions. These enabling events are
curiously in the quasi-transcendental position of Kantian conditions
of possibility.

Laughter. For Freud an outburst of laughter is not fully under conscious control or voluntaristically strategic since it is related to the
release of repressed forces. (Indeed there is a subtle range of experiences of laughter, with differing relations to possible control or strategic use, from the coy smile or ironic chuckle to "contagious" hilarity
and the belly laugh.) We in some sense experience laughter, which
may even have critical and therapeutic effects. And laughter bears on
identities and subject positions. It often, perhaps typically, works
with, and possibly against, invidious distinctions, at times touching
on the desirable possibility of a joke without a butt or at least with a
floating butt that undoes or contests itself. Hence its relation to prej-

udice and discrimination is complex and internally divided. So is its relation to realism and reason, going counter at least to the sustained sobriety of certain of their prominent forms. In any case laughter is not reducible to realism or reason, and it is similar to trauma in its status as an experience that does not conform to certain prevalent, perhaps idealized, conceptions of experience (experience as conscious, linked to agency, epistemocentric). Yet laughter may be bound up with learning experiences and may not be incompatible with reason and certain forms of realism (grotesque and critical realism, for example), although it may be incommensurable with reason and at least a limited, systematically reasonable realism. It may also have a sociopolitical role in both criticizing certain policies and practices or their proponents and in creating bonds within a group.

A few jokes may help to bring home the points I have just made abstractly and all too reasonably. First, an old joke that made the rounds some time ago, indeed so long ago that a younger generation may not have heard it. Question: "What do you get when you cross a Mafioso with a deconstructionist?" Answer: "Someone who makes you an offer you can't understand." When I would tell this joke, I would try to undo a fixated butt by adding: "This joke affects me personally in at least two ways." The delayed effect of the additional statement depended, of course, on my not specifying the two ways, which, after a brief time lapse, became evident.

I shall paraphrase from memory two more jokes from the repertoire of the stand-up comic Rita Rudner. The first is about sharing experiences across different subject positions. Rudner tells of giving birth, with her husband standing next to her, urging "push, push." She asks: "Is that really sharing the experience? I'd at least want him stretched out on a table next to me getting his legs waxed." A second, slightly modified Rudner joke juxtaposes dissonant experiences of a partner in view of creating an empathic relation to the self. "Men with pierced ears make better partners because they have had two essential experiences: they have bought jewelry, and they have felt pain."

Subject Positions.   One may have a subject position without experiencing it, and often one's experience of it depends on a recognition, at times an insulting recognition, coming from others. But subject positions are crucial for both experience and identity. *Identity formation might even be defined in nonessentialized terms as a problematic attempt to configure and, in certain ways, coordinate subject positions–in-process.* This attempt would involve a limited, variable, but significant role for the responsible agency of individuals and groups, with the possibility of creating new subject positions (ones not beholden to victimization, for example). With respect to subject positions and their role in social life, one may ask whether there has ever been a politics that has not in some significant sense been an identity politics and whether criticisms of certain forms of identity politics are, often implicitly, made in favor of other (often idealized past or utopian) forms of identity politics (for example, a nostalgia for the 1960s idealized or selectively remembered as a period of universalistic values and alliance politics).

Among the standard subject positions that one has to take into account in any discussion of identity are the following (which may themselves be multiple or internally divided): sexuality, gender, family, language, nationality, ethnicity, class, "race," religion or secular ideology, occupation, and at times disciplinary affiliation. Debates about identity and identity formation often concern the actual and desirable prioritizing or, more generally, the relation and possible coordination or integration of subject positions. They also concern the possibilities of communication and cooperation or conflict between subject positions within the self or distributed among different individuals or groups. It is more difficult to change some subject positions than others. For example, for most people a sex-change operation, with all of the attendant modifications it involves, reaches very deep into identity as most of us presently understand it. A change of occupation would be less telling, although a drastic change (from wealthy banker to vagrant, say) would entail major changes in identity.

I would observe that, in his influential article, John Toews does not consistently relate the concept of experience to that of subject position or elaborate a distinction among subject positions with respect to experience—both subject positions of historians and subject positions of their objects of study. Here I would raise a series of difficult questions: Should the historian make explicit his or her own subject positions to the extent that they are pertinent to research and argument? Does it matter, for example, if the historian of the Holocaust is a survivor, a child of survivors, a child of a perpetrator, an Israeli, a Palestinian, a Gentile, and so forth? Could one make a stronger case for auto-ethnography than for a more narrowly individual, at times narcissistic, autobiography? Should the historian treat in the same way perpetrators, victims, bystanders, collaborators, rescuers, and so forth, especially with respect to extreme or limit events that involve trauma? To what extent can one determine what precisely in the work of the historian is to be related to his or her own experience? How does one relate one's own experience to the experience of those one studies? Is it desirable, in research and in social life, to attempt to work out subject positions not identical to those one studies, for the latter often tend to depend on processes of victimization? These questions do not arise within an abstract theoreticist approach to problems. Nor do they arise within a neopositivisitic approach or within a historiography that relies on a conventional, self-contained research model. Even when they do arise, they may be addressed in a dubious manner, notably when a relation to the other is established not critically and through an empathy that recognizes alterity but through incorporative or projective identification and fictionalizing, as is the case in Daniel Jonah Goldhagen's *Hitler's Willing Executioners*.[23]

I noted at the outset that the problem of how to relate one's experience to that of others does not seem pertinent for, and is often not salient in the work of, someone who studies his or her own group or people.[24] But there is an important sense in which it should be of critical interest. There are always more or less significant and subtle differentiations between oneself and those one studies as well as differences within oneself (and within others) that both render problematic any identity and may enable one to address identity in more subtle and cogent terms, indeed to envisage and work toward different subject positions and identities. I have intimated that identity formation is a matter of recognizing and coming to terms with one's

[23] *Hitler's Willing Executioners: Ordinary Germans and the Holocaust* (New York: Alfred A. Knopf, 1996). See my discussion in *Writing History, Writing Trauma*, chap. 4.

[24] It should of course be observed that the study of one's own group is justified to the extent it has been neglected, downplayed, or tendentiously represented and its study is part of a broader process of putting forward legitimate claims, particularly with respect to oppressed or subaltern groups. Moreover, a dubious form of self-directed if not narcissistic study has been typical of dominant groups, which have taken their own activities to be either the primary or even exclusive object of concern or the center to which all else is referred. Canons as well as various area studies, even when presumably directed at the investigation of others, have often had this self-directed orientation as one of their most questionable features.

subject positions, coordinating them, examining their compatibility or incompatibility, testing them, and either validating them by a process of reproduction and renewal or transforming them through questioning and related work on the self and in society. Any resultant identity would have at most an internally dialogized and self-critical coherence. Moreover, insofar as experience is a (if not the) basis of identity, the problematics of experience carry over into identity.

I have also remarked that a useful concept is signifying practice and that language is a crucial signifying practice (or congeries of signifying practices) but not the only one. Often language is privileged in our culture in ways one may want to interrogate. It (like reason or even affect) is one of the criteria invoked to differentiate humans from nonhumans, typically in an invidious fashion, and people become uneasy when the differentiation is rendered unstable (as it should be). And we typically make language pivotal by using it to discuss all other signifying practices and to limit, see as second-best, or exclude the use of other signifying practices to comment on one another or on it. (Everyone would be more than surprised—and I most of all—if I started to dance or play a musical instrument, much less if I occasionally growled, in the attempt to address the problem of experience and identity.)

It is worth noting that in Toews, experience and meaning remain the basic if not the foundational concepts. In his triangulation, language—perhaps signifying practice in general—is located on what seems to be a significantly different level: it is a mediation. (One is led to picture a triangle with meaning and experience as its base angles and language at its apex, with language transforming experience into meaning.) This gesture serves the fruitful function of not privileging language, albeit at the expense of leaving both experience and meaning undefined. But how then does one situate the often complex experience of using language itself—say, the experience of speaking, listening, reading, or writing? Take, for example, the experience of a lower-class child speaking in an upper-class environment, of the lone woman speaking in a meeting of executives, or of a bi- or multilingual person addressing a monolingual official (or reader) complacently competent only in the dominant language. For many academics, writing, or speaking in public, may be an arduous experience as demanding as many others. In addition, the constraining processes in learning to speak and, perhaps even more, to read and write involve arduous, albeit in part empowering, undertakings for anyone, particularly for the oppressed or disabled.[25] (The legitimate deconstruction of the binary opposition between speech and writing should not be made to obscure the "experiential" demands and exigencies of acquiring literacy in any culture.) Why are these experiences not as experiential as any other experience, such as listening to music? I have intimated that the problem of using language to discuss music (invoked by Zammito) presents difficult issues in translation, intersubjectivity, and objectivity that are not addressed by the seemingly self-evident assertion that listening to Mozart is not—or at least not exclusively or primarily—a linguistic event. How does objectivity apply to the analytic and critical discussion of music? In what sense is music a signifying practice? To what extent may it be seen as an articulation of subjectivity? Or is the conjunction of experience, emotion, and subjectivity, as well as the explicit or implicit privileging of subjectivity and the subject, basically misguided?[26] If one retains the concept of subjectivity, what is required of a seemingly paradoxical "objective" history of experience that includes—and in some uses seems identical to—subjectivity? Should certain explicitly problematic concepts, including that of subject position, be understood as destabilizing and criticizing a notion of the subject and of subjectivity as unified and privileged?

[25] See, for example, Peter Carruthers and Jill Boucher, eds., *Language and Thought: Interdisciplinary Themes* (Cambridge: Cambridge University Press, 1998); Mary Klages, *Woeful Afflictions: Disability and Sentimentality in Victorian America* (Philadelphia: University of Pennsylvania Press, 1999); Joseph P. Lash, *Helen and Teacher: The Story of Helen Keller and Anne Sullivan* (New York: Delta/Seymour Lawrence, 1980); and Jeffrey Moussaieff Masson, *Lost Prince: The Unsolved Mystery of Kaspar Hauser* (New York: Free Press, 1996). See also the excellent article by James Berger, "Helen Keller and Implementation H[elen]," *Arizona Quarterly* 58 (2002): 109–37, in which Berger provides a sensitive and broad-ranging analysis of the life of Helen Keller as prototype or intertext for the creature of artificial intelligence in Richard Powers's novel, *Galatea 2.2*.
[26] See the argument in Rei Terada, *Feeling in Theory: Emotion after the "Death of the Subject"* (Cambridge: Harvard University Press, 2001). Although I do not agree with all of her complex and subtle argument, I do in qualified ways agree with aspects of it, including the crucial contention that "experience [including emotion or affect] is the experience of self-differentiality" (156). I find somewhat forced her admittedly ingenious concluding reading of the replicant's tears in *Blade Runner* as the occasion that "dramatizes the fact that destroying the illusion of subjectivity does not destroy emotion, that on the contrary, emotion is the sign of the absence of that illusion" (157). As intimated earlier, I would read this scene more broadly as delegitimating the appeal to emotion as a differentiating criterion between human and other-than-human. More generally I would argue that there is no such decisively differentiating

Empathy. I already referred to empathic response, and I think that any historiographical, sociological, or theoretical appeal to experience is inadequate without an account of the problem of empathy as it bears on the relation of the inquirer to the experience of those studied. It is significant that neither Toews nor Zammito even refers to this problem—a kind of missing link in their arguments. Empathy has in general tended to drop off the historical agenda in part because of its earlier "romantic" or even somewhat "mystical" uses and because of the professionalization of history under the banner of objectivity, often narrowly defined as objectivism. (By "objectivism" I mean the exclusive use of narrowly empirical and analytic techniques in the representation of the other as object sharply separated from the self as subject, inquirer, or observer.) The notions of transference and observer-participation question objectivism, and they should also lead in historiography to a critical reexamination of empathy and the role of affect in historical understanding. More generally, they may also be seen as raising the question of trust and its role as an experience whose presence or absence opens or closes other possibilities. Trust is a significant issue in all social relations, and it has a bearing on one's initial inclination to acknowledge or affirm the credibility of an interlocutor. And traumatization typically involves the betrayal of trust. These problems are of course further connected to the issue of subject positions, including the subject positions of historians and of those they study. We may initially tend to trust those with similar subject positions and, even more so, those with similar articulations of subject positions into broader identities. Others may have to undergo special tests over time to be deemed trustworthy or reliable. And it is difficult to see how an other who is accepted as empathic would not also be accepted as trustworthy. With respect to historiography, trust is an obvious component in one's response to colleagues' research and arguments—one's inclination to accept their reliability prima facie—and in a more virtual sense it may also apply to one's relation to the past and its dead. One may at least initially trust or not trust an interpretation depending on the historian's "track record" in the field and one's belief that he or she has a good understanding of

---

criterion, and any criterion one postulates invariably serves invidious purposes and forecloses concern with the problem of victimization.

the problem at issue or is at least questioning existing understandings or orientations in a way one finds challenging or worthy of consideration.

Empathy is especially problematic in the case of traumatic events and the relation of perpetrators and victims to them. Empathy is too often conflated with identification, especially with the victim, and this conflation leads to an idealization or even sacralization of the victim as well as an often histrionic self-image as surrogate victim undergoing vicarious experience. (One may note certain effects of this conflation in aspects of Shoshana Felman's contributions to *Testimony* and Claude Lanzmann's role as interviewer in *Shoah*.)[27] Empathy is, I think, a virtual but not a vicarious experience in that the historian puts him- or herself in the other's position without taking the other's place or becoming a substitute or surrogate for the other who is authorized to speak in the other's voice.[28] Empathy involves affective response to the other, and affective response interacts with difference as well as critical distancing and analysis in historiography. It implies what I am terming empathic unsettlement in the secondary witness, including the historian in one of his or her roles or subject positions. This unsettlement should, I think, have nonformulaic stylistic effects in representation, for example, in placing in jeopardy harmonizing or fetishistic accounts that bring unearned spiritual uplift or meaning— something that tends to occur in certain hermeneutic approaches (in certain ways, for example, in Charles Taylor's *Sources of the Self* or,

---

[27] See Shoshana Felman and Dori Laub, M.D., *Testimony: Crises of Witnessing in Literature, Psychoanalysis, and History* (New York: Routledge, 1992), as well as my discussion of Felman in *History and Memory after Auschwitz*, particularly her treatment of Lanzmann's *Shoah*.

[28] The question of whether there should be an empathic response to certain perpetrators is difficult. Absolute denial of such response or of its desirability is not a safeguard against unconscious processes of identification or voyeuristic engagement and may even facilitate them. I would be inclined to argue that a limited empathic response is defensible for trying to understand, in however unsettled, inadequate, or even consciously constrained a manner, the motivation and behavior of even blatant, extreme perpetrators, and that the "virtual" basis of such an attempt is the acknowledgment that one might oneself be led to perform comparable extreme acts in certain circumstances—or at least that one cannot be certain about how one would act, especially if one has not been tested by those circumstances and their experiential dimensions. Such an acknowledgment or realization may of course be a good reason for resisting the genesis of such circumstances or situations that facilitate victimization. It is not desirable to have all experiences or incur all "tests," particularly those involving victimization.

more blatantly, in various representations of the Anne Frank story).[29] At the very least the empathic unsettlement of the secondary witness with respect to trauma brings out the dubiousness of a quest for closure or full dialectical synthesis.

Memory. The concept of experience also raises the problem of memory and of the relation between history and memory. What we refer to as experience is typically the memory of experience. Memory has recently become a "hot" topic among historians, often generating more heat than light. Debates about it are like fallout from the culture wars, and when memory is mentioned, identity and identity politics are never far behind. But historians, I think, often ignore the role of what might be termed disciplinary identity politics, which they may enact without thematizing as a problem or addressing critically. Indeed critiques of identity politics in society are often themselves instances of disciplinary identity politics that attempt to shore up the professional identity of historians, often by contrasting their enlightened, rational, or objective methods with the political motivations and quest for symbolic capital of those they analyze critically. This dynamic is quite evident in Peter Novick's *The Holocaust in American Life*, Joyce Appleby, Lynn Hunt, and Margaret Jacob's *Telling the Truth about History*, Richard Evans's *In Defense of History*, or Gérard Noiriel's *Sur la "crise" de l'Histoire*.[30] Indeed in *Telling the Truth about History*, multiculturalism and poststructuralism are presented as destroying a putative earlier consensus on how to narrate the past of the United States, while in Noiriel it is Americans (that is, foreigners) who are destroying the authentic unity of the Annales school of historiography in France—in spite of the fact that it is often those affiliated with that school who are raising some of the most pointed questions. In brief, recent tendencies justify a certain skepticism about the seaworthiness of at least some ships that sail under the banner of professional historiography or even under that of a chastened, ascetically self-denying objectivity.

[29] *Sources of the Self: The Making of the Modern Identity* (Cambridge: Harvard University Press, 1989). See my discussion of this book in *Representing the Holocaust*, 183–87.

[30] Joyce Appleby, Lynn Hunt, and Margaret Jacob, *Telling the Truth about History* (New York: W. W. Norton, 1994); Richard Evans, *In Defense of History* (New York: W. W. Norton, 1997); Gérard Noiriel, *Sur la "crise" de l'histoire* (Paris: Belin, 1996).

Since memory is a prominent part of (indeed at times a metonym for) experience, the problem of the relation between history and memory is a somewhat smaller scale version of the problem of the relation between history and experience. I would simply reiterate the point I develop at length in the first chapter of *History and Memory after Auschwitz*. History and memory should neither be opposed in binary fashion nor conflated. Their relations are complex. One key argument I make is that historiography most directly impinges on the public sphere and is not purely professional or technical in nature when it touches on problems of memory, including of course problems of forgetting, repression, and avoidance.[31] At its best historiography contributes to the public sphere a critically tested, accurate memory that groups in society may possibly internalize as the remembered past. In any case, memory as part of the experience of a group is bound up with the way that group relates to its past as it bears on its present and future. One may deny the status of shared memory as a mode of experience in relating to the past if one takes up a neo-Adamic individualistic, if not anarchistic or narrowly presentist, so-called pragmatic point of view. I find this denial with its premises to be more questionable than what it criticizes. I would also observe that experience of a certain sort, including differentially shared or collective memory, initially enables one to speak in certain voices and can give one a prima facie claim to knowledge and understanding, including their role in scholarship—something that includes but goes beyond narrow cognition in the sense of facts, dates, and their analysis. But this prima facie claim has to be spelled out and argued for in a larger discursive context.[32]

Hyperbole. Zammito is not alone in the historical profession in having a profound suspicion of hyperbole. Still, he becomes transferentially hyperbolic in attacking hyperbole—his attacks on hyperbole

[31] Robert Paxton's *Vichy France: Old Guard and New Order, 1940–1944* (published in English in 1972 and in French translation in 1973 as *La France de Vichy, 1940–1944*) might be taken as a paradigm case of a book—interestingly written by a nonnational—that brought professional historical research into live contact with a sensitive problem of national memory, amnesia, and self-understanding. For a discussion of its role in France, see Henry Rousso, *The Vichy Syndrome: History and Memory in France since 1944*, trans. Arthur Goldhammer (Cambridge: Harvard University Press, 1991), esp. 252–56.
[32] I think this is a basic point that Linda Martin Alcoff, sharing a perspective with Satya Mohanty, develops at length in "Who's Afraid of Identity Politics?"

are at times hyperbolically unqualified. I would agree with him that unchecked hyperbole is of dubious value, especially when it is joined to an all-or-nothing logic that eliminates or sees as superficial all transitional or mediating processes, even when they do not pretend to closure or higher "dialectical" unity. Still, hyperbole (even opacity, or at least a difficult style that is not simply obscurantist) is in certain contexts necessary, and it is important to examine whether hyperbole (or difficulty) is warranted, how it works, and the extent to which it is discursively related in a given account to countervailing forces or voices. Hyperbole may have a provocative, agonistic, and fruitful role in emphasizing what one believes is granted insufficient weight at a given time in the ongoing attempt to articulate possibilities in a discipline, in the academy, or in the broader culture. In this sense, I think it may, for example, be justifiable, at a certain point in the history of historiography, to stress the role of rhetoric and performativity insofar as they are indeed largely ignored or downplayed, as long as one does not present them as eliminating or denigrating the importance of truth claims and research or as constituting the exclusive generative, constructivist, or self-referential basis of language and of a conception of the past. Moreover, while hyperbole (as well as a certain kind of opacity or stylistic involution) may arguably be at times overdone in recent critical theory, it hardly runs rampant in historiography. (Witness the antihyperbolic plain style of *Telling the Truth about History* or the journalistic pace and synoptic sweep of *In Defense of History*.) Encompassing or general judgments about the state of a discipline or area are always contestable, but I think one would be hard-pressed to argue that the role of rhetoric or performativity in historiography has been broadly acknowledged or even discussed—much less hyped— among modern historians, especially before the mid-1980s.[33]

[33] Here a personal experience is pertinent. In 1983 I submitted to the Program Committee of the American Historical Association a proposal for a panel on "Rhetoric and the Writing of History" to be held at the annual convention. The proposal was rejected. One member of the committee, sympathetic to the proposal, wrote the following in a letter to me: "I am particularly interested in talking to you after reading your recent letter in the AHR and your proposal to the AHA Program Committee. I fought valiantly for your proposal, but the rest of the Committee did not understand why you wanted to do what you wanted to do because they could not understand (perhaps refused to understand) your proposal. In any case I thought it enormously important and said so to no avail. (I even said I would chair, comment, or read a paper if it would help, but so much for my influence.)" This historian might indeed have been expected to have had some influence, since he was an extensively pub-

I do not think that arguments or forms of hyperbole that were justified fifteen or even ten years ago are still as necessary in order for points to register, and they may now require further qualification and counterargument because of developments in historiography and related areas. In this essay, for example, I have tended to stress the role of affect and empathy—elsewhere I have stressed the role of truth claims—in historiography—not the role of rhetoric or even performativity, although they are indeed important and have intricate connections to affect, empathy, and truth claims. In any case, one has to historicize one's approach to hyperbole and be attentive to the varying uses of, or resistances to, hyperbole over time in the work of an individual, a group, or a profession. On a general level, I would argue that one significant function of hyperbole is to attest—both as symptom and possibly in part as constructive response—to the fact that one is affected by, or at least recognizes the significance of, trauma (or, more generally, excess) and that one empathically responds to it. I would also note that signaled and framed hyperbole is not simply hyperbolic. And one may defend hyperbole while nonetheless countering excess through specific, context-related appeals to normative limits. In any event, a hyperbolic, overly generalized or categorical reading of hyperbole may be unable to take account of its possible value, make distinctions among its uses, or be sensitive to ways in which hyperbole is not unchecked or unqualified.

I intimated earlier that utopian affirmation always goes imaginatively beyond existing experience, hence tends to be hyperbolic. A uniform realism, reasonableness, or discursive style that rejects all hyperbole may be deceptively reassuring. Reality-testing is necessary if utopianism is not to turn into wishful thinking, but a certain systematic realism and reasonableness can itself be an unimaginative form of utopianism that curtails other possibilities, including any disconcerting insight that agitates thought and opens options by going beyond existing experience and what is judged to be reasonable on its basis. As I intimated earlier, it may be useful to shift the defense of realism toward the process of reality-testing in its tense relation to

---

lished, well-established figure at a major research institution with all the *signes extérieurs* of professional legitimacy. That the Program Committee did not consider his defense or my proposal worthy of acceptance is itself a significant statement about the state of the discipline at the time.

the imagination and hyperbole. One might also raise the related issue of the often unsettling role of a traumatic realism that attempts to come to terms with extreme events that call both for a response involving hyperbole and for the articulation of empathic unsettlement with more comprehensive efforts to work through problems.[34]

Objectivity. Here an important issue is the possibility and limits of objectification and the relation of objectification to other modes of signification, notably stylistic variations elicited by the attempt to address traumatic, limit events. Objectification is a process through which the other is positioned as an object of description, analysis, commentary, critique, and experiment. It distances one from the experience of the other, notably in terms of empathic or compassionate understanding, and it restricts one's own experience in the production of knowledge to the process of objectification itself, hence to aloofness and at times ironic or critical detachment. What I earlier termed objectivism carries this process to extremes and makes it the exclusive basis of valid knowledge, particularly within certain disciplinary contexts. It also excludes other countervailing modes of signification. A postpositivist orientation remains neopositivistic if it confines itself to objectification and does not engage the problem of other modes of signification that may complement, be intimately bound up with, and also test objectification as well as place in question the binary opposition between objectivity and subjectivity (or the external and the internal).

Objectification is connected with certain forms of predication generally recognized as conveying knowledge about the other. Processing information is often construed as an objectifying procedure. With respect to extreme or traumatizing events and experiences, objectification not only functions to produce knowledge but also serves as a protective shield for the investigator, which may be necessary in warding off possibly disorienting types of identification. But, in its unmitigated form, it may also impede empathy and affective response in general, thereby putting the investigator in the untenable or at least questionable position of the bystander if not the fully knowledgeable subject (the "subject-supposed-to-know" analyzed and criticized by Lacan). Unmitigated objectification or objectivism may render one

[34] See Michael Rothberg, *Traumatic Realism: The Demands of Holocaust Representation* (Minneapolis: University of Minnesota Press, 2000).

insensitive to the problem of the transferential implication of the investigator in the object of investigation, including the tendency (typically acted out in objectivism) to repeat processes operative in, or projected into, that object.

One always has some tendency to project or to identify (whether positively, negatively, or ambivalently), and one may also be tempted to repress or deny any involvement in the other. Objectivity in a desirable sense should be seen as a process of attempting to counteract identificatory and other phantasmatic tendencies without denying, or believing one can fully transcend, them. Rather, limited but significant objectification should be cogently related to other discursive and signifying possibilities depending on the nature of the object of study and how one is able to negotiate one's own subject positions. Objectification is bound up with reality-testing that does not eliminate affect or involvement in one's responsive attempt to understand the other but may check unmediated identification and related modes of phantasmatic investment, including the sense of being haunted or possessed by the other (something I indicated may be inevitable for victims of trauma and perhaps for those empathically unsettled by their experience). Moreover, the distance required for critical analysis becomes deceptive if it is not itself tested and contested by an empathic attempt at understanding others and their contexts of behavior. The relation between critical analysis and empathic or compassionate response, as well as their articulation with more comprehensive forms of sociopolitical and historical explanation, raises complex questions of language use, voice, and subject position that vary with disciplinary perspectives but are not simply determined by them. In any case, questions of voice, subject position, affect, and empathic response complicate, without simply contradicting, affirmations of realism and objectivity and require a sustained engagement with a set of problems often absent in a restricted epistemological treatment of issues.[35] They also situate the role of experience in knowledge of self and other and thus assist in estimating its significance and limits. Attention to such issues may be the next step in trying to elaborate a postpositivist perspective that critically and fruitfully engages poststructural initiatives.

[35] There is an initial attempt to address issues raised in this section in my *Writing History, Writing Trauma*, esp. chaps. 1 and 6.

CHAPTER TWO

History, Psychoanalysis, Critical Theory

The normative experience for a professional psychoanalyst is the training analysis, which has certain characteristics of a rite of passage. For most historians the normative-experience-cum-rite-of-passage is work in the archives, including the perils of "archive fever." For the literary critic and the philosopher, it is probably some combination of close reading and theoretical reflection. For the anthropologist it has been the field experience, although the disappearance or destruction of the "field" with the advance of global capitalism has turned quite a few recent anthropologists in a textual and theoretical direction. The latter orientation is shared by intellectual and cultural historians whom feverishly archival historians for that reason may consider marginal to the profession, unless intellectual and cultural historians offer primarily contextual accounts of the genesis, functioning, or reception of thought or meaning.[1] Whether scholars in various areas with an interest in psychoanalysis should undertake a training analysis or have clinical experience is an open question. It clearly is not required or normative, and whether it is desirable or diversionary is subject to debate.

[1] My own view is that contextualization is an altogether necessary but not sufficient condition of historical understanding, particularly in intellectual and cultural history, where dialogic and critical issues of reading and response are also pertinent. See my *History and Reading: Tocqueville, Foucault, French Studies* (Toronto: University of Toronto Press, 2000), chap. 1, and *Writing History, Writing Trauma* (Baltimore: Johns Hopkins University Press), chap. 1.

My own interest in psychoanalysis is specific and limited, and, unlike certain members of the postmodern mafia whose *Alltags-geschichte* (everyday life) is chronicled in a famous television series, I have not had the psychoanalytic experience, training or otherwise. Moreover, I would distinguish the approach I am exploring from standard forms of psychohistory that apply psychoanalytic theories or concepts to individuals or groups in the past, for example, by analyzing Max Weber's Oedipal complex or the aggressive fantasies of the *Freikorps* or the Nazi youth cohort.[2] Nor do I attempt to provide psychoanalytic readings of historical events or cultural artifacts in a manner that is by and large theory-driven and inadequately informed by the procedures, concerns, and substantive research of professional historians. My "metahistorical" interest is rather in creating a mutually informative and challenging exchange between psychoanalysis and historiography as a process of inquiry, especially one that renders history more self-reflexive and self-critical in its approach to problems.[3]

I would also maintain that it is mistaken to believe that psychoanalytic concepts apply first and foremost to individuals and not at all or only by analogy to collectivities. Such a belief attests to the power of individualistic ideologies, which are in fact often existentially accompanied by extreme dependence on others, particularly in times of crisis. The basic concepts of psychoanalysis are pertinent—and problematic—in comparable ways with respect to individuals and collectivities. (This assertion applies to the concepts on which I later focus: transference, trauma, acting-out, and working-through.) In other words, they undercut the standard opposition between the individual and the collectivity, may help us to rethink that opposition, and are to variable degrees applicable in individuated or collective ways

---

[2] For a particularly thought-provoking approach to psychohistory, see Klaus Theweleit, *Male Fantasies*, trans. Erica Carter and Chris Turner in Collaboration with Stephen Conway, 2 vols. (1978; Minneapolis: University of Minnesota Press, 1987, 1989). There are many contestable elements in Theweleit's own theoretical and political assumptions, particularly the notion that one may viably oppose fascist rigidity and paranoid fantasies through an uncritical reliance on a utopian, Deleuzian conception of anarchistic, flowing, indiscriminate desire.

[3] The notion of metahistory I am invoking, in its emphasis on the dialogic, mutually questioning relation between theory and historical practice, is different from the more formalistic and constructivist view in Hayden White, *Metahistory: The Historical Imagination in Nineteenth-Century Europe* (Baltimore: Johns Hopkins University Press, 1973).

depending on contexts and situations.[4] Such a conception of basic psychoanalytic concepts is epistemological. It does not rely on the belief in a biologically transmitted "archaic heritage" or on the idea that ontogeny recapitulates phylogeny. It is also not based on a simple, typically shaky, analogy between the individual and society.

In a manner showing certain similarities to Freud's "talking cure," especially with respect to the attempt to work through problems, historiography itself may in significant measure be understood as an exchange or complex dialogue both with the past and with others inquiring into that past.[5] One of the key concepts to describe the ways in which such an exchange functions is *transference*. My use of the concept is revisionary and easily misunderstood when construed in more or less orthodox Freudian terms. Without excluding the significance of interpersonal or intergroup relations (for example, those between teachers and students), by "transference" I mean primarily one's implication in the other or the object of study with the tendency to repeat in one's own discourse or practice tendencies active in, or projected into, the other or object. For example, one may have a ritualistic, phobic response to ritual, may replicate a scapegoat mechanism in an analysis of scapegoating, may repeat Nazi terminology in an analysis of Nazism, or may manifest fanaticism in a critique of religion. This dimension of transference is, I think, less developed in the literature than the interpersonal bond, which is often seen in Oedipal terms and centered overmuch on the relation between psychoanalyst and analysand.

Transferential processes are most pronounced and difficult to manage with respect to the most traumatic, affectively charged, or "cathected" issues, for example, the Holocaust, slavery, or (until recently in France) the French Revolution (more recently, Vichy or the

---

[4] For a limited attempt to analyze in psychoanalytic terms the mutually reinforcing, more or less collective responses of certain scholars to the discovery of Paul de Man's wartime journalism, see my "Paul de Man as Object of Transference," in *Representing the Holocaust: History, Theory, Trauma* (Ithaca: Cornell University Press, 1994), chap. 4.

[5] Unlike Freud, I do not rely on the concepts of normality and pathology but object to the way they encrypt unargued normative assumptions that typically conflate normativity with normalization (or take as normative the statistically prevalent or dominant, for example, heterosexuality or the family). Instead I insist on the need to make normative concepts and orientations explicit and subject to criticism. Any analogue of therapy would share this insistence and be directed primarily at collectively pertinent forms of working through problems.

Algerian war). I think that clinical, Oedipally centered transference is best understood as a subcase of this broader tendency to repeat. Although Oedipal relations have an obvious importance in a society in which the nuclear family remains important, transference extends beyond the Oedipal relationship. Indeed its confinement within that scenario (or within the analytic context that relates psychoanalyst and analysand) amounts to a domestication or territorialization that may well divert attention from one's implication in broader problems, institutions, and social relations that extend beyond but of course do not exclude, and even help to shape, the family.

One might, however, contend that the range of applicability of the concept of transference is limited insofar as it does not apply to psychosis. If one agrees with this Freudian view, one may, with a touch of irony, conclude that transference does not apply either to psychotic objects of research or to psychotic historians doing research. My own inclination is not to make use of pathologizing concepts that typically encrypt normative judgments but instead to insist on the role of norms (in historical understanding and elsewhere) and to attempt to make those norms explicit and thereby open to critical inspection, discussion, and debate. One may, however, reformulate the possible limits of transference in nonpathologizing language by raising the question of whether there are—or may be—aspects of the other that in their opacity are on first encounter inaccessible to transference and empathy (for example, with respect to the polar, extreme cases of the *Muselmann* or abject victim reduced to living death, and the perpetrator who fashions conditions in concentration and death camps that lead to the emergence of the *Muselmann*). This possibility of blocked transference with respect to limit cases and experiences may induce dubious projective identification, as in the approach of Giorgio Agamben with respect to the *Muselmann* or Daniel Jonah Goldhagen with respect to perpetrators (phantasmatically seen through the eyes of victims).[6] This possibility may also be obscured or covertly generalized in the tendency of neopositivists and at times structuralists and formalists to deny or dismiss out of hand the very notion of transference and rely instead on a one-sidedly objectifying methodology often

[6] See Giorgio Agamben, *Remnants of Auschwitz: The Witness and the Archive*, trans. Daniel Heller-Roazen (New York: Zone Books, 1999); and Daniel Jonah Goldhagen, *Hitler's Willing Executioners: Ordinary Germans and the Holocaust* (New York: Alfred A. Knopf, 1996). I discuss Goldhagen's book in *Writing History, Writing Trauma*, chap. 4.

simplistically identified with critical, secular rationality. Such denial conveniently occludes certain problems both personal and professional, including the self-reflexive question of how research procedures are bound up with practices of identity formation, for example, an identity as a professional historian or an objectifying structural analyst.

Forms of objectification may well be necessary for research in the valid attempt to reconstruct the past. Moreover, dialogic exchange, which calls for critical self-reflection, and reconstruction of the past or the object, which requires research and related conventional procedures of professional historiography, are complementary but at times tensely related aspects of historical understanding. Especially with respect to charged, value-laden, extremely difficult topics or disconcerting limit events, objectification may even be necessary for the protection of the researcher, particularly in resisting the tendency to take transference to the point of identification with the object of study and hence to compulsively relive what others have experienced. There may well be a tendency to identify with the victim and undergo secondary traumatization and surrogate victimage, or even to identify (perhaps unconsciously) with the perpetrator and exacerbate one's own tendencies toward victimization of others. One may of course also identify with more complex, ambiguous figures in Primo Levi's gray zone and go so far as to project their plight into a rashly generalized paradoxicalism, zone of indistinction, or double-bind sensibility (as does Giorgio Agamben). But these tendencies should not in my judgment simply be indulged. Nor should the necessary resistance to them and the generation of counterforces lead to the opposite extreme of objectification devoid of affect, self-implication, and empathic response.

Empathic or compassionate response may be seen as distinguishable from incorporative or projective identification and as involving a heteropathic mode of identification in which the difference between self and other is recognized. However it is figured, empathy, in the sense I am using the term, takes one out of oneself toward the other without eliminating or assimilating the difference or alterity of the other. It is in this sense "ecstatic" rather than being a projection of what one has experienced onto the other. Neither should empathy be conflated with an incorporation of the other into one's own (narcissistic) self or understood instrumentally as a means of discovering one's own "authentic" identity. On the contrary, it induces one to recognize one's internal alterity or difference from oneself—one's own opacities and gaps that prevent full identity or self-knowledge and prompt a readiness to temper, qualify, or even in certain cases suspend judgment of the other. Empathy in this sense is enabled by internal alterity (or the unconscious) and based on one's being open to the other, who is constitutive of the formation of oneself. It is not a facile passe-partout but an affect crucial for a possible ethical relation to the other and hence for one's responsibility or answerability. The notion of conscience as the call of the other in oneself (recapitulated in the notion of the superego and its relation to the affect-laden or "cathected" voice and injunctions of the parents) attests to the constitutive relation to the other. So does the need of a witness in order that a testimony or act of bearing witness be effective or even possible. It is this need that helps validate the notion of a secondary witness—a witness to the witness, a witness who does not speak for the witness or simply identify with the victim in becoming a surrogate victim. More broadly, empathy is one significant dimension of moral affect or sentiment that is often ignored in overly abstract, objectifying, legalistic, or rule-bound conceptions of ethics (notably those in the Kantian tradition). It should also be related to an understanding of affective and ethical response that does not substitute for sociopolitical action but instead is viably articulated with it.

Objectification of an extreme sort is found both in neopositivism and in formalism, which, on other levels, may be opposed, for example, in the standoff between neopositivistic historians and someone like Hayden White when he espouses a relativistic, radical, but objectifying constructivism in which all structures or modes of emplotment are seen as fictive projections of the historical mind, and the object or the past is reduced to raw material that itself poses no resistance to the constructivist or form-giving—but seemingly affectless, information-processing—imagination of the historian. What neopositivism and formalism may also share is both a certain type of ironic distance, which masks or denies one's investment in the object of study, and a misdirected skepticism, especially with respect to the use of such concepts as transference and trauma, at least insofar as they address unconscious and affective dimensions of experience—a skepticism that may make valuable critical questioning slide indiscriminately into querulousness.

At the same time one should recognize that transference is related to a certain excess in relations between self and other that calls for understanding and representation yet is not fully open to mastery or knowledge. In this sense one cannot say exactly what one means by transference if by "exactly" one means a definition or set of criteria that provide surefire methodological procedures, adequate knowledge, and a full grasp of the problems involved. Such a definition of transference would eliminate the problem of transference. One can only be as precise and comprehensive as the problems allow. And one can also call for greater reflection and self-reflection about them on the part of those implicated in them—reflection that may revise, supplement, or contest one's own formulations and even lead one to change one's mind. This transferential excess perforce produces anxiety and, in its extreme form, raises the problems of traumatization and of more or less questionable attempts to transfigure it into a sublime or apocalyptic revelation. But anxiety may also be validated as fostering self-questioning and preventing disciplinary identity from reaching illusory closure. It may also prompt one to raise the question of how certain problems exceed or cut across existing disciplines and whether they call for a reformulation or transformation of disciplines and, at the limit, a cross- or even transdisciplinary mode of thought.

The relation between excess and normative limits is, I think, a crucial (if not the crucial) problem of ethics (including professional ethics), and the way one attempts to bind or control transference through normative limits is of the utmost importance. Hence psychoanalysis in the clinical setting includes the normative requirement that there not be a sexual involvement between analyst and analysand during the professional relation, and one of the most serious ethical charges against a psychoanalyst is that he or she abuses transference and the power it brings over someone in a vulnerable position. Something like transference is operative in the teacher/student relation and serves to raise the issue of an ethics of sexual relations between a teacher and his or her students. And there is a sense in which the ethics of transference is at issue in appropriative, radically constructivist refashionings or uses of the past, which might be seen as an abuse of interpretive power or an extreme disempowerment of the object of study—at the very least an unwillingness to listen to and possibly learn from the other, however much one's understanding of past texts or phenomena is transformed by belated recognitions. Of course it would be illusory to believe one could—or even should try to—eliminate all transferential dynamics in relations with others, and interpretations or readings that open newer perspectives perforce have an active, participatory, performative dimension. Still, one may call for a greater caution and sense of responsibility with respect to transference and insist on the role of normative processes involving limits that to some extent control—without ever fully mastering—its operation and effects.

The analogue to a responsible coming-to-terms with transference in relation to the object of study would be the heuristic readiness and the obligation to be attentive to the manner in which the object can in some sense answer one back and pose resistances to the interpretations or fashionings one would like to make of it. The less metaphoric analogue of this process is the willingness to engage the different, at times markedly divergent, approaches others take to a set of problems, whether they be inquirers in the same or in different fields. (Past approaches need not be reduced to objects of antiquarian interest, and the relevant reference group should not be restricted to the living or to the most recent contributors to a line of inquiry, as is often the case in professional historiography and seminars on methodology.) Such attentiveness and willingness are components of a dialogic relation with the object or the other that tries to stave off abusive readings or interpretations. A sign of excessive professionalization of a discipline is the unwillingness to take seriously and try to come to terms with the views of commentators or critics who are not within one's own guild, and such a tendency may mark both epistemologically conservative scholars and those who take themselves to be radical or avant-garde. One might even argue that there should be internalized ethical limits and resistances to the ability of any strong methodology or reading technology to simply reprocess the object of study in its terms—to become an all-purpose tool or intellectual Cuisinart. Especially with respect to high-intensity problems having a collective dimension, these limits and resistances have an obvious political or ethicopolitical valence. Neopositivism explicitly attempts to eliminate but may merely conceal the responsive dimension of understanding, while radical formalism or constructivism tends to be "responsive" to the point of overwriting or not listening attentively to the other—not recognizing limits or resistances, even rationalizing a disregard for them through a legitimation of a will-to-power, appropriative, or unchecked performative dynamics. The latter stresses only strategies of deployment and presentist uses and functions, for example, those related to contemporary political or aesthetic interests.[7] At the limit the past is reduced to raw material or ground down into a kind of particleboard or Chicken McNugget subjected to our power and contemporary desires or ideologies.

I would argue that readings or interpretations, to the extent they claim to be relevant to historical understanding, must recognize the resistances posed by the object of study—indeed the way it heuristically may be said to answer one back—and not take performativity to the point of "free" variations that take a past text or phenomenon as little more than a pretext for one's own undoings and refashionings. But a normative sense of legitimate limits does not in itself determine the status of framed stylizations, reorientations, rewritings, or even riff-like improvisations in which a text is explicitly taken as an other in an interaction or intervention. Such an approach, common in Derrida or Barthes, may provide newer insights into the object or add something of interest on the level of the rewriting or refashioning itself. Still, one's response to active rewritings or refashionings can raise ethical, aesthetic, and political issues that might differ by situation or discipline. For example, there is a difference between rewriting Hegel to accentuate submerged aspects of his thought and rewriting the ideologically saturated, early antisemitic journalistic articles of Paul de Man to show that they are *really* self-deconstructive and even close to resistance. A further issue is raised when a reorientation or rewriting is not explicitly framed but simply enacted as one's reading. Here the question, to which there is no simple answer, is what is required of an attempt to work through a transferential relation in a critical and self-critical manner—rather than simply enact it or act it out. Such a question should at the very least create a self-critical hesitancy in the way one reads texts or analyzes problems as well as make one sensitive to the problematic nature of conflating performativity with the acting-out of an unmedi-

---

[7] One finds this tendency in Hayden White's "The Politics of Historical Interpretation: Discipline and De-Sublimation," *Critical Inquiry* 9 (1982), reprinted as chap. 3 in *The Content of the Form: Narrative Discourse and Historical Representation* (Baltimore: Johns Hopkins University Press, 1987). One also finds it in Bill Readings, *The University in Ruins* (Cambridge: Harvard University Press, 1996).

ated "writerly" or "creatively" free-indirect response, including one that goes with the flow of desire.

The transferential relation helps one to understand the so-called contagiousness of trauma—the way it can spread even to the interviewer or commentator. But "contagiousness" is a medicalized concept and as such is dubious. I think its mechanism is the process of projective and/or incorporative (perhaps altogether confused) identification. Hence identification is crucial in transferential relations in general and especially in the accentuated case of trauma both for its victims and in various and different ways for those relating to them. One may even come to relive or reexperience posttraumatic symptoms of events (such as the Holocaust or slavery) one never lived through. This reliving (or secondary traumatization) sometimes happens to children of victims or perpetrators, and the transmission of trauma may occur in largely unconscious ways, notably when certain events become secrets (at times more or less open secrets) and are not explicitly discussed.[8] To some extent it may even occur in those who at some level desire to be victims or to identify with them, for example, in different ways in Claude Lanzmann as interviewer and filmmaker in *Shoah* and in Binjamin Wilkormirski as "wannabe" Holocaust survivor and author of the false memoir *Fragments: Memories of a Wartime Childhood*.[9] And it is a possibility for someone who is in intimate contact with traumatized victims, and even for those who work closely with texts or films conveying their experience.

It is often very difficult for an intimate of a victim to work through secondary trauma. But an empathic relation to the other on the part of a historian or other analyst or commentator, which brings a certain necessary unsettlement (what I term empathic unsettlement), need not lead to identification, secondary traumatization, or surrogate victimage. Such identification and suffering are moving and may even be seen as sublimely beyond ethical or political judgment. Certainly, a nonsurvivor is in no position to comment critically on the response of a survivor who has such a relation to lost intimates or friends and who may even experience a posttraumatic "symptom," such as a recurrent nightmare, as a memorial or gift that binds one to lost others. But survivors may move to some extent beyond victimhood

[8] See Nicolas Abraham and Maria Torok, *The Shell and the Kernel*, vol. 1, ed. and trans. Nicholas Rand (1987; Chicago: University of Chicago Press, 1994).

[9] Trans. Carol Brown Janeway (1995; New York: Schocken Books, 1996).

or even the status of witnesses to suffering or abjection by becoming engaged in social and political activity. And there is a question whether identification with the traumatized victim and the assumption of the position of witness are sufficient for the nonsurvivor (or one born later). Such identification, even the role of witness if it becomes all-consuming, may exclude forms of social responsibility and political activity that are incumbent on someone who is fortunate enough not to have lived through certain extreme, traumatizing events. Of course any unqualified judgment is out of place in such a fraught area of feeling, thought, and behavior, and within oneself there may well be an interaction of contending forces that varies over time.

Still, other responses should not be denigrated, and forms of working through the past need not be seen dismissively as signs of insensitivity or of a dubious ideal of total health or ego identity. In those traumatized by their experience of extreme events and even in those empathically responding to them, at times to the point of identification, working-through may never transcend acting-out or reliving the past, and any unilinear schema of achieving "health" or a "cure" would be deceptive. Working-through may nonetheless render possible forms of activity that relate witnessing or giving testimony to broader sociopolitical processes that are oriented to achieving desirable change, including the elimination of contexts conducive to the oppression and traumatization of discrete, typically scapegoated groups of victims. Moreover, one may see performativity both in relation to a complex, critical notion of working-through and in a necessary relation to the constative, contextualizing, representational dimension of understanding involving research and critical thought and practice. Indeed the idea of pure performativity as found in extreme, radical constructivism amounts to a kind of secular creationism in which the powers of a transcendent divinity are transferred to humans, who are deceptively endowed with abilities to create ex nihilo, to transfigure disempowerment or abjection into sublimity, and to transcend or annihilate the past, at times in an apocalyptic manner that repeatedly calls for the coming of the utterly new or the radically other. I would suggest that, while it may never fully transcend acting-out and the repetition compulsion, working-through involves another modality of performativity more closely bound up with respect for the alterity of the other (which itself need not be seen as total otherness) and with critical thought and practice, including a critical relation to the self (or the group) and its desires and ambitions.

Recognizing transferential tendencies should ideally enable one to resist uncritical identification with the other and the derivation of one's identity from others in ways that deny their otherness. Such identification occurs when one becomes a mimetic disciple projectively reprocessing phenomena or texts in terms of a methodology or reading technology. Recognizing the force of, and trying to come to terms with, transference also enables one to appreciate both the insistence of tendencies toward identification and the limitations of objectification that ignores such tendencies, forecloses the problem of the investigator's subject positions, and denies the other's voice and the questions it poses for oneself and one's approach. Here a crucial issue is the extent to which one comes to terms with transference through acting-out and working-through.

I would like to turn to an important recent book that helps to render more concrete and bring into focus the issues I have touched on concerning the relation of history to psychoanalysis and critical theory: Ruth Leys's *Trauma: A Genealogy*.[10] Although I shall attempt to indicate some of its contestable features, I think this book is an altogether basic contribution that must be engaged by those studying, or even making use of the concept of, trauma. In contrast to the approach I elaborate, Leys does not explicitly employ psychoanalytic concepts in her own voice. For her purposes, she treats them only as objects of analysis, and she does not explore the relations between history and critical theory in general. In appealing to Foucauldian genealogy for guidance, she asserts that "as a historian or genealogist of trauma my project has been to reveal and investigate the tensions inherent in the mimetic-antimimetic structure, without for a moment attempting to settle those tensions or—except in the most general way—to take sides. . . . By the same token, the argument of my book does not yield a meta-position from which to assess the messy and intrinsically painful conundrums of the field" (306–7). Hence, like Foucault, Leys keeps psychoanalysis at a distance and does not fully articulate the relations between it and her own approach to problems. But, unlike Foucault (and like many historians), she feels it is not incumbent on her to elaborate a theoretical perspective and to think through the

[10] (Chicago: University of Chicago Press, 2000).

problems she treats in order to work out a better articulation of their assumptions and possibilities. (Whether one terms this perspective a meta-position or not, one need not see it as a dubious form of "taking sides".)

The absence of an explicit inquiry into the implications of psychoanalysis for one's own project brings with it the risk of a relatively unself-conscious enactment of transferential relations. In Leys's case, one form this enactment takes is the use of symptomatic dimensions of trauma, and of certain theories of trauma, as unmediated components of her own analytic framework, to wit, the categories of the mimetic and the antimimetic. Perhaps understandably given its goals, the book also eliminates the more tangled yet self-questioning theoretical or philosophical dimensions of Foucault in order to adapt him to a history of concepts and disciplinary or subdisciplinary constellations.[11] In general it bases its impressive reading and research on analytic or theoretical assumptions that may not have undergone sufficient critical scrutiny. And, at least from a certain perspective, a principal omission is any sustained exploration of the concept of working-through and the way it could have implications for historiography that has an explicit, dialogic relation to psychoanalysis and critical theory.

Leys clearly sees the way theories of trauma themselves displace or repeat, with more or less significant and distinctive variations, the features of their object, trauma itself. But she does not explore the question of her own inevitable implication in that process or how to respond to it. In not explicitly and critically exploring the question of transferential implication in the object of study along with the need to work through that implication, Leys is led to draw what would seem to be a fatalistic conclusion from her research: "Current debates over trauma are fated to end in an impasse, for the simple reason that they are the inescapable outcome of the mimetic-antimimetic oscillation that has determined the field of trauma studies throughout this century" (305). Participating in the more or less self-conscious tendency to relegate one's own approach to a form of enlightened disempowerment, Leys, from a seemingly secure vantage point in

[11] For an attempt to explore more fully this problem with special reference to Foucault's *Histoire de la folie*, see my *History and Reading: Tocqueville, Foucault, French Studies*, chap. 3.

science studies, confines trauma studies (like trauma itself) to symptomatic acting-out and excludes any attempt to work through problems in a manner that would not simply be tantamount to compulsively repetitive or "fated" oscillation. Such a gesture restricts her ability to elicit aspects of the history she tells and the thought of figures she treats that might contribute to that attempt, including the very concept of working-through itself. Moreover, although she appears to be deconstructing or even debunking the concept of trauma to a degree that might seem to jeopardize any viable use of it, she nonetheless wants to affirm the importance of trauma as an experience in those undergoing it and to resist the extension of the concept in ways she plausibly sees as misguided or fraudulent. She even begins the book with a Foucauldian shock effect: a stark contrast between kidnapped and abused children in Uganda who can be said to have really been traumatized and Paula Jones in her questionable if not utterly specious appeal to PTSD (posttraumatic stress disorder) and demand for compensation for Bill Clinton's alleged sexual harassment.

What is the mimetic/antimimetic polarity that both structures the story she recounts and provides the analytic framework for Leys's own narrative account? Mimesis is identification to the point of identity with the other and full absorption in the traumatic experience. Identification here is the very mechanism of trauma, and the victim may be deceived about events but, on the mimetic theory, not a conscious liar. Or if there is lying or "fabrication," it is constitutive of traumatic experience. Antimimetic theories present trauma as befalling a passive but sovereign, conscious subject who is the victim of some purely external event such as a train accident but who may also theatrically simulate or even fake trauma.

Here is a portion of Leys's own summary of the mimetic theory:

> The first or *mimetic* theory holds that trauma, or the experience of the traumatized subject, can be understood as involving a kind of hypnotic imitation or identification in which, precisely because the victim cannot recall the original traumatogenic event, she is fated to act it out or in other ways imitate it. The idea is that the traumatic experience in its sheer extremity, its affront to common norms and expectations, shatters or disables the victim's cognitive and perceptual capacities so that the experience never becomes part of the ordinary memory system.

She continues:

> An aspect of the mimetic theory that should be stressed is that it leads
> to doubts about the veracity of the victim's testimony: to the extent that
> the traumatic occurrence is considered never to have become part of
> the victim's ordinary memory, it is unclear how she can truthfully
> testify to what befell her. There is even a sense in which she cannot
> quite be said to have experienced the trauma in question (another way
> of putting this is to say that the victim is imagined as having been
> absent from the traumatic event). Moreover, because the victim is
> understood as traumatized into a state of imitative-hypnotic
> suggestibility, the mimetic theory cannot escape worrying about the
> question of hypnotic suggestion and the "fabrication" of more or less
> false memories. Finally, since the mimetic theory posits a moment of
> identification with the aggressor, the victim is imagined as
> incorporating and therefore sharing the feelings of hostility directed
> toward herself. (298–99)

Here is Leys on the polar opposite, the antimimetic theory:

> The second, or *antimimetic*, theory also tends to make imitation basic to
> the traumatic experience, but it understands imitation differently. The
> mimetic notion that the victim is hypnotically immersed in the scene of
> trauma is repudiated in favor of the antithetical idea that in hypnotic
> imitation the subject is essentially aloof from the traumatic experience,
> in the sense that she remains a spectator of the traumatic scene, which
> she can therefore see and represent to herself and others. The
> antimimetic theory is compatible with, and often gives way to, the idea
> that trauma is a purely external event that befalls a fully constituted
> subject; whatever the damage to the latter's psychical autonomy and
> integrity, there is in principle no problem of eventually remembering or
> otherwise recovering the event, though in practice the process of
> bringing this about may be long and tortuous. And in contrast to the
> mimetic theory's assumption of an identification with the aggressor, the
> antimimetic theory depicts violence as purely and simply an assault
> from without. (299)

Are these really two theories or at best two partial descriptions of
the more or less dissociated aspects of a traumatized person's expe-

rience? In any case, it would seem that, until they reach the point of mutual exclusivity and extreme assertion, the two putative theories replicate one of the two split-off dimensions of traumatic experience itself: the disempowered, infantlike self that experiences or feels without being able to represent, is trancelike or "hypnotically" suggestible, and tends to identify with the aggressor; and the spectatorial, objectifying (possibly aggressive or sadomasochistic) self that numbly or, in a sense, objectifyingly represents the event without being able to feel. Although I make no pretense to a God's-eye metaposition, I do not find it impossible for a more comprehensive "theory" of trauma to account for and situate as symptomatic the mimetic and the antimimetic perspectives, notably with respect to the elusive experience of trauma, with its intrusive and uncontrollable aftereffects, and the possibility of an objectifying, aloof representation of the traumatizing event. Moreover, the very polarity of the opposition is threatened not only by the fact that each pole may characterize one (unstable) side of a traumatized person's situation or plight but because theatricality or performativity (as well as sadomasochistic aggressivity) falls on both sides of the polarity, albeit as quasi-hypnotic, absorptive performativity (or being fully into one's role) in one case and uninvolved, rhetorically distant, lucidly theatrical performativity in the other.[12]

The polar opposites of Leys's own theoretical framework, the mimetic and the antimimetic, are employed in a manner that may obscure the role of concepts and processes that have a more critical, less symptomatic, relation to the difficult problems she treats. I have mentioned working-through (which, unlike acting-out, does not appear in Leys's index, although there are a few references to it in the text). Leys can get at the problem of the actual or phantasmal status of the traumatic event (which beleaguered Freud in his so-called seduction theory) only through the opposition between mimetic and

---

[12] One of course has here a replication of the classical "paradox" of the actor or comedian who may be seen either as entirely "into" or identified with his role or as playing it in a distant, aloof manner (or both in some obscure or oscillating manner). One may also note that the approach in Leys's last two chapters is significantly different from that in the rest of the book, which tends to be more objectifying and detached. In treating Bessel van der Kolk and Cathy Caruth, however, Leys's response is extremely judgmental and affectively charged. Although aspects of the work of van der Kolk and Caruth may be subject to criticism, Leys does not acknowledge that they too may be grappling with intractable problems in ways that may have valuable or instructive dimensions.

antimimetic theories, with the actual event relegated to the antimimetic side of the polarity. But the issue of the status and effects of traumatic (or "traumatogenic") events also arises with respect to issues grouped under the mimetic pole. For example, is trauma generally more severe when there is an actual and not only a phantasmal event, even if one maintains that there must be some phantasmatic investment for an event to become traumatic? Moreover, is acting out or compulsive repetition of posttraumatic symptoms equally likely in mimetic and antimimetic responses? Is it less subject to criticism (at times even suspending it) when it occurs in analytic sessions or, in a different register, in the art or writing of traumatized individuals or, at times, their intimates than when it is manifested in secondary-witness or third-party activities (say, those of a filmmaker or commentator) or in certain areas of public life (for example, in politics or social action)? Are the responses of victims or survivors more open to critical analysis when they comment on media events or aspects of public life than when they address their own experience and how they try to cope with it? In these respects, one may also note that Leys may not devote sufficient attention to identification and alternatives to it with respect to the issue of postmemory (the acquired memory of experiences one did not oneself live through) and the related questions of posttraumatic symptoms in those who did not directly experience the traumatic events, including the different cases of intimates of trauma victims, therapists, and "wannabe" survivors. She treats in a justifiably critical manner only the dubious, indiscriminate generalization of trauma to the post-Holocaust world.

I would also mention the problem of the transhistorical (or structural) and historical dimensions of trauma.[13] Leys interestingly touches on this problem when she writes: "What is striking about them [theories of trauma] is their irruptive character; when the same or similar issues recur, they do so as if for the first time and almost with the same quality of shock or disruption that has been attributed to trauma itself, though of course it is also true that each episode bears the distinctive imprint of its historical moment. Throughout this study I try to do justice to the historical specificity of the cruxes I discuss. But my approach, by avoiding the assumptions implicit in a continuous narrative, enables us to see what is recurrent, and in an important sense structural, in the difficulties and contradictions that

[13] I try to address this problem in *Writing History, Writing Trauma*, chap. 2.

have tormented conceptualizations of trauma throughout the century" (10).

In the terms I have myself been using, theories of trauma have a transferential relation to the dynamics of trauma, which they often tend compulsively to repeat or act out rather than work through. And a crucial problem is to distinguish analytically and trace the articulations between transhistorical (or structural) and historical dimensions of trauma. Leys's own analysis might be extended into an attempt to trace these articulations and to indicate the importance of working-through as well as to point to the role of working-through in certain theories that provide clues to counteracting acting-out and the force of the repetition compulsion. In certain ways Freud attempted to provide such articulations, notably in the very concept of working-through, even though he did not devote to the latter the theoretical attention it warranted.

Here one may also mention Leys's extremely valuable discussion of a dimension of Sándor Ferenczi's thought: his notions of originary and postoriginary trauma (which to some extent may be mapped onto the transhistorical and historical dimensions of trauma). Leys sees Ferenczi as caught up in slippage between these concepts rather than able to articulate their relations. One might point out that in any specific event or case, the two do intermingle and that the distinction is analytic but nonetheless important for critical understanding and even for social and political action. The confusion of the two may, for example, lead to the impossible quest for a return to the putative originary, pretraumatic condition of full unity, identity, or communion, for example, by way of apocalyptic politics or social action—action that may turn violent and traumatizing, notably through the attempt to get rid of groups to which the obstruction or prevention of such originary identity is falsely and projectively imputed. In Ferenczi the originary trauma was the abrupt move out of the assumed pretraumatic state of identity or identification with the mother into the subject/object split and relation. (Of course the originary condition of identity with the mother may itself be seen as a phantasmatic projection from the postoriginary position whereby an absence of full identity is construed as a loss or lack with respect to some imaginary, presumably originary, pretraumatic condition.)

The postoriginary (or historical) trauma in Ferenczi would, paradoxically, be a violent return to the putative originary condition of identity that now shatters the articulations of the postoriginary world, including the subject/object relation and the ability to predicate, make judgments, and be an agent with any degree of credibility. Hence the postoriginary trauma might induce both the victim's "regressive" self-identification as helpless infant (which Leys does not explore) and identification with the perpetrator or aggressor inflicting injury on the victimized self. This dual identification might further be related to a splitting or dissociation of the self between the victim who (like an infant) could feel or experience traumatic suffering without knowing or representing it and the "numbed" self who could objectifyingly (perhaps aggressively) represent the traumatic event without feeling it on an experiential level. Moreover, the traumatized person would be uncertain about his or her own judgments and credibility, rein-forcing the suspicion that the victim was self-deceived if not a liar and that the experience was faked. The hypnotic, suggestible condition of the traumatized victim facilitates identification, and the use of hyp-notic therapy could at best get the victim to act out (real or phantas-mal) trauma. I would add that the reliance on hypnotic, cathartic, or abreactive therapy alone tends to conflate acting-out with working-through, and Freud's rejection of hypnosis was related to his realiza-tion that acting-out was not sufficient for working through problems. However, one might argue, as Ferenczi was inclined to do, that abre-action (a "cathartic" feature of acting-out) enables the release of fixated affectivity and in this way is necessary (albeit not sufficient) for the process of working through trauma, or more precisely, post-traumatic symptoms.

I have reformulated Leys's account of Ferenczi in a manner that accentuates certain of its dimensions. The reformulation enables one to resolve or at least get a different perspective on something she tends to see in terms of pure aporia or even contradiction when she asks: "Why did Ferenczi's project reach such an impasse? A close reading of his *Clinical Diary* demands that we confront at least two possibilities: (1) The nature of trauma is such that it can never be con-sciously experienced and hence remembered; (2) Hysterics tend to lie, which is why the truth of their pasts can never be known with confi-dence" (124).

The second possibility leads to the theory of trauma as simulation that is brought about in a purely conscious and performative manner in the very diagnostic and therapeutic relation between therapist and patient (a kind of simulated *folie à deux*). This of course takes one in the direction of the recovered memory syndrome. It also takes one to the later, antipsychoanalytic thought of Mikkel Borch-Jacobsen, who holds a special place in Leys's account. Leys, however, is closer to the early Borch-Jacobsen with his notion of unconscious identification or mimesis, which his later thought repudiates, denies, or forecloses. Leys at times suggests that the suspicion of fraudulence concerning the traumatized may be related to their own self-doubts and incredulity about the things that happened to them—things that at times they can hardly bring themselves to believe. Of course the problem remains of whether the events in question actually happened in historical reality or were phantasmal. As I noted, Leys may not highlight this problem even though it is intimately related to the issues she discusses, in good part because her attention is directed at the mimetic/antimimetic polarity.

Leys does devote sustained attention to the first possibility she finds in Ferenczi—the possibility that trauma as such "can never be consciously experienced and hence remembered"—which seems to pose an irresolvable dilemma. As she puts it with reference to Ferenczi: "As he recognized, by the very terms of his own analysis, a patient who attempted to heal her split state by verbally narrating or representing the event to herself and others could achieve a conscious, *intellectual* knowledge of the event, but such knowledge necessarily lacked the *affective* experience required to give it validity. By the same token, if she attempted to reexperience the emotions associated with' the trauma by sinking into a trance state, she felt the suffering involved but on 'waking' had no confidence in the reality of the reexperienced or reconstructed trauma" (133–34).

Here one may note a number of issues. It is interesting that when Leys refers to trauma victims, especially in cases when she takes trauma as an appropriate term for the experience, the victim is gendered as feminine. (The intellectual and ideological implications of this gesture are unclear: does it follow common forms of reversal in pronomial usage, reinforce unfortunate stereotypes of abjection with respect to women, highlight victimizing tendencies in men, or have other significations?) In addition, the concept of "validity" is curious when applied to the reliving of affective experience in cases where it amounts to excruciating suffering, and where the "confidence" of the person reexperiencing trauma would be directed at the "reality" of the event, not at the experience. Leys herself, in referring to trauma, often tends to use "event" and "experience" interchangeably in a manner that may be confusing. The above passage is useful in this respect. A trauma victim may remember *events* in a conscious manner related to the split-off self that numbly perceived the events while they occurred. But one may only act out or compulsively repeat the *experienced affect* in the manner of the disempowered victim who returns to the condition of the helpless infant. One might suggest that working through the trauma requires the ability to empathize with, or feel compassion for, oneself as victim in the past, but it should not simply be collapsed into full identification with that fixated, anguished "self" and the endless reliving of its affect or experience.

Working-through, in its complex, nonlinear relations to acting-out or compulsive repetition, is a difficult, undertheorized concept, especially in academic approaches to psychoanalysis. Here I would note that, with respect to trauma, one should not conflate working-through with the impossible attempt to consciously remember and fully master the affective experience that was not fully conscious at the time of the traumatizing events—indeed to square the circle by somehow fully transforming such affect into cognition or a narrative memory. Nor does working-through provide a specious integration of representation and the affect involved in traumatic experience. Rather working-through involves work on posttraumatic symptoms, specifically, the attempt to counteract their compulsive repetition by generating counterforces to them (including the ability to distinguish—not dichotomize—between past and present with nonfatalistic openings to the future). In other words, it requires the achieved ability to make certain distinctions as well as to explore ways in which they are problematic. It also involves attempting to link or integrate representation and affect in the present and future—an attempt that in the severely traumatized may call for repeated effort because of the inability to fully overcome the dissociation and the tendency to act out related to trauma. In this sense the notion of working through trauma is somewhat misleading shorthand if it leads one to believe that one can fully overcome or transcend trauma by bringing together or integrating what was split apart in the past and that one can rewrite history or make it appear as if the traumatic had never happened at all. It is also misleading to believe that one can somehow convert dissociated affect into cognition in a manner that "masters" it and enables one to be fully liberated from the past (or from "the burden of history"). (In this respect *Vergangenheitsbewältigung*—mastery of the past—is an unfortunate, misleading term.) The split between affect and cognition related to trauma, including the reliving or acting-out of traumatic scenes, may never be totally or definitively overcome, and it may even become the template for subsequent experience, especially of an intimate or highly cathected sort. Or one may more or less explicitly attempt to subdue violence and acquire some perspective on the past by "theatricalizing," ritualizing, or transfiguring such traumatizing scenes, at best in a manner that over time may assist in the attempt to counteract uncontrolled and intrusive forms of acting-out or even to overcome certain posttraumatic symptoms.

Leys provides a largely nonpsychoanalytic history of a concept important in psychoanalysis. She does not treat in any extended manner postmemory and the belated effects of trauma in those not directly involved in the traumatizing events—those who were not there: children and other intimates of victims, those who share with victims certain significant subject positions (for example, that of Jew, Palestinian, or Romany) as well as so-called secondary witnesses (including historians or other commentators in one of their roles). Peter Novick has written what might be seen as a pendant to Leys's *Trauma*. In his important book, *The Holocaust in American Life*, he offers an antipsychoanalytic reading of a traumatizing limit event in which he by and large denies the relevance of the concept of trauma to the "American" experience of the Holocaust.[14] For him the only group to which it may apply is the group of actual survivors.

Novick is convincing in signaling the dubiousness of facile identification through sacralization or memorialization of the Holocaust, and much of the information he furnishes, especially about the tendentious political role of certain organizations, is valuable. But he tends to believe that there is a simple choice between acknowledging the pressure of the past and recognizing the ways present interests shape approaches to it. Or to put the problem in nominal terms, he postulates a simple choice between Freud and Halbwachs (as Novick reads him) on the problems of memory and the interaction between past and present. In focusing exclusively on the way current political and ideological interests determine the uses and abuses of the Holocaust in American Jewry, he believes he must opt for Halbwachs

[14] (Boston: Houghton Mifflin, 1999).

over Freud in a manner that in effect denies the pressure of the past on the present, including certain effects of a disturbing, at times haunting, heritage on those living within it. Novick explicitly rejects the possible role of secondary trauma, postmemory, and the transmission of posttraumatic symptoms to those who were not there. In important ways he is close to the later, antipsychoanalytic Borch-Jacobsen in focusing on synchronic scenes and present interests.

In fact it is interesting to read Novick's book along with Henry Rousso's *Vichy Syndrome* on France and Tom Segev's *Seventh Million* on Israel, because they tell very much the same story even though the interpretive frameworks differ.[15] Segev takes a somewhat journalistic approach and has a valid political and polemical purpose when he criticizes official Israeli uses of the Holocaust in the context of the Israeli-Palestinian conflict. Rousso provides important information and probing analyses concerning responses to Vichy but his under-conceptualized, often pathologizing use of psychoanalytic categories to label periods does not contribute enough to our understanding of problems. Indeed, as he sometimes intimates, the very understanding of temporality in psychoanalysis would raise questions about discrete periods (except as pragmatic, rough, but at times useful approximations) and suggest more complex, uneven developments involving more or less varied repetitions and attempts to work through them. And Novick rejects psychoanalysis and trauma as "overall" irrelevant to the "American" reception of the Holocaust, instead fixing his sights on the way present concerns, especially in terms of identity politics, determine memory and its manipulations. The more demanding problem that is not sufficiently elucidated in these works is how to understand the interplay between trauma, posttraumatic effects, and the pressure exerted by the past on the one hand, and such issues as identity (including memory) politics or the uses and abuses of the past, including its strategic role as symbolic capital in the service of contemporary interests on the other.[16]

[15] Henry Rousso, *The Vichy Syndrome: History and Memory in France since 1944*, trans. Arthur Goldhammer (Cambridge: Harvard University Press, 1992); Tom Segev, *The Seventh Million: The Israelis and the Holocaust* (1991; New York: Hill and Wang, 1993).

[16] Although numbers do not make a case, they are significant for Novick. Here one may point out that Novick himself indicates that around 150,000 survivors came to the United States. If one counts their spouses (say, another 50,000 people, allowing for the tendency of survivors to intermarry), their children (say, 300,000 people) and

A significant issue here is the experience of individuals and groups with respect to the Holocaust. Novick, like Segev and Rousso, provides little research on, or analytic insight into, experience. Categories such as memory and trauma tend to remain abstract concepts or political pawns whose actual functioning in people remains outside the scope of inquiry. There is, for example, no use of testimonies, case histories, oral history, or works of art to address how people experience events and whether there is evidence of symptomatic behavior in children or other intimates of survivors as well as those who relate to survivors and their experience in intensely cathected ways. One instance of a critical and insightful exploration of these problems is of course Art Spiegelman's *Maus*—a text, curiously, not even mentioned by Novick. *Maus* may be argued to contest Novick's approach to problems or at least his tendency to rashly generalize the applicability of his thesis.[17] I think there are many other significant attempts to come to terms with trauma and posttraumatic experience as well as the problems they pose for identity and memory, which cannot be accounted for by a reduced and at times misleading idea of identity politics, for which the relation of present to past is a one-way street paved with narrow self-interest and symbolic capital.

Still, one should not lessen the importance of the sociopolitical uses and constructions of trauma. Nor should one amalgamate all forms of experience related to traumatic limit events or valorize, even sacralize, secondary forms of traumatization that depend on unmediated, at times uncritical, modes of identification. The events of September 11 (2001) and their aftermath bring out the complexity of these problems in an accentuated way. The suicide bombings of the World Trade

---

other intimates, including friends and family members (a conservative estimate of 500,000 people), one has a group of about a million people, not all of whom may be assumed to be traumatized but who do have some direct experiential relation with the Holocaust or with its survivors. Given the symbolic importance and cultural role of this group in the recent past, one might make a case for the relevance of trauma to the role of the Holocaust in U.S. life, including the problem of the intergenerational transmission of traumatic memory to intimates. This problem does not simply disappear when one moves to the generation of grandchildren, where postmemory (or culturally acquired memory) comes into play. In any case this set of issues presents a more cogent starting point in an investigation of the possibly traumatic impact of the Holocaust in the United States than Novick's carte blanche assertion that, with respect to the Holocaust, trauma has "overall" no application to "American life."

[17] For an analysis of *Maus* see my *History and Memory after Auschwitz* (Ithaca: Cornell University Press, 1998), chap. 5.

Center and the Pentagon were traumatic—clearly for intimates of those killed and apparently for many others. There have been many and varied attempts to remember and mourn the victims of these events, both popular responses such as the emergence across New York City of shrines to the victims, and media-driven ones, such as the cover of *US News and World Report* for the week of November 12. With the titles "Altered States of America" and "Coping with Life after 9/11," the issue features a photograph of two grief-stricken women whose heads lean or are propped against each other. One of them has eyes reddened by tears; the other has a look of forlorn reverie. Their relation to the events of September 11 is not specified. They simply seem to be Americans, albeit very fair-skinned, young, attractive Americans appropriately gendered for grief and mourning—the traditional task of women. The photo also includes a somewhat blurry but resolute male face in the background. He may have cried but he is now ready to do something about the events.

This conventional representation is typical of much dominant media coverage and underlines the more questionable side of media-driven uses of trauma and mourning. These uses reinforce the effort to construct and experience September 11 as a consensual national trauma, something all Americans (perhaps all good people) must feel—indeed a trauma that helps define what it is to be an American (or perhaps even a good person called upon to fight against the forces of evil). In the wake of understandable heightened anxiety about terrorism that affected the American "homeland" and even led to the establishment of a cabinet-level Department of Homeland Security, this construction was aligned with an administration-sponsored, politicized state-of-emergency mentality that even led to the idea that the "war" against terrorism is a constantly intensifying, never-ending enterprise. Unfortunately, such a mentality lends itself both to a blurring of distinctions (especially between Muslim, Arab, and terrorist) and to a deceptive clarity and precision in defining the United States's new enemy and the object of its new war—terrorists (the more homogeneous the category the better). Indeed terrorism and the terrorists, along with the "Axis of Evil" and Iraq as its primary pivot (at least until recently), have slipped all too readily into the space left vacant by the end of the Cold War and then filled more uneasily by drugs and drug lords or by multiculturalism and identity politics—although the latter may well be swept along if not up into the terrorist net as un-American activities. The Bush administration has taken pains to disavow and deny the idea that the war against terrorism is a war against Islam. And Norman Mineta, secretary of transportation, explicitly condemned racial profiling, drawing on his own experience as a child interned during the Second World War with other Japanese Americans. These efforts complicate the picture and attempt to counteract extreme effects of a state-of-emergency mentality that the administration has in other ways fostered, for example, through the authorization of military tribunals to try non-U.S. citizens charged with terrorist activities and through the president's own unselfconscious reference to a crusade. Racial profiling has in fact taken place in areas such as airports, where there has been a swing from near total laxity before September 11 to near paranoia after it. Indeed the force of the denial itself attests to the strength of the inclination to employ racial profiling and to conflate terrorists, Muslims, and Arabs, indeed many people of color—a tendency that existed before 9/11 and was exacerbated by it.[18] And the war against terrorism eventuates in a shifting condensation or particularization of its elusive object onto concrete targets. The entire state-of-emergency mentality, the division of the world into "good" friends and "evil" enemies of the endless war against terrorism, and the resurgence of a McCarthyite

[18] The tendency to see Muslims as the enemy and, after September 11, to localize the enemy even further as terrorists perceived as agents of a civilization alien to the West, is also furthered by the type of thinking illustrated if not epitomized in Samuel Huntington's *Clash of Civilizations and the Remaking of World Order* (New York: Simon and Schuster, 1996). For Huntington modern politics, including global politics, is basically cultural politics. And the most basic form of culture is civilizational. Civilizations tell us who we are and what we stand for. And civilizations clash. They are shaped by and need enemies in crucial ways. For Huntington we are the West. And the West is declining, threatened internally by multiculturalism and divisive identity politics in groups that refuse to assimilate. Hence identity politics is a misguided form of cultural politics close to un-American activity. The West is also threatened externally, especially by Islamic and Asian civilizations that are exploding demographically and/or "expanding their economic, military, and political strength." Indeed "the survival of the West depends on Americans reaffirming their Western identity and Westerners accepting their civilization as unique not universal and uniting to renew and preserve it against challenges from non-Western societies" (20–21). Huntington's style might be characterized as free, indirect, and diagnostic, blending seeming hypotheses, foregone conclusions, a pronounced if not near apocalyptic sense of emergency, and advocacy in his own performative or even prophetic voice. In content his argument is not too distant from Oswald Spengler or other "civilizational" thinkers of the early twentieth century, especially in Germany. And claims to uniqueness aside, it is also on one level not too distant from Osama bin Laden or Mullah Omar with their variant of the clash of civilizations.

atmosphere attest to the force of attraction as well as the dangers of a political construction of trauma rendered subservient to certain uses. Such a construction is all the more dubious in a context in which there is an official policy of preemptive strikes on perceived threats that, often with the compliance of the media, leads to quick-on-the-trigger bellicosity, prejudicial stereotyping of critics, and heightened instability in the name of security.

As the brief and inadequate reference to September 11 and its aftermath makes evident, the interest in the use and abuse of memory and trauma, both in the academy and beyond it, is not reserved for the Holocaust. You find similar concerns in the study of Japan (for example, the work of Robert J. Lifton), France (the entire debate over the French Revolution, Vichy, and the Algerian war), and the United States (not only the Holocaust but the Vietnam war, the heritage of slavery, and the treatment of American Indians). Work on the Holocaust has for a variety of contingent reasons given rise to some of the most advanced, albeit at times contestable, theorizing about the problem of trauma and limit events, but this work can have—and is having—mutually informative interactions with work in other areas, including study of the *testimonio* in Latin America and elsewhere. It is altogether diversionary to see these problems and approaches in terms of a zero-sum game or a grim competition for first place in victim status.

I would also note that an interest in ethics or normativity in general (importantly including the relations among ethics, art, and politics) has recently become prevalent, but it requires further elaboration in ways few if any of us has been professionally equipped to engage in a cogent manner. I have intimated that working-through itself, along with its ethicopolitical implications, remains a relatively underdeveloped concept in academic appropriations of psychoanalysis. I think one should try to take ethics out of a purely individualist, subjective, or personal frame of reference and consistently relate it to interpersonal, social, and political problems. One thereby inflects the concept of working-through by linking the ethical and the sociopolitical rather than conflating them or construing them as essentially different or even opposed categories. An insistently individualistic approach, including certain psychologizing orientations related to a therapeutic or "feel-good" outlook on life, often does dissociate ethics from social and political problems. Of course there is a crucial individual or rather singular dimension to ethics that involves responsibility toward others, and there are aspects of decisions—especially very difficult decisions—that are not programmed in terms of norms. But one need not postulate an antinomy or incommensurability between the decision in its singularity and the social or political norm or value. Such a postulation, however radical or anarchistic in intent, may reinforce the standard opposition between the individual and the collectivity. Norms do not simply program events or decisions in a way that takes the decision out of decision, but they do set limits and pose resistances to excess or pure decisionism. These limits are not absolute but have varying degrees of solidity or force. Moreover, institutions are nodal points of collective, normatively regulated or guided activity. They should not be seen in purely bureaucratic terms or even construed as unfortunate precipitates of the evil demon. Rethinking ethics and politics requires the difficult and contested effort to rethink institutions, including the university and the role of disciplines and administrative units such as departments within it.

Ethical debate that is socially and politically relevant should obviously address issues of this sort. For example, in what ways do aporias become paralyzing or compulsively repeated objects of fixation and how do they indicate problems (including traumas) that have not been worked through, even helping to point the way to newer formulations and possibilities for action? To what extent and in what ways are various binding limits, including those provided by norms in institutional settings, also flexible and enabling? To take but one example: even defenders of pornography will typically set different limits for adults and for children, both in viewing pornography and in its subjects and performers (with child pornography typically being seen as unacceptable or even taboo). And while one may be inclined to defend the legitimacy of a course on pornography, involving the viewing of pornographic material, in college, one might resist defending it in grammar or even in high school. In other words, one may in certain cases lucidly defend rather strict limits and even believe that they should be ingrained in the personality with the force of a taboo. But one need not generalize this perspective to all ethical limits or bounds. Indeed one may argue that certain dimensions of life, such as sexuality, are in general overregulated while others, notably economic activity, are severely underregulated. One may also consistently raise the question of whether certain limits are illegitimate and based on prejudicial grounds typically related to forms of social and political dominance.

With respect to art, it is problematic, especially at the present time, to see it as a discrete, autonomous, purely aesthetic sphere that is simply beyond truth claims and ethical considerations. Rather there is a complex interaction between art, truth claims, and ethics (including the ethicopolitical). The implication is not state censorship but the expansion of the range of critical discourse and the ability to have two-way or multiple forms of critical exchange. Art may pose questions to history or ethics, and vice versa. It may also serve as a relatively safe haven for experimental ventures, including the exploration of the complex relations between acting out and working through problems.

For example, Thane Rosenbaum's novel *Second Hand Smoke* (like Toni Morrison's *Beloved*) may be read as suggesting to historians and other analysts the need for a closer, critical examination of the intergenerational transmission of trauma and compulsively haunting presences, or revenants, related to forms of oppression and victimization.[19] In its parodic and self-parodic dimensions, *Second Hand Smoke* may also be read as posing the ethicopolitical question of the use of humor in coming to terms with a fraught past. In addition, it may be seen to ask whether and in what way a legacy involving culturally acquired memory should or should not become a basis of identity for individuals and groups in the present, including such political issues as reparation for past wrongs that in certain ways affect later generations. Conversely, one may address historical questions to works of art in a manner that critically inquires into the way they imaginatively re-create, supplement, or transform—at times avoid or repress— historical issues relevant to their operations.

Roberto Benigni's 1998 film *Life Is Beautiful* may be questioned on the basis of historical research into camp life. In light of this knowledge one may argue that the representation of camp life in the second part of the film is either too unrealistic or not unrealistic enough. In other words, what happens in the father's attempt to protect the child is so out of keeping with historical possibility that it seems ludicrous if not offensive. Yet the film, despite its all-too-obvious relation to

---

[19] *Second Hand Smoke* (New York: St. Martin's Griffin, 1999); *Beloved* (New York: Pantheon, 1988).

fantasy and the fantastic, also retains too many links to standard modes of realistic representation (including by-now familiar techniques of "magical" realism) to enable its counterimage (opposing paternal protection of the vulnerable child to Nazi abuse of vulnerability) either to effectively engage extreme forms of historical reality (including the overwhelmingly obscene nature of Nazi abuse) or to challenge our understanding of it in truly disconcerting, even surrealistic or fantastic ways. As it is, camp life in the film as it affects the father-son relation tends to create an imaginary world that simply floats free of actual camp conditions and seems to express not the world of the child but the dissociated, projective fantasies of the good-natured, ingratiating, bumbling, indeed escapist father. One might contend that what the film needed was a stronger combination of traumatic realism and surrealism as well as gallows humor. In the latter respect it is not the presence of humor in the film but the type of humor it employs that is dubious: it is altogether too benign (or too "Benigni"—too much like that in his other films) for the extremity and challenge of the problems the film addresses. Yet the success of the film is itself significant in signaling the quasi-realistic, romantic, ingratiatingly amusing memory (or forgetting) of the past that many apparently desire.

The implication of what I have been saying is that there may well be a significant element of uncertainty, uncanniness, or undecidability in art (or "literary language") but that element varies, and one should not simply equate art or the literary with uncertainty, uncanniness, and undecidability—or aporia, self-referentiality, autonomy, and so forth—equations that I think still remain within a postromantic frame of reference that excessively privileges an aesthetic of the sublime and uncritically displaces a radically transcendent religious problematic (that is, art is the beyond—beyond history, beyond ethics, beyond politics, beyond beyond—a secular beyond, or postapocalyptic metabeyond, that displaces a relation to an otherworldly but now dead, unavailable, absent, self-cancelling, aporetic divinity).

I would also note that much can be gained by taking the concepts of "acting-out" and "working-through" from Freud and from psychoanalysis, and then developing them in a way that makes them especially significant for use in historical studies related to critical theory. I see acting-out and working-through as two interrelated ways of coming to terms with transference, or with one's transferential implication in the object of study. Of course the two may be both combined in various subtly hybridized ways and mediated by complex processes of working over as well as playing out relations. Indeed play is important. A certain ability to engage in play—to joke or to acquire distance (to some extent a safe haven) through explicit dramatization or simulation that frames itself as such—may in certain cases indicate a critical relation to haunting or possessive events and may be related to an attempt to counter acting-out with working-through. (As I intimated, my doubts about Benigni's film do not extend to play in general but to the nature of the humor and the kind of play with history in which the film engages.) The notion of "work" in working-through (including memory work) is also important, for one does in some sense perform work on the self and on one's material. But work should not be understood in a narrowly literal, exclusive, or instrumental manner and locked in a binary opposition with pure expenditure or free play. There is also a place for play that interacts with work in its seriousness and its limits—play that cannot be adapted to a hierarchy or to a "from ... to" scenario, including the putative movement from a restricted economy of (instrumental) work to a general economy of play or *dépense* (wasteful or useless expenditure). One may recall that Thomas Mann, echoing Goethe, defined art as jesting in earnest—a definition one may relate to Clifford Geertz's notion of "deep play"—play concerning matters of life and death.

Working-through may be least successful when it is a purely or predominatly individual or even one-on-one process. It has greatest chances of at least relative success when it is a social process. (In this sense clinical, one-on-one relations, even group therapy in a restricted orbit, have but limited chances of sustained effectiveness even for the individual, much less with respect to the social and political causes of certain problems.) Mourning itself can be a form of deep play, as in the wake. It becomes impossible or loops endlessly back into melancholy when it is a process of isolated grieving (or metametaphysical meditation). It is important to see the possible role of mourning as a social or even a ritual process that is not confined to the individual or the inner psyche (the context in which even Freud understands it in his essay "Mourning and Melancholia").[20] Indeed,

[20] *The Standard Edition of the Complete Works of Sigmund Freud*, vol. 14, trans. James Strachey (London: Hogarth, 1957), 237–60.

in certain contexts, whom one deems worthy of mourning is a political issue. Of course in modern society, secular groups may not have collective forms of mourning but may be largely confined to discursive or media-driven variants of it. The point is not simply to replicate symptomatically this cultural and social condition in one's own mode of analysis or sense of possibility but to inquire critically into its possibilities and limits.

Working-through may be conceived as an articulatory process that generates countervailing forces to acting-out and the repetition compulsion, and it should raise the question of sociopolitical practice and the actual and desirable role of institutions as normatively guided forms of collective life. For the academic, it raises the question of the university as an institution, its "inner" articulations and workings, and its relation to the larger society and polity. Prominent among these questions is the role of an ethics of transference, for example, in one's relations with students as well as with colleagues. It is, for example, an altogether necessary and salutary blow to one's narcissism to realize that affective responses on the part of those in positions of lesser power and knowledge, particularly when they are very impressionable, may well be far in excess of what is called for by one's personal qualities or attributes. In terms of textual analysis, working-through implies the need explicitly to pose and explore the question of one's own transferential implication and the tendency to repeat or act out processes active in, or projected into, one's object of study. It also requires an attempt to formulate problems in a more critical manner that may counteract symptomatic, unself-conscious acting-out. Moreover, in criticizing the encrypted normativity involved in concepts of normality and pathology, one should not reject all normativity or conflate it with dubious normalization (which identifies the dominant or the statistically general as normative). Instead one should try to take psychoanalysis in explicitly normative, ethical and political, directions where one's claims may be open to argument and criticism. This of course does not mean blaming the victim, but it does mean seeing working-through as a desirable process with ethicopolitical force.

In working-through, the person tries to gain critical distance on a problem and to distinguish—as well as explore the interactions—between past, present, and future. And working-through is intimately bound up with the possibility of being an ethical and political agent, which, in victims of extreme events, involves the arduous process of moving from victim to survivor and agent while perhaps never totally transcending the effects of victimization. Moreover, especially in an ethical sense, working-through does not imply avoiding, harmonizing, simply forgetting the past, returning to a status quo ante, or submerging oneself in the present. (There is a sense in which Benigni's film is the aesthetic analogue of a posthypnotic suggestion to forget the reality of the past and imagine it in some more uplifting way.)[21] Working-through involves coming to terms with extreme events, including the trauma that typically attends them, and critically engaging—but not simply reinforcing—the tendency to act out the past while nonetheless recognizing why acting-out may be necessary and even compelling.

In any case certain wounds from the past—both personal and historical—cannot simply heal without leaving scars or residues—in a sense archives—in the present. There may even have to remain open wounds, even if one strives to counteract their tendency to swallow all of existence and incapacitate one as an agent in the present. One of the most difficult aspects of working-through is to undertake it in a manner that is not tantamount to betraying the trust or love that binds one to lost others—that does not imply simply forgetting the dead, distorting what they went through, or being swept away by current preoccupations. The feeling of trust betrayed or fidelity broken (however unjustified the feeling may in fact be) is one of the greatest impediments to working through problems. As noted earlier, the posttraumatic symptom may be experienced as a bond with the dead, and its dissolution, while in some sense liberating, may also be felt—and resisted—as a loss or a betrayal.

It should be evident that the acting-out/working-through distinction is not itself a polar opposition, binaristic dichotomy, or separation into totally different categories. It is an analytic distinction between interacting processes. And of course it applies in significantly different ways to people in different situations or occupying different subject positions. It should not be employed indiscriminately to imply

---

[21] There may be a sense in which Benigni and Giorgio Agamben are inverted mirror images of one another: the latter generalizes an unrelentingly abject and hopeless image of the concentration camp as the prototype of modern life, while the former reimagines the camp as a Disney World of projective fantasy relatively untouched by traumatic dimensions of historical reality.

that everyone is equally a survivor or a trauma victim. But it is one way of trying to get back to the problem of the relationship between theory and practice and to counter the prevalent relegation of thought to a form of enlightened disempowerment at times combined with blank utopian hope for the radically other. Working with certain distinctions, and more generally with psychoanalysis construed not simply as individual self-understanding or therapy but as a mode of critical theory, is also a way of approaching dimensions of history that cannot be reduced to the nonetheless necessary components of a research model that enjoins a reconstruction of the past that is as validated and as substantiated as possible. Vital dimensions of historical understanding not encompassed by a restricted research model include one's implication in the object of study, affective or emotional response (notably including the role of empathy), and coming to terms with that response in an attempted dialogical exchange with the past and with other inquirers into it in a manner that bears on the present and future.

CHAPTER THREE

Trauma Studies:
Its Critics and Vicissitudes

In certain areas of the humanities and social sciences, trauma, along with the specific form of recall termed traumatic memory, has, in the last ten years or so, become a center of concern, even leading to the emergence of the field or subdiscipline of what is called trauma studies.[1] Especially in light of the relation of trauma to extreme or limit events such as the Holocaust, other genocides, terrorism, slavery, aspects of colonialism, and so forth, one would think trauma and its aftermath would be of marked interest to historians. But, with some exceptions (for example, Saul Friedlander and myself), the interest in trauma and, perhaps even more so, in dimensions of the posttraumatic has thus far not been pronounced in the work of historians, and

---

[1] In this respect see, for example, Paul Antze and Michael Lambek, eds., *Tense Past: Cultural Essays in Trauma and Memory* (New York: Routledge, 1996); Elizabeth J. Bellamy, *Affective Genealogies: Psychoanalysis, Postmodernism, and the "Jewish Question" after Auschwitz* (Lincoln: University of Nebraska Press, 1997); Cathy Caruth, ed., *Trauma: Explorations in Memory* (Baltimore: Johns Hopkins University Press, 1995); Cathy Caruth, *Unclaimed Experience: Trauma, Narrative, and History* (Baltimore: Johns Hopkins University Press, 1996); Hal Foster, *The Return of the Real: The Avant-Garde at the End of the Century* (Cambridge: MIT Press, 1996); Geoffrey Hartman, *The Longest Shadow: In the Aftermath of the Holocaust* (Bloomington: Indiana University Press, 1996) and *Scars of the Spirit: The Struggle against Inauthenticity* (New York: Palgrave Macmillan, 2002); Michael Rothberg, *Traumatic Realism: The Demands of Holocaust Representation* (Minneapolis: University of Minnesota Press, 2000); Eric Santner, *Stranded Objects: Mourning, Memory, and Film in Postwar Germany* (Ithaca: Cornell University Press, 1990); Ernst van Alphen, *Caught by History: Holocaust Effects in Contemporary Art, Literature, and Theory* (Stanford: Stanford University Press); Nancy Wood, *Vectors of Memory: Legacies of Trauma in Postwar Europe* (Oxford: Berg, 1999); Barbie Zelizer, *Remembering to Forget: Holocaust Memory through the Camera's Eye* (Chicago: Univer-

there has even been some suspicion of attempts to conceptualize trauma and its aftermath.[2]

Here a crucial question is whether in culture there is a sense in which Jean-Baptiste Lamarck was right—a sense in which there is the "inheritance" of acquired characteristics. This "inheritance," more precisely repetition or reproduction, occurs through some combination of more or less conscious processes such as education as well as critical practices, including various signifying practices, which may enact changes on what is inherited, and unconscious or less controlled processes such as identification or mimeticism, including the incorporation and symptomatic acting-out or compulsive repetition of posttraumatic effects.

I have already referred to Peter Novick's extreme wariness concerning the concept of trauma and its posttraumatic aftermath, particularly the transmission of posttraumatic symptoms to others through repetition, identification, or mimesis. Novick even asserts that, except for Holocaust survivors themselves, "the available evidence doesn't suggest that, overall, American Jews (let alone American gentiles) were traumatized by the Holocaust, in any worthwhile sense of the term" (3). Novick implicitly dismisses the relevance

---

sity of Chicago Press, 1998) and Barbie Zelizer, ed., *Visual Culture and the Holocaust* (New Brunswick: Rutgers University Press, 2000). A collection of essays by a group of historians in England, stemming from a 1996 conference in Manchester, has been published as *Traumatic Pasts: History, Psychiatry, and Trauma in the Modern Age, 1870–1930*, ed. Mark S. Michale and Paul Lerner (Cambridge: Cambridge University Press, 2001). As the title indicates, the discussion, despite its value for the early history of trauma, does not extend past the 1930s and hence does not centrally address either later phenomena or the role of the concept of trauma both in post–World War II social life and in intellectual discourse. See also the informative discussion of the tense relations among rendering justice, representing traumatic history, serving memory, and attending to the testimonial voices of victims in Holocaust-related trials such as Nuremberg (Adolf Eichmann, Klaus Barbie, John [Ivan] Demjanjuk, and Ernst Zundel) in Lawrence Douglas, *The Memory of Judgment: Making Law and History in the Trials of the Holocaust* (New Haven: Yale University Press, 2001). See as well the contributions to *History, Memory, and the Law*, ed. Austin Sarat and Thomas R. Kearns (Ann Arbor: University of Michigan Press, 1999).

[2] See Peter Novick, *The Holocaust in American Life* (Boston: Houghton Mifflin, 1999); and Ruth Leys, *Trauma: A Genealogy* (Chicago: University of Chicago Press, 2000), esp. 305, as well as the discussion in the preceding chapters. Suspicion is at times warranted, for example, toward the uses of the Holocaust as "symbolic capital." In this respect, see also the contributions to *Witness and Memory: The Discourse of Trauma*, ed. Ana Douglass and Thomas A. Vogel (New York: Routledge, 2003), especially the editors' substantial introduction.

of what has been called postmemory and the intergenerational transmission of trauma, as does in quite explicit and trenchant terms the
historicizing literary critic Walter Benn Michaels, concerning the aftermath of slavery.[3] Benn Michaels even reads Toni Morrison's *Beloved*
as uncritically feeding into self-serving identity and memory politics
rather than as an exploration of postmemory and the intergenerational transmission of trauma or of posttraumatic symptoms as haunting revenants. Postmemory is the acquired memory of those not
directly experiencing an event such as the Holocaust or slavery, and
the intergenerational transmission of trauma refers to the way those
not directly living through an event may nonetheless experience and
manifest its posttraumatic symptoms, something especially prominent in the children or intimates of survivors or at times perpetrators
who are possessed of, and even by, the past and tend to relive what
others have lived.[4] Even those not the intimates of survivors or perpetrators may through identification come to manifest posttraumatic
symptoms, sometimes with dubious effects in the public sphere
if they pose as actual survivors, the apparent case of Binjamin
Wilkomirski, author of *Fragments: Memories of a Wartime Childhood*.[5]

In part as a reaction or overreaction to phenomena epitomized by
Wilkomirski, a number of historians—such as Lucy Dawidowicz,
Charles Maier, Arno Mayer, Henry Rousso, and Yosef Hayim
Yerushalmi—draw a sharp distinction, even an opposition, between
history and memory in general, often viewing memory, including testimony, only as an object of study and critique or at best as an unreliable source of facts for history—a view that threatens to render
testimony redundant since whatever it discloses has to be checked

[3] See "'You Who Never Was There': Slavery and the New Historicism—Decon-
struction and the Holocaust" in *The Americanization of the Holocaust*, ed. Hilene
Flanzbaum (Baltimore: Johns Hopkins University Press, 1999), 181–97.
[4] On these problems, see Nicolas Abraham and Maria Torok, *The Shell and the
Kernel*, ed. and trans. Nicolas T. Rand (Chicago: University of Chicago Press, 1994);
Marianne Hirsch, *Family Frames: Photography, Narrative, and Postmemory* (Cambridge:
Harvard University Press, 1997); Thane Rosenbaum, *Second Hand Smoke* (New York:
St. Martin's Griffin, 1999). Also relevant are James Berger, *After the End: Representa-
tions of Post-Apocalypse* (Minneapolis: University of Minnesota Press, 1999); and Satya
Mohanty, *Literary Theory and the Claims of History: Postmodernism, Objectivity, Multicultural Politics* (Ithaca: Cornell University Press, 1997). Both these books include readings of Morrison's *Beloved* that may be contrasted with Benn Michaels's.
[5] Trans. Carol Brown Janeway (1995; New York: Schocken Books, 1996).

against what are presumed to be more reliable documents.[6] This is a very limited conception of testimony that does not explore its specific relation to experience as distinguished from events. In addition, certain scholars have seen a radical parting of the ways between sociopolitical analysis and critique on the one hand, and interest in trauma (or what John Mowitt dismissively terms "trauma envy") on

---

[6] See Lucy Dawidowicz, *The Holocaust and the Historians* (Cambridge: Harvard University Press, 1981); Charles Maier, "A Surfeit of Memory? Reflections on History, Melancholy, and Denial," *History and Memory* 5 (1993): 136–51; Arno Mayer, *Why Did the Heavens Not Darken?: The "Final Solution" in History* (New York: Pantheon, 1988); Henry Rousso, *The Vichy Syndrome: History and Memory in France since 1944*, trans. Arthur Goldhammer (1987; Cambridge: Harvard University Press, 1991); and Yosef Hayim Yerushalmi, *Zakhor: Jewish History and Jewish Memory* (Seattle: University of Washington Press, 1982). On these issues see my *History and Memory after Auschwitz* (Ithaca: Cornell University Press, 1998) and *Representing the Holocaust: History, Theory, Trauma* (Ithaca: Cornell University Press, 1994), esp. chap. 3 on Mayer. Gabrielle Spiegel returns to these problems in terms that accord with the approaches of Maier and Yerushalmi. See her "Memory and History: Liturgical Time and Historical Time," *History and Theory* 41 (2002): 149–62. In the same issue of *History and Theory*, Wulf Kannsteiner provides a discussion of history and collective memory focusing on the media and reception in his "Finding Meaning in Memory: A Methodological Critique of Collective Memory Studies" (179–97); and Carolyn Dean, in her "History and Holocaust Representation" (239–49), offers a thought-provoking, critical but appreciative analysis of Michael Rothberg's *Traumatic Realism* that raises in a particularly insightful manner the issue of the relations between history and theory as well as between historiography and other fields such as literary studies. Kannsteiner provides many interesting observations concerning the reception of the Holocaust on German television. On the one hand, he fully accepts Halbwachs's view that individual memory is shaped by collective forces, indeed that autonomous individual memory is a dubious abstraction. Moreover, he thinks that processes studied in psychoanalysis, such as repression, apply to collectivities. On the other hand, he denies that psychoanalysis itself applies to collectivities, not noticing that processes such as repression would then have a greater chance of operating without critical control. He also asserts that collectivities do not suffer psychic damage from repression. One might agree with Kannsteiner that psychoanalysis should not be applied in a manner that obscures or diverts attention from crucial social, political, and ethical processes and problems. One might also argue that, with respect to large collectivities, such as nations, the significant issue is not psychic damage but the political, social, and ethical consequences of not coming critically and self-critically to terms with a past in which one is implicated. And one might well insist that the application of psychoanalysis to collectivities has a speculative dimension that should be subjected as much as possible to responsible cognitive control, especially through specification of how and to what the psychoanalytic categories and processes apply. For example, one might argue that in Israel after World War II there was a prevalent repression of the plight of victims and survivors of the Holocaust in line with a redemptive Zionist narrative and the desire to construct a new nationally based identity for the Jew as a fighter. In this respect, the Eichmann trial might be seen as a fraught return of the repressed, and how to work through the past and arrive at a different, more self-critical, "post-

the other.[7] Indeed there has recently been a backlash against trauma as well as Holocaust studies, a backlash that has largely symptomatic interest and that includes a tendency to oversimplify diverse and at times divergent approaches to both trauma and the Holocaust. In his article Mowitt himself misleadingly sees "trauma studies" as a unified rather than an internally contested field and understands trauma primarily in terms of Wendy Brown's notion of "wounded attachments." The latter amount to an envy-filled, *ressentiment*-laden form of identity politics, which in turn are construed as a symptom of liberalism conflated with global capitalism. In rather predictable old-left fashion, which nonetheless at times seems dangerously close to reactions on the far right (notably in the appeal to envy and resentment), Mowitt also sees any ethical turn—at times linked to the interest in trauma— as perforce a turn away from politics and socioeconomic criticism. The latter view is prevalent on the left and is in evidence even in Alain Badiou's *Ethics: An Essay in the Understanding of Evil.*[8]

In her book *Aftermath: Violence and the Remaking of a Self*, Susan Brison points to a suspicion of trauma among Anglo-American philosophers.[9] Whereas historians tend to rely on objectification and contextualization within a restricted research paradigm, philosophers (at least analytic philosophers), for Brison, manifest a decided preference for an acontextual or decontextualized variant of an impersonal approach to problems. This approach dichotomizes between the empirically contingent—especially the personal (what historians also

---

Zionist" national narrative in a complex political and international context is a recurrently insistent problem in Israel.

[7] John Mowitt, "Trauma Envy," in the special issue edited by Karyn Ball on "Trauma and Its Cultural Aftereffects" of *Cultural Critique* 46 (2000): 272–97. See also Ball's significantly different approach to trauma in her own essay, "Disciplining Traumatic History: Goldhagen's Impropriety" (124–52) as well as in her substantial introduction, "Trauma and Its Institutional Destinies" (1–44) in which she investigates the reasons for the recent interest in trauma. In her introduction Ball nonetheless tends to historicize trauma in overly circumscribed terms as an interest of the 1990s that has come, crested, and all but gone. Perhaps defensively, she thus contributes to the questionable tendency to see trauma studies, or even the study of trauma itself, as yet one more academic fad with a very short life. This view obscures how inquiry into trauma, conducted in a certain way, may provide new insight into extreme events and experiences, notably those figured as catastrophe, crisis, or radical break with the past. With respect to these problems, see my *Writing History, Writing Trauma* (Baltimore: Johns Hopkins University Press, 2001).

[8] Trans. Peter Hallward (1998; London: Verso, 2001).

[9] (Princeton: Princeton University Press, 2002).

tend to suspect as "ego-history")—and the philosophical. Philosophers for Brison also tend to downplay the significance of narrative
as a medium of philosophical thought, oppose (at times in gendered
terms) the cognitive to the affective or emotional in understanding
(the affective being coded as feminine), prefer sometimes far-fetched
imaginary examples to actual experiences of trauma and violence
(where facts may go beyond the imagination), and ignore certain
problems such as rape or relegate them to the sphere of the non-
philosophical. (Brison herself attempts to combine a narrative of her
own rape and near death by strangulation with a philosophical meditation on the problem of trauma.)

To the extent Brison's depiction of analytic philosophy is accurate
(a depiction she qualifies with respect to countercurrents especially
prominent in feminist thought), one might see a neo-Aristotelian division of labor between philosophy and history based on larger shared
premises: a division between the conceptual and the empirical or
contingent, the far-fetched imaginary and the soberly realistic, the
analytic and the narrative—but based on a shared tendency to exclude
affect (notably empathy) from understanding and to protect a
restricted idea of reason and rationality from contact with what might
upset it and the self-image of those basing their own identity on it,
notably trauma, its aftermath, and its possibly unsettling effects on
those who inquire into it. Even theorists closer to Continental philosophy, such as Jean-François Lyotard and Giorgio Agamben, may at
times not explore the problematic, mutually questioning relation
between history and theory but instead see the historically specific,
such as Auschwitz, simply as an instantiation, illustration, sign, or
singular epiphany of the transhistorical, theoretical concept or
concern such as sublimity, the differend, or the split, abject subject.[10]
(Here one repeats, in the guise of theory, a traditional philosophical
reduction of, even prejudice against, history.)

[10] Jean-François Lyotard, *Heidegger and "the jews,"* trans. Andreas Michel and Mark
S. Roberts (1988; Minneapolis: University of Minnesota Press, 1990); Giorgio
Agamben, *Remnants of Auschwitz: The Witness and the Archive*, trans. Daniel Heller-
Rosen (New York: Zone Books, 1999). See also Georges Bataille, "Concerning the
Accounts Given by the Residents of Hiroshima" in *Trauma: Explorations in Memory*,
ed. Cathy Caruth (Baltimore: Johns Hopkins University Press, 1995), 221–35. Bataille
offers an ecstatic discussion of the bombing of Hiroshima in terms of an inner core
of darkness, a sublime idea of wasteful expenditure beyond reason and profit, and a
collapse—or at least relegation to the level of the superficial and irrelevant—of the
distinction between natural disaster and human agency.

Critiques of "trauma studies" may in important respects be justified when such critiques are specific, focused, and self-critical. When sufficiently qualified, these critiques pose a challenge. The challenge is to develop a differential, careful approach to the study of trauma and the posttraumatic, especially in relation to extreme or limit events and experiences—an approach that does not become merely psychologizing, consumingly theoretical, oblivious to larger social and political problems, subservient to the quest for heritage or narrowly self-serving forms of identity politics, or the object of a fixation whereby history is simply identified with trauma and one tends indiscriminately to see trauma everywhere.

My general point in what follows is that all significant, "cathected" or emotionally charged distinctions are problematic, but some distinctions are more problematic than others. And the critique of a use or dimension of a distinction, for example, the gendering of the private/public distinction or the ethnocentric use of the universal/particular distinction, does not ipso facto delegitimate or undo all uses or dimensions of the distinction. Furthermore, the salutary deconstruction of binary oppositions or dichotomies, which is politically and ethically important insofar as it unsettles or undoes the bases of a scapegoat mechanism, need not eventuate in the blurring of all distinctions or in a notion of thought as generalized astigmatism or conceptual meltdown. Rather it heightens the importance of how to make problematic distinctions and weigh their actual or desirable strength or weakness, thus explicitly raising the issue of which distinctions ought to be effaced, which preserved, and which refashioned or transformed.[11] In line with these views I would like not to dichotomize but to distinguish, however problematically, among the traumatizing event or events, the experience of trauma, memory, and representation. Such a distinction among dimensions of trauma that are often elided is important for a number of reasons. (Typically the terms "event" and "experience" are used interchangeably, for example, by both Caruth and Leys, despite the latter's critique of Caruth.) One reason the distinction is important is that a person may

[11] For example, one might well argue in normative terms that gendered dimensions of distinctions should indeed be radically blurred or effaced while nonetheless recognizing their empirical and historical role. (This argument would raise the larger problem of one's very understanding of what Lacan terms the symbolic along with the attempt to ground it in gendered distinctions or even oppositions that function inter alia to delegitimate nontraditional families, as in the view of certain opponents of the PaCS [Pacte de Solidarité Sociale] in France.) But such an argument does not

take part in the event without undergoing the experience of trauma. For example, while there may be traumatization of the perpetrator, Nazi ideology and practice were geared to creating perpetrators able to combine extreme, traumatizing, radically transgressive acts with hardness that, when it succeeded in functioning as psychic armor, foreclosed traumatization of the perpetrator. One finds similar tendencies in Ernst Jünger and others, where violence and possible trauma are transfigured into the occasion for an ecstatic experience of the sublime, notably in the *Fronterlebnis*, the experience of fighting on the front in World War I.[12] (The colonial experience might function in

---

apply uniformly to all other dimensions or uses of distinctions, at least if one does not take up an indiscriminately antinomian approach to problems (at times linked to extreme anarchistic utopianism). I think there is a questionable tendency, apparent in the work of Agamben for example, to believe that the only two basic options in thought are dubious binaries on the one hand, and the blurring of all distinctions or radical indistinction on the other. Hence all distinctions, however guardedly analytic or self-critical, are conflated with binary oppositions that separate reality into discrete realms or spheres, and the deconstruction of binaries is understood to lead inevitably to the blurring, undoing, or confusion of all distinctions. Curiously, this orientation may lead to a paradoxical metabinarism in the restriction of options to binaries on the one hand, and indistinction or generalized blurring on the other. Avoided are the problems of both analyzing closely the actual historical role of binaries (including the compulsively repeated tendency to construe all distinctions in binaristic terms) and attempting to rearticulate distinctions—including newer distinctions—when binaries have been deconstructed and displaced. These problems raise ethical and political issues. I would further note that the belief that the deconstruction of binaries eventuates inevitably in the radical blurring or collapse of distinctions may induce the generalization of what Primo Levi termed the gray zone such that everyone involved in extreme events becomes complicitous as perpetrator-victims. What the collapse of the perpetrator-victim distinction brings about is an inability to distinguish between different situations in terms of various degrees of complicity, innocence, and guilt. For Levi, in the Holocaust there was a very large group of victims who were innocent and did not deserve the treatment they received from a group of perpetrators who themselves were not victims in any significant way in their role as perpetrators. Between these groups there was a variously shaded gray zone of perpetrator-victims, including members of Jewish councils and the *Sonderkommando* (one might add other groups such as certain kapos in camps epitomized by the case of Tadeusz Borowski). Of course it would be desirable to get beyond the perpetrator/victim distinction by overcoming the entire grid of victimization involving perpetrator, victim, bystander, rescuer, gray zone, and so forth. But this would involve an explicitly normative, ethicopolitical initiative to transform society and culture in basic ways and not a generalized blurring of existing historical distinctions accompanied at best by empty (post)apocalyptic hope.
[12] On Jünger, see, for example, the discussions in Jeffrey Herf, *Reactionary Modernism: Technology, Culture, and Politics in Weimar and the Third Reich* (New York: Cambridge University Press, 1984), chap. 4; Karl-Heinz Bohrer, *Die Ästhetik des Schreckens: Die Pessimistische Romantik und Enst Jüngers Frühwerk* (Munich: Carl Hanser, 1978); and Klaus Theweleit, *Male Fantasies*, vol. 2, trans. Erica Carter and

a comparable manner.)[13] Conversely, one may experience aspects of trauma or undergo secondary traumatization, at least through the manifestation of symptomatic effects such as extreme anxiety, panic attacks, startle reactions, or recurrent nightmares, without personally living through the traumatizing event to which such effects are ascribed. As I suggested earlier, this is the case in the intergenerational transmission of trauma, notably through processes of identification with the (actual or imagined) experience of intimates. Secondary traumatization may even occur in those reacting only to representations of trauma, apparently the case for Wilkomirski with respect to his childhood viewing of a Holocaust documentary film. In his 1985 novel *Writing the Book of Esther*,[14] Henri Raczymow describes a young woman, named after an aunt who died in Auschwitz, who attempts to reexperience what she herself has never lived through: the intense suffering and traumatization of life in the camps. In an *imitatio* of the victim, she undergoes surrogate victimage and dresses in camp clothing, shaves her head, undergoes periods of starvation, and finally gasses herself. Uncertainty of subject position and voice affect not only Esther's younger brother, Mathieu, but even the narrator with respect to both Mathieu and Esther herself.[15] Such processes help to illuminate and provide critical perspective on the plight of imaginary survivors who may actually manifest posttraumatic symptoms comparable to those of survivors of events such as the Holocaust. In religious history we are familiar with something that would appear analogous in the extreme form of the imitation of Christ leading to stigmata, which might be seen as posttraumatic, symptomatic, somatic effects of crucifixion in one who has not been crucified. This

---

Chris Turner in collaboration with Stephen Conway (1978; Minneapolis: University of Minnesota Press, 1989).

[13] See the discussion in Sven Lindqvist, *"Exterminate All the Brutes,"* trans. Joan Tate (1992; New York: New Press, 1996).

[14] Trans. Dori Katz (1985; New York: Holmes & Meier, 1995). The original French title of the novel is *Un cri sans voix.*

[15] At the end of the novel Mathieu determines that he will not pass on Esther's legacy and curse to his child: "My child must live, not simply survive. It's my duty as a father to allow him his life to which he's entitled. No direct line from Esther to this child. Except maybe through this book. But only a book, nothing more" (*Writing the Book of Esther*, 204). It is noteworthy that before her death Esther falls madly in love with a filmmaker—"a new god, a god for the eighties, perfect for the eighties" (189)—who is making a film about the camps. The narrator, this time in the person of Esther's husband, Simon, is quite ironic about the filmmaker and his project.

inexact example is pertinent insofar as it also brings up the issue of the transformation of trauma into a foundational experience (or event), the very basis of an existence, with the possibility that trauma will be sacralized or transvalued into the sublime.[16]

Here I would add a further consideration: one's deepest experiences of suffering, disturbance, loss, or even ecstasy may not stem from living through traumatizing events, to which they are at times mistakenly attributed, such as the putative modern loss of authentic memory, true community, or oneness with Being. Such "losses" are, I would suggest, better conceptualized as absences related to what might be termed structural or transhistorical trauma as an unsettling condition of possibility that is generative of anxieties or vulnerabilities. The latter, which apply to everyone, may be dubiously fixated and hypostatized when they are projectively derived from putative events (the exile from Eden, the primal crime) or ascribed to the nefar-

---

However, like Claude Lanzmann (who would seem to be the obvious model for the filmmaker in the novel), the narrator of *Writing the Book of Esther* at times discusses the Shoah in tones of negative sacralization and sublimity. For example, Mathieu (who is closest to the narrator in general if not to the author) reflects: "The absolute before. Followed by an absolute afterward. . . . This instant in time, this nothingness, is called Auschwitz. Auschwitz is the name of this nothingness. This 'nothingness' is very much like God. Perhaps it is his ultimate name" (156).

[16] The distinction between event and experience provides a way to emerge from, or at least better situate, impasses that have prevented or discouraged many historians from using testimonies in composing their own historical narratives. Especially when dealing with testimonies concerning extreme, disconcerting events and traumatic experience, the obvious issue is how the testimony is employed in a historical account. In this respect, one should obviously recognize that the memory of experience, while always of historical interest, bears a problematic relation to experience during the events and, even more so, to the events themselves—even though there is no simple binary that opposes event and experience. Testimonies may well contain accurate factual statements concerning events, but their accuracy does not derive only from the further fact that the person recounting them actually lived through the events in question. The experience might be seen as lending a certain "authenticity" to the testimony, including its account of events, which should not be simply conflated with its factual accuracy (or "truth value" in a delimited, empirical sense). Whether an experience can be termed authentic (or "true" in other than a delimited empirical sense) when it involves factual inaccuracy (for example, when it refers to a fantasized event that did not empirically take place or to one that took place in a different form) is an issue that is both semantic and evaluative. In any case, testimonies always supplement facts with experience and performative qualities that at times constitute their primary interest both for the historian and for others. Of course when testimonies are the only sources for certain facts, they may have a *faute de mieux* claim to credibility, and cross-checking them when possible is a partial test of their accuracy.

ious role of particular people (immigrants, Jews, and so forth). Moreover, the attempt to narrativize the structural or transhistorical dimension of trauma is always mythological or fictive. And it may feed into the structure of prejudice. There are no discrete, differentiated victims in transhistorical or structural trauma, but there may be in historical trauma or, misleadingly, in the historicization and narrativization of the transhistorical, for example, when woman is scapegoated in the exile from Eden or Jews in the fall from the *Volksgemeinschaft*.

Indeed one might speculate that a misrecognition is at the basis of the tendency to experience as loss the type of absence related to structural or transhistorical trauma (that is, the all-too-common feeling that one has lost what one never really had—such as true community, paradise, authentic memory, or Being). This misrecognition distorts or disguises both the nature of transhistorical trauma related to absence (notably the absence of ultimate foundations) and the dynamics of the intergenerational transmission of trauma and indeterminate feelings of guilt (for example, when such transmission is read or misread as original sin or its secular displacements, for example, in certain understandings of the primal crime or originary melancholia, shame, guilt, or violence).[17] Such a tendency to experience absence as loss (as well as the tendency to displace an actual loss—such as Wilkomirski's loss of his mother—onto a fantasized one) may become attached to actual events such as those of the Holocaust, particularly by someone not living through them, and (along with identification) may be another factor in accounting for the phenomenon of "wannabe" or imaginary survivors who may even come to believe that they were indeed there. It may also lead to the conflation of a putatively transhistorical condition of abjection with the specific problem of victimization, thereby both adding to the allure of victimhood and obscuring the status of discrete historical victims and the perpetrator's role in the perpetrator-victim dynamic.[18]

In historical trauma (or in the historical, as distinguished from transhistorical, dimension of trauma), the traumatizing events may at least in principle be determined with a high degree of determinacy

[17] I would note that, from this perspective, one may belatedly recognize the "death of God" as perhaps the historically necessary experience of an absence as a loss. Conversely, one may see belief as the figuration of absence in terms of a hoped-for presence.

[18] The problem of thinking through the complex, overdetermined relations of the transhistorical and the historical, including the intergenerational, is very difficult and important. For an attempt at a fuller treatment, see my *Writing History, Writing*

and objectivity. These would include the events of the Holocaust, slavery, apartheid, child abuse, or rape. In practice the determination of such events in the past poses problems of varying degrees of difficulty for the obvious reason that our mediated access to such events is through various traces or residues—memory, testimony, documentation, and representations or artifacts.

The experience of trauma poses even greater difficulties, perhaps difficulties of a different order of magnitude. Trauma is itself a shattering experience that disrupts or even threatens to destroy experience in the sense of an integrated or at least viably articulated life. There is a sense in which trauma is an out-of-context experience that upsets expectations and unsettles one's very understanding of existing contexts. Moreover, the radically disorienting experience of trauma often involves a dissociation between cognition and affect. In brief, in traumatic experience one typically can represent numbly or with aloofness what one cannot feel, and one feels overwhelmingly what one is unable to represent, at least with any critical distance and cognitive control. Here one has an aporetic relation between representation and affect with the possibility of uncontrolled oscillation between poles of a double bind. Indeed one might postulate that an aporia marks a trauma that has not been viably worked through, hence inducing compulsive repetition of the aporetic relation. One might also maintain that, in the terms used by Walter Benjamin (at least as I am appropriating them), trauma as experience is *Erlebnis* rather than *Erfahrung*.[19] As *Erlebnis* trauma is a shock to the system and may be acted out or compulsively repeated in so-called traumatic

---

Trauma, chap. 2. I would note that the distinction between the transhistorical and the historical is itself analytic and that the two intersect and interact in complex fashion in actual, historical cases of traumatization. The distinction is important, however, in counteracting the tendency simply to derive one dimension of trauma from the other—to see the historical (such as the Holocaust) simply as an instantiation or illustration of transhistorical trauma (original sin or the Lacanian real, for example) or, conversely, to attribute all dimensions of trauma or its analogues (Heideggerian thrownness, anxiety, and being-toward-death, for example) only to specific events or contexts. While I am acknowledging something like a transhistorical dimension of trauma, I can understand the hesitation to use the same term for it as for historical trauma, although such use would be supported, for example, by the force of the phantasmatic and related processes of identification that may contribute to the historical or "empirical" traumatization of those who have not actually lived through certain limit or extreme events.

[19] On this distinction in Benjamin, see John McCole, *Walter Benjamin and the Antinomies of Tradition* (Ithaca: Cornell University Press, 1993), esp. 2.

memory. *Erfahrung* involves more viable articulations of experience allowing openings to possible futures.

The problem of working through trauma or, more precisely, its recurrent symptoms, is to move from *Erlebnis* to *Erfahrung* to the extent that this movement is possible. (Narration, including experimental narrative, plays an important role here, especially in engaging posttraumatic symptoms of limit events and experiences, but so may other forms such as the lyric or essay as well as performative modes including ritual, song, and dance.)[20] The experience of trauma is thus unlike the traumatizing event in that it is not punctual or datable. It is bound up with its belated effects or symptoms, which render it elusive.[21] Its elusiveness—or what Cathy Caruth terms its unclaimed quality—makes the historical experience of trauma distinguishable only with difficulty from structural or transhistorical trauma, hence facilitating in certain cases the confusion of the imaginary or vicarious experiential identification with certain events and the belief that one actually lived through them (so-called recovered memory).[22] Moreover, as I have already indicated, working through trauma does not imply the possibility of attaining total integration of the self, including the retrospective feat of putting together seamlessly (for

[20] See, for example, the discussion of "black music" in Paul Gilroy, *The Black Atlantic: Modernity and Double Consciousness* (Cambridge: Harvard University Press, 1993), chap. 3.

[21] Those living through limit events generally have limit experiences. But one may have a limit experience without living through a major limit event in history. One may even place oneself intentionally in a high-risk or near-death situation in order to undergo a limit experience with the attendant possibility of "sublime" elation. Such activity may be defended insofar as it does not victimize others (including nonhuman animals) and is entered into with the consent of all participants. One may even see such activity as an attempt to confront structural or transhistorical trauma and provide a setting in which it may be engaged or played out. By contrast historical traumas involving victimization (such as genocides) may be understood in part as ways in which perpetrators avoid or deny such engagement in its relation to their own anxiety and vulnerability.

[22] In one sense recovered memory might be seen as a localization and condensation of the transhistorical in the historical and of the general in the particular. Hence from the belief that the human condition is one of originary sinfulness or abjection, I conclude that I have been sinned against or rendered abject by a parent or a particular group. Or from the belief that child abuse is prevalent in my society, I conclude that I have been a victim of child abuse. Of course intermediary processes of imaginary identification or transposition, at times involving interaction with a therapist, might be necessary in the unfolding of such a practical syllogism. For example, in the complex, contested case of Binjamin Wilkomirski, he identified with Holocaust victims, reacted to a film seen early in life, transposed the loss of the mother, and participated in therapeutic sessions.

example, through a harmonizing or fetishistic narrative) the riven experience of the past trauma. Any such retrospective "suturing" would itself be phantasmatic or illusory. *Working-through means work on posttraumatic symptoms* in order to mitigate the effects of trauma by generating counterforces to compulsive repetition (or acting-out), thereby enabling a more viable articulation of affect and cognition or representation, as well as ethical and sociopolitical agency, in the present and future. Hence, at least as I am using the term, working-through does not mean total redemption of the past or healing its traumatic wounds. Indeed there is a sense in which, while we may work on its symptoms, trauma, once it occurs, is a cause that we cannot directly change or heal. And any notion of full redemption or salvation with respect to it, however this-worldly or deferred, is dubious. But, at least in trauma's historical dimension, we can work to change the causes of this cause insofar as they are social, economic, and political and thereby attempt to prevent its recurrence as well as enable forms of renewal. Insofar as trauma is transhistorical, we can only learn how to live better with its attendant anxiety and not mystifyingly attribute it to an event as its putative cause or project responsibility for it onto a discrete group of scapegoats.

Traumatic memory (at least in Freud's account) may involve belated temporality and a period of latency between a real or fantasized early event and a later one that somehow recalls it and triggers renewed repression, dissociation, or foreclosure and intrusive behavior. But when the past is uncontrollably relived, it is as if there were no difference between it and the present. Whether or not the past is reenacted or repeated in its precise literality (which figures such as Cathy Caruth and Bessel van der Kolk at times maintain but that I doubt), one experientially feels as if one were back there reliving the event, and distance between here and there, then and now collapses. One may, as at times in Caruth, closely approximate or even conflate the event and the experience of trauma for a distinctive reason: a belief that traumatic recall or the posttraumatic symptom, for example the nightmare or flashback, is literal in the dual sense of being, or at least deriving from, a precise replication or repetition of the event and constituting something incomprehensible, nonsymbolizable, or unreadable. (Van der Kolk bases this belief on the questionable idea that the traumatic event leaves a neural pathway or imagistic imprint in the amygdala and that the problem of symbolization or verbalization is based on the lateral "translation" of the dissociated image from the amygdala to the verbal centers of the brain.)[23] In a particularly intriguing statement, Caruth is led to indicate ways in which understanding and working-through entail what she sees as losses:

> The trauma thus requires integration, both for the sake of testimony and for the sake of cure. But on the other hand, the transformation of the trauma into a narrative memory that allows the story to be verbalized and communicated, to be integrated into one's own, and others', knowledge of the past, may lose both the precision and the force that characterizes traumatic recall. . . . Yet beyond the loss of precision there is another, more profound, disappearance: the loss, precisely, of the event's essential incomprehensibility, the force of its *affront to understanding*. It is this dilemma that underlies many survivors' reluctance to translate their experience into speech. . . . The possibility of integration into memory and the consciousness of history thus raises the question, van der Kolk and van der Hart ultimately observe, "whether it is not a sacrilege of the traumatic experience to play with the reality of the past."[24]

[23] This literalized notion of lateral dissociation is the basis of van der Kolk's dubious rejection of repression and the Freudian unconscious at least with respect to trauma.

[24] Cathy Caruth, "Recapturing the Past: Introduction," in *Trauma: Explorations in Memory*, 154. Tending to conflate historical trauma with, or simply subsume it under, a transhistorical notion of trauma (such as the Lacanian real), Slavoj Žižek, in *The Plague of Fantasies* (London: Verso, 1997), is close to Caruth (or even Felman and Agamben) when he writes of Lanzmann's *Shoah*: "This example also brings home the *ethical* dimension of fidelity to the Real *qua* impossible: the point is not simply to 'tell the entire truth about it,' but, above all, to confront the way we ourselves, by means of our subjective position of enunciation, are always-already involved, engaged in it" (215). Elaborating his "example," Žižek states: "Let us clarify the key point apropos of trauma and the Real. Claude Lanzmann's film *Shoah* alludes to the trauma of the Holocaust as something beyond representation (it can be discerned only via its traces, surviving witnesses, remaining monuments); however, the reason for this impossibility of representing the Holocaust is not simply that it is 'too traumatic,' but, rather, that we, observing subjects, are still involved in it, are still a part of the process which generated it (we need only recall a scene from *Shoah* in which Polish peasants from a village near the concentration camp, interviewed now, in our present time, continue to find Jews 'strange,'—that is, repeat the very logic that brought the Holocaust about . . .)." I would certainly agree that there is a strong, perhaps inevitable, tendency to repeat aspects of the traumatic past and that historical trauma is not squarely in the past but implicates "us" to varying degrees depending on our relation to that past and our present practices or even possibilities—indeed that this "transferential" implication is one of the most important considerations with which we have to come to terms in studying the past. I would also acknowledge the inclination of the trau-

Caruth here seems dangerously close to conflating absence (of absolute foundations and total meaning or knowledge) with loss and even sacralizing, or making sublime, the compulsive repetition or acting-out of a traumatic past. I have already indicated that working-through need not be understood to imply the integration or transformation of past trauma into a seamless narrative memory and total meaning or knowledge.[25] Narrative at best helps one not to change

---

matized to experience posttraumatic symptoms not simply as pathological traits to be transcended but as marks of devotion if not monuments to dead intimates. Along with this recognition, I would affirm the need to empathize with survivors such as Charlotte Delbo who did indeed experience a "fidelity" to traumatic experience or to those who were consumed by the events related to it. But I would hesitate to affirm the indiscriminate identification Žižek enacts between "us" and the Polish peasants or the related notion that historical trauma is simply the instantiation of the transhistorically traumatic real. (Žižek does not observe that Lanzmann often distances himself radically from Polish peasants, whom he at times treats with disdainful irony, and enacts an identification between himself and victims, something I argue facilitates his tendency to pose obtrusive questions to survivors in a desire to have them relive—so that he too may "relive"—the traumatic past that he did not directly experience. See my *History and Memory after Auschwitz*, chap. 4.) Moreover, as Žižek at times recognizes, the notion of an ethics of psychoanalysis in terms of a "fidelity" to the traumatic real has the value of enjoining the acknowledgment of a transhistorical dimension of trauma that should not be converted into historical trauma, notably through the operation of a scapegoat mechanism. But, when this notion is hyperbolically made into the basis of ethics in general, it threatens to eventuate in a "sublime" aestheticization of ethics that is dubious in its implications for social and political life in that it ignores or downplays the significance of working through problems and subordinates ethics to a tragic or posttragic vision without sufficiently elaborating the tense, intricate relations between the two. One would also think that a crucial dimension of an ethics of psychoanalysis would be directed at the problem of transference, its uses, and abuses.

[25] Nor should belated recognitions, often associated with working through the past, be conflated with teleology. Belated recognitions, through which one is able to understand or read differently a past phenomenon because of the occurrence of intervening events, may be related both to a qualified sense of historical necessity and to the way a future anterior is active in the past. Without undermining all efforts at contextualization, such recognitions also bring out the illusoriness of attempts to understand something purely and simply in its own terms and its own time (as if the past were not as riven and problematic as the present or future). But the conflation of belatedness with teleology constitutes a dubious attempt to provide full meaning or explanation to a past in relation to the present and future, thereby giving rise to foregone conclusions or a notion of historical inevitability. For example, one may read Nietzsche differently and be attentive to certain dimensions of his thought (its elitism, its invocation of the *Übermensch*, its gestures in the direction of eugenics, its sometimes oracular, ecstatic style) because of Nazi uses and abuses of it. But the conclusion need not be that there is some inevitable link between Nietzsche and the Nazis. Indeed one may also belatedly be particularly aware of aspects of Nietzsche's thought that run

the past through a dubious rewriting of history but to work through posttraumatic symptoms in the present in a manner that opens possible futures. It also enables one to recount events and perhaps to evoke experience, typically through nonlinear movements that allow trauma to register in language and its hesitations, indirections, pauses, and silences. And, particularly by bearing witness and giving testimony, narrative may help performatively to create openings in existence that did not exist before. But a more basic point may be that Caruth's argument represents a displacement of some long-standing religious views relating to a radically transcendent, inscrutable divinity and his mysterious, nonsymbolizable, unreadable, or unrepresentable ways. In secular terms, one is in the vicinity of an aesthetic of the sublime. Caruth's views resonate in certain ways with those of others, such as Theodor Adorno, who at times believed that any mitigation, mediation, or modification of the utterly unacceptable and catastrophic was indicative of unmerited consolation and co-optation by the dominant system, indeed, that it amointed to joining in the SS-dictated music played at Auschwitz to accompany the suffering of victims. Although there are significant countertendencies in Caruth (and in Adorno) that indicate the desirability of working-through,[26] views such as those in the above-quoted passage at times shade into a rather prevalent valorization, even a negative sacralization or rendering sublime, of trauma—a sublimation in a peculiar sense. There may also be a resistance to working-through—working-through often understood (I think mistakenly) in extreme terms both as total transcendence of trauma and as a betrayal of it.[27]

---

counter to Nazi appropriations of it, for example, its self-directed playfulness, irony, and humor or its disdain for scapegoating in general and antisemitism in particular.

[26] See especially Adorno, "What Does Coming to Terms with the Past Mean?" in *Bitburg in Moral and Political Perspective*, ed. Geoffrey Hartman (Bloomington: Indiana University Press, 1986), 114–29. (Adorno's essay was first published in 1959.)

[27] See, for example, Colin Davis, "Levinas on Forgiveness; or, the Intransigence of Rav Hanina," in *PMLA* 117 (2002): 299–302. Davis objects to Julia Kristeva's attempt to elaborate a notion of working-through with respect to forgiveness and opposes it to what he sees as the preferable approach of Levinas "in his darkest and most uncompromising moments" (302). Invoking a particular exegesis to make an argument of a very general if not universal nature, Davis in effect insists on the sublimely intransigent nature of acting-out and, in the process, may even unself-consciously act out or repeat in his own analysis the aggressive pattern he presents a younger rabbi enacting toward Rav Hanina. In the story Rav Hanina refuses to grant forgiveness to the younger rabbi who, after an act that Hanina, in classically Oedipal fashion, interprets

Caruth's as well as Shoshana Felman's form of trauma theory (in *Testimony*) may, at least on one significant level, be read as a fascinatingly subtle, often disguised displacement of Paul de Man's variant of deconstruction in which the terminology changes (with unreadability becoming the incomprehensibility of trauma) but the aporetic and paradoxical discursive strategies recur with some variation.[28] I shall later indicate an interesting way in which Caruth's approach may also resonate with the writing practice of important figures such as Beckett and Kafka. (Felman herself discusses Paul Celan among others.) Without denying the force of considerations theorists such as Caruth and Felman bring forward, one may nonetheless maintain that a noncaricatural, nontotalizing form of working-through is desirable, especially in social and political life, in that it does not transcend but sets up counterforces to the compulsive repetition that remains within—or manifests an uncanny fidelity to—trauma.[29] Working-through also counteracts the tendency to sacralize trauma or to convert it into a founding or sublime event—a traumatic sublime or transfigured moment of blank insight and revelatory abjection that helps to create a compelling, even disabling sense of betrayal if one departs from a "fidelity" to it or at least to those who were destroyed by the events to which it is related. Moreover, the conception of working-through I have proposed may constitute one component of a nondecisionist understanding of ethics and politics.[30]

---

as aggressive, requests it of him. Davis concludes: "Rav Hanina's intransigence hints that to be human is to remain unforgiven" (ibid.). There are of course many ways to be human, and Davis elicits and affirms only one of them. One might also observe that Hanina would not even have been confronted with the problem of forgiveness had he interpreted the younger rabbi's supposed attempt to outshine him as a compliment to the effectiveness of his school's and his own teaching.

[28] The conjunction of trauma theory and deconstruction becomes altogether explicit and valorized in Petar Ramadanovic, *Forgetting Futures: On Memory, Trauma, and Identity* (Lanham, Maryland: Lexington Books, 2001), which dismisses or collapses the distinction between historical and transhistorical or structural trauma.

[29] Žižek puts forward the tragic (or posttragic) fidelity to the traumatic "real" as the "ethic" of Lacanian psychoanalysis. (See, for example, *The Ticklish Subject: The Absent Centre of Political Ontology* [London: Verso, 1999], esp. chap. 6.) This construction represents one way to read Lacan's own "ethical" injunction: Don't give up on your desire (Ne cédez pas sur son désir). See Jacques Lacan, *Le Séminaire VII: L'éthique de la psychanalyse 1959–1960* (Paris: Editions du Seuil, 1986).

[30] Decisionism is the view that all values and ethical judgments ultimately lead to, or are based on, pure subjective decisions. One finds such a view in Max Weber or Carl Schmitt as well as in varieties of existentialism. At times Hayden White seems

In her account, Susan Brison claims to have a fairly accurate memory of the event and even to have raised questions for herself concerning how to understand what was going on as the assault was happening, leading her to criticize Caruth's notion of trauma as an unclaimed or elusive experience. She indicates that her experience may be common in the case of single, in contrast to repeated, traumatizing events, and she asserts that, with respect to the former (a rape, for example), dissociation between mind and body, resulting in an out-of-body experience, is not typical. Brison nonetheless does show signs of a dissociation between affect and cognition with attendant numbness or aloofness and the need to work toward a convergence or viable articulation of feeling and knowledge. In her account one might also detect the elusiveness of the experience in contrast to the event, in the sense that the experience cannot be narrowly localized or dated and constitutes a past that will not pass away—a past that belatedly invades the present and threatens to block the future. The event may be "history" in one common, overly restricted sense of the word, that is to say, over and squarely in the past. But the experience is not "history" in this sense, evidently with respect to traumatic memory and more generally in the case of experience related to events carrying an intense affective and evaluative charge such as those of the Holocaust, other genocides, slavery, or apartheid.

---

to go in this direction in terms of the primacy of decision and the will. The concept of working-through might provide a larger framework for ethical thought, including a crucial role for reasoning. This would not deny the way concrete decisions, especially in controversial cases, cannot be simply deduced from norms or values. But it would make our understanding of ethical judgment more complex, with subjective elements interacting often inextricably with principles or norms. Decisionism still seeks some ultimate foundation for values even if that "totalizing" foundation is subjective, radically relativistic, or idiosyncratic. A notion of working-through would not provide an ultimate foundation or solve all ethical and political problems, but it could be related to a conception of practical reason and forms of social or political action that involve questions of value. This approach would be bound up with the idea that working-through should not be seen purely in terms of individual therapy. Rather it raises larger ethical, social, and political questions. Such a view would not imply that one could fully conflate the ethical and the political, but it would argue for complex relations between the two. For example, the provision of venues and receptive audiences for the testimony of victims as well as perpetrators, indeed for hybrid victim-perpetrators, would itself be a significant political event as well as a phenomenon bound up with broader political issues, such as the role of acknowledging and coming to terms with the past as a condition of a viable democracy. I think one finds this approach to problems as one aspect of the Truth and Reconciliation Commission, however limited its implementation may be in practice.

I have intimated that the experience of trauma may be vicarious or virtual, that is, undergone in a secondary fashion by one who was not there or did not go through the traumatizing events themselves. In the vicarious experience of trauma, one perhaps unconsciously identifies with the victim, becomes a surrogate victim, and lives the event in an imaginary way that, in extreme cases, may lead to confusion about one's participation in the actual events (which, as noted earlier, may conceivably have been the case of Binjamin Wilkormirski with respect to the Holocaust)[31] (One may of course also have this vicarious relation to the perpetrator or to other subject positions in the grid of victimization.) In the virtual (in contrast to the vicarious) experience of trauma, one may imaginatively put oneself in the victim's position while respecting the difference between self and other and recognizing that one cannot take the victim's place or speak in the victim's voice. Such virtual experience may be connected with what I have termed empathic unsettlement, which, I would argue, is desirable or even necessary for a certain form of understanding that is constitutively limited but significant.

[31] See my discussion of Wilkomirski's *Fragments: Memories of a Wartime Childhood*, in *Writing History, Writing Trauma*, 207–9. I argue that one should empathize with, and be unsettled by, Wilkomirski and *Fragments* but nonetheless criticize the text for social and political reasons, notably the way it confuses subject positions and may feed misplaced doubts about other testimonies. In this sense, Wilkomirski's disconcerting plight as enacted in his text, including the challenges it poses to the reader, should not simply be conflated with the role of his text as a phenomenon in the public sphere. See also Stefan Maechler, *The Wilkomirski Affair: A Study in Biographical Truth*, trans. John E. Woods (New York: Schocken Books, 2001). For a very different approach to Wilkomirski and his text, see Ross Chambers, "Orphaned Memories, Foster-Writing, Phantom Pain: The *Fragments* Affair," in *Extremities: Trauma, Testimony, and Community*, ed. Nancy K. Miller and Jason Tougaw (Urbana: University of Illinois Press, 2002). Chambers approaches *Fragments* through the categories of asyndeton (disconnectedness) and hypotyposis (vividness). And he sees Wilkomirski as a cultural symptom of collective repression of the Holocaust and thereby haunted or even possessed by ghosts that "we" have not laid to rest. In a sense, Wilkomirski becomes the almost saintly if not sublime bearer of the phantom pain and the haunting posttraumatic symptoms others have repressed, even a possessed writer whose confusion or collapse of genres (memoir and fiction) conveys "truth as a cultural symptom" (99)—indeed "the recognizable truth that arises from the readability of the figural" (109). The difficulty with Chambers's rhetorically intricate and psychologically sensitive analysis is that it tropes away from specificity and may obscure, rather than illuminate, historical, sociopolitical, and ethical issues. Perhaps as a result of his identificatory, free-indirect style, the collectivity to which he refers remains free-floating and unspecific, and his use of psychoanalysis threatens to conflate issues and become speculative in a critically uncontrolled manner. Indeed one might question Chambers's argument with a contrasting view. Wilkomirski was Swiss and an orphan. At

One may, however, believe that affect and cognition or even understanding are utterly incommensurable and that any articulation (or compromise formation) conjoining them is impossible. In this view affect is by definition unbound and excessive. One may also believe that the secondary witness can only (indeed ought to) respond to the experience (or even the texts) of the victim or survivor in an uncontrolled affective manner. On the basis of these beliefs (or assumptions), which are at times operative in certain variants of psychoanalysis, working-through, in however limited or qualified a form, is itself impossible, and the point is to "work through" working-through to the recognition that one is always already—indeed can only be—acting out or participating compulsively in the "contagiousness" of trauma. Transference not only invariably occurs; it is all-consuming and untransformable. In certain variants of this approach, there is a conflation between transhistorical and historical dimensions of trauma, and the intractability of the former is transferred without mediation onto the latter. And there are no significant differences between the victim, the survivor, and the secondary witness since all are (at least in the "post-Auschwitz" world) (post)tragically and (post)apocalyptically within the death drive or the compulsive repetition, acting out posttraumatic symptoms and uncontrolled affect. Binjamin Wilkormirski may be figured as (the idealized avatar of) everyman, and certain distinctions—between victim and survivor, between victim-survior and secondary witness,

---

least in terms of sociocultural stereotypes, to which Wilkomirski was apparently very sensitive, these subject positions did not provide a sufficiently clear and substantial identity. By the time Wilkomirski had his experience of recovered memory and wrote his "memoir," the Holocaust was not simply a collective ghost that had not been laid to rest. (How the Holocaust may have "haunted" Switzerland is not raised by Chambers, despite recent disclosures about Swiss banks, and he does not even pose as a problem how "haunting" does not apply in the same way to all nations or groups.) By the time Wilkomirski wrote his book and may actually have come to undergo secondary traumatization and believe he was (or even came to be "born again" as) a Holocaust victim and survivor, the Holocaust had become in many ways a basis for an affirmative identity as a founding trauma bringing with it a great deal of "cultural capital." If Wilkomirski was a cultural symptom, it might well be that he was symptomatic of the Holocaust as a transnational metaphor and icon of victimhood transfigured into an identity that could be affirmed and (at times vividly) enacted, thereby serving both to anchor anxiety and to compensate for the lack Wilkomirski experienced as an orphan. This analysis may remain rather speculative, but it at least serves to bring out the limitations and counter certain dimensions of less controlled, unframed speculation.

between acting-out and working-through—are to be collapsed or radically blurred.[32] Any type of representation or signification must itself become impossible or even sacrilegious, and it can go forward only in the agonizing form of a recurrent, even compulsively repetitive, insistence on its very impossibility or aporetic, abyssal nature.[33]

Here one touches on extremely difficult problems that are not amenable to facile resolution. I have been arguing for certain problematic but important distinctions that touch on very basic assumptions about thought, ethics, politics, and the relation between thought and practice. And differences in orientation may reach toward very ingrained assumptions related both to more or less displaced religious

[32] Hence, in part on the basis of a misreading, Ann Cvetkovich writes: "I refuse the sharp distinction between mourning and melancholy that leads Dominick LaCapra, for example, to differentiate between 'working through,' the successful resolution of trauma, and 'acting out,' the repetition of trauma that does not lead to transformation. Not only does the distinction often seem tautological—good responses to trauma are cases of working through, bad ones are cases of acting out—but the verbal link between 'acting out.' and ACT UP suggests that activism's modes of acting out, especially its performative and expressive functions, are a crucial resource for responding to trauma." "Legacies of Trauma, Legacies of Activism. ACT UP' Lesbians," in Loss, ed. David L. Eng and David Kazanjian (Berkeley: University of California Press, 2003), 434. One might be surprised by the appeal to verbal association in the last sentence, and one might also argue that certain political tactics are not simply modes of acting-out but may involve attempts to work through problems on a collective level—more generally, that the relations between acting-out and working-through are not simple or unilinear. As I clearly state in an early formulation to which Cvetkovich explicitly refers: "I would emphasize that the relation between acting-out and working-through should not be seen in terms of a from/to relationship in which the latter is presented as the dialectical transcendence of the former. I have noted that, particularly in cases of trauma, acting-out may be necessary and perhaps never fully overcome. Indeed, it may be intimately bound up with working through problems. But it should not be isolated, theoretically fixated on, or one-sidedly valorized as the horizon of thought or life" (Representing the Holocaust, 205). Cvetkovich may well tend in the direction indicated in the last statement insofar as she adamantly resists any notion of working-through and conflates performativity with acting-out. My own inclination would not be to conflate with acting-out the carefully staged, typically strategic enactments of ACT UP, but instead to see homophobic responses to ACT UP as typical instances of acting-out. In any case there are questions here on which disagreement is possible or even likely, but it should be related to an accurate understanding of the view to which one takes exception. Moreover, while it would be deceptive to see the relation between acting-out and working-through on the model of a simplistic division between "good" and "bad" objects, the issues to which these concepts are related do indeed raise difficult normative issues at times involving judgment—issues that are misleadingly encrypted in prevalent concepts of normality and pathology.

[33] It might seem that one has a paradigm case of this insistence in the final words of Samuel Beckett's Unnamable: "You must go on, I can't go on, you must go on, I'll go on, you must say words, as long as there are any, until they find me, until they

views and to one's relation to recent theoretical currents that themselves have tangled relations to religion and its displacements. (I have indicated one possible instance of this relation to religion or its displacements regarding the work of Cathy Caruth.) And certain cases are extremely complex. For example, Primo Levi, a few months before his death (which some believe was a suicide), is reported to have indicated to a friend that he had stopped having his recurrent nightmare related to his experiences in Auschwitz.[34] If indeed his death was a suicide, one might speculate that the nightmare was experienced by him as more (or even other) than a pathological symptom—that the "symptom" had become a ritual activity or memorial binding him to those "drowned" in the camps and that its loss could have been experienced as a genuine loss if not a betrayal. (Charlotte Delbo at times explicitly sees her own "symptoms" in this light.)[35]

In this sense a posttraumatic "symptom" would itself exist in a tangled relation to acting out or compulsively repeating the past and attempting to work through it. Writing—or more generally signifying

---

say me, strange pain, strange sin, you must go on, perhaps it's done already, perhaps they have said me already, perhaps they have carried me to the threshold of my story, before the door that opens on my story, that would surprise me, if it opens, it will be I, it will be the silence, where I am, I don't know, I'll never know. In the silence you don't know, you must go on, I can't go on, I'll go on" (*Three Novels by Samuel Beckett: Molloy, Malone Dies, The Unnamable*, trans. Patrick Bowles in collaboration with the author [New York: Grove Press, 1955], 414). It is nonetheless significant that the structure of this passage, which might be read as addressing what I earlier termed absence and not only loss, resembles a dislocated, incantatory, call-and-response prayer or litany.

[34] See Elspeth Probyn, "Dis/connect: Space, Affect, Writing," paper given in "Spatial Cultures Conference," University of Newcastle, Australia, June 2, 2001. Online at http://home.iprimus.com.au/painless/space/elspeth.html. Probyn argues that Levi's suicide (which she believes others deny was indeed a suicide because of their desire for uplift) was caused by his no longer being able to endure the trauma "reenacted" in his writing. She thus sees writing in terms of unmediated acting out of affect and ignores the possibility that the posttraumatic symptom may be ritualized as a bond with the dead whose loss may itself be destabilizing. Probyn is extremely critical of what she understands (I think reductively or even inaccurately) to be my view of working-through, which she thinks simply denies the effects of trauma in secondary traumatization. She advocates "affective" writing on the part of the secondary witness, who seems very close in her account to identifying with the voice of Levi or other victim/survivors. Her understanding of the relations among trauma, affect, and representation or signification, as well as between victims, survivors, and secondary witnesses is, however, far from clear.

[35] See the excellent article by Thomas Trezise, "The Question of Community in Charlotte Delbo's *Auschwitz and After*" MLN 117 (2002): 858–84.

practices, including bearing witness or giving testimony—would in different but related ways themselves mediate that tangled relation and help to prevent its dissolution in the direction of either uncontrolled repetition or deceptive closure. Indeed maintaining such a tense, even tangled relation may be crucial in the movement from victim to survivor—a movement that is not linear but subject to unpredictable returns and uneven developments. But a question is whether the secondary witness can or ought to have a mimetic or unmediated identificatory relation to the "symptoms" of victims and survivors. I have indicated that I think secondary traumatization is indeed possible. To judge whether it is desirable would entail considering how ethical, social, and political issues applied and whether they were preempted by higher-order considerations that were religious or "ethical" in some revised sense related to the quasi-religious. A somewhat similar issue arises with respect to an analogy I made earlier to the imitation of Christ. A believer who identifies with Christ to such an extent that he or she leads a life of absorbed, melancholic devotion and may be unable to perform ordinary social or political duties is a deeply problematic and at times moving or captivating figure. Such an intense "affective" or lived response may in certain important respects be uncontrollable, but one may also help to induce it "performatively" by lowering critical defenses, opening oneself to certain experiences, immersing oneself in certain practices, and internalizing certain ideological and "theoretical" perspectives. Responses to Claude Lanzmann as figured in his film *Shoah* are at times imbued with the kind of awe that might be evoked by a prophet or even a saint bearing stigmata.[36] Some initiatives may be contestable, especially insofar as they obscure problems, for example, the way that Lanzmann's seeming identification with the victim (notably the former barber at Treblinka, Abraham Bomba) may induce him to pose intrusive, insensitive, insistent questions that do not respect what a person may have good reasons not to disclose, especially to an inter-

---

[36] See, for example, Elisabeth Huppert, "Voir (*Shoah*)", 150–56; and Sami Naïr, "*Shoah*, une leçon d'humanité," 164–74, in *Au sujet de Shoah: le Film de Claude Lanzmann*, ed. Michel Deguy (Paris: Belin, 1990). Huppert writes: "To attach the term *prophet* to Claude Lanzmann is embarrassing but not to do so is a lie" (151). Discussing the exchange between Lanzmann and Abraham Bomba, which he sees as "worthy of the greatest tragic works," Naïr validates identification with (or *imitatio* of) the victim in asserting: "For there is no other way than this, *to relive in one's flesh the tragedy of tortured victims*" (172, emphasis in the original).

viewer making a film.[37] On the other hand, Lanzmann is indeed disconcerting, and one may well have inhibitions about criticizing him related to one's own sense that certain forms of identification with the victim may approach a quasi-religious experience that resists ethical and political judgment. Such an identification may occur in ordinary life to the point of leading someone to stop eating, washing, or fulfilling obligations (caring for children or meeting other legitimate expectations). A person in this state, like Raczymow's Esther, entering into profound melancholia and even undergoing secondary traumatization, may be compelling or at least unsettling (indeed "strangely disconcerting" or uncanny). Without being immune to the compelling force of the tragic, one may still ask whether one may attempt to provide guardrails or preventive possibilities, for example, when approaching certain issues (even the viewing of videos and documentaries) or attempting to work through problems when they arise.

It is nonetheless important not to reify the concepts of acting-out and working-through or to see them as pure binaries, components of a linear process, or exhaustive of all possible responses to traumatic events and experiences. Nor should one pathologize the concept of acting-out or valorize in one-dimensional terms the process of working-through. There are many subtle modulations of response and complex interactions between more or less compulsive repetition and work or play on symptoms bringing about significant variations on what is repeated. Moreover, the very meaning and significance of processes vary with context and subject position. A theorist or commentator who (I think questionably) speaks for the victim, or transforms the traumas of others into the occasion for a discourse of sublimity, should not be conflated with a victim who experiences a symptom as a binding memorial to dead intimates, or even with a person possessed by the dead and "mimetically" speaking in their voices. In the latter two cases one might restrict oneself to an attempt at compassionate understanding and suspend judgment or realize that one does not have a subject position that enables worthwhile commentary. In the case of a theorist or commentator one may indeed be warranted in offering criticism. Moreover, the conversion of trauma into other modalities may take many forms, for example, the

---

[37] For an elaboration of this argument, see my *History and Memory after Auschwitz*, chap. 4.

transformation of the compulsive repetition of the symptom into a ritualized repetition, which may occur in a sociocultural process of mourning, memorialization, pilgrimage, or prayer. How such conversions function in a larger sociopolitical context may be ambiguous and varied, in any case not subject to an overly general analysis or judgment. And the slippage between the transhistorical and the historical dimension of trauma is at times compelling, perhaps irresistible, particularly for the severely traumatized or those identifying with them.

In the attempt to represent traumatizing events and traumatic or posttraumatic experience, testimony, fiction, and history may share certain features, for instance, on the level of narrative, but they also differ, notably with respect to truth claims and the way that an account is framed. Testimony makes truth claims about experience or at least one's memory of it and, more tenuously, about events (although one clearly expects someone who claims to be a survivor to have lived through certain events in actuality). Still, the most difficult and moving moments of testimony involve not truth claims but experiential "evidence"—the apparent reliving of the past, as the witness, going back to an unbearable scene, is overwhelmed by emotion and for a time unable to speak.[38]

History makes truth claims about events, their interpretation or explanation, and, more tenuously, about experience. It may take certain leads from testimony and critically test memory without

[38] Kriss Ravetto misses the point of my argument and confuses distinctions I try to draw when she asserts that I criticize Lanzmann's *Shoah* "for expressing the presence rather than the *pastness* of the trauma of the Holocaust" (*The Unmaking of Fascist Aesthetics* [Minneapolis: University of Minnesota Press, 2001], 35). My argument in no way denies the importance of Lanzmann's awareness of the "presence" of past trauma or its posttraumatic symptoms, but it does question the means and motivation through which he at times leads survivors (such as Abraham Bomba) to become victims again by reexperiencing their traumas so that he too may "relive" them and presumably transmit them to viewers of his film. I have indicated that one should distinguish between the tendency of certain victims and survivors to manifest a "fidelity" to traumatic experience and lost intimates, which may involve a sacralization or memorialization of trauma, and the transfiguration of trauma into the sacred or the sublime on the part of commentators. Moreover, the orientation of perpetrators may be attended by the valorization of extreme transgression or unheard-of atrocity in a manner that conflates the sublime with "radical evil" (which conceivably could be seen as an extreme, negative version or inversion of the sublime). This conflation may well be part of the "fascination" exerted by fascism and by limit events in general. Here one has extremely difficult problems for the commentator who attempts to analyze this complex of problems, including problems of terminology,

becoming identical to them. Indeed in trying to account for or evoke experience, history must turn to testimony, oral reports, inferences from documents such as diaries and memoirs, and a carefully framed and qualified reading of fiction and art. Fiction, if it makes historical truth claims at all, does so in a more indirect but still possibly informative, thought-provoking, at times disconcerting manner with respect to the understanding or "reading" of events, experience, and memory. (There is a reading of the aftermath of slavery in Morrison's *Beloved*, and it may suggest hypotheses for historians and social scientists, for example, concerning the process of the intergenerational transmission of trauma within a group.) Especially in the recent past, fiction may well explore the traumatic, including the fragmentation, emptiness, or evacuation of experience, and may raise the question of other possible forms of experience. It may also explore in a particularly telling and unsettling way the affective or emotional dimensions of experience and understanding. Vicarious experience, linked to processes of identification, may lead to the extreme blurring or effacement of these distinctions insofar as one who was not there comes (or is moved) to believe he or she was indeed there and presents fiction as if it were testimony or historical memoir. Or, to put it another way, in phantasy the specificity of fiction is effaced, and the event and the experience are collapsed. The experience—real, "really" phantasized, simulated, or some combination thereof—becomes enough for the postulation of the event. By contrast, virtual (as distinguished from vicarious) experience and, more specifically, empathy in the sense I am using the term (a sense that does not conflate it with projective or incorporative identification inducing vicarious victimage), are related to the recognition and enactment of certain distinctions (including the distinction—not the binary or total opposition—between self and other).

I have touched on the perplexing question of how to represent and relate to extremely transgressive or limit events typically associated with traumatic experiences such as those of the Holocaust. (Only recently has one formulated explicitly the problem of the relation

---

voice, and perspective. One danger of an overly participatory account or a generalized free-indirect style is the role of unintentional movements in voice and perspective through which the quest for an "intellectual high" may engender indiscriminately elated "sublimations" of trauma that bring identification not only with victims but with dimensions of perpetrators.

between the limit event and trauma.) Let me insert here that one may initially define a limit event as an event that goes beyond the capacity of the imagination to conceive or anticipate it. Before it happened, it was not—perhaps could not be—anticipated or imagined, and one does not quite know what is verisimilar or plausible in its context. At the very least there was extreme resistance to envisioning its possibility. Hence such an event (or series of events) must in some sense be traumatic or traumatizing, and what would call for special explanation is the nontraumatization of one who had experienced it. Even after its occurrence, such an event may still test or possibly exceed the imagination, including the imagination of those not experiencing it directly (those who were not there). Here the facts may go beyond one's powers of imagination and may even seem incredible—something that is grist for the mill of negationists or deniers of these events.[39] The seemingly unimaginable nature of the limit event is also a reason why fictional or artistic treatment of such events may seem unsatisfying or lacking. This excess of event or fact over imaginative power—this beggaring of the imagination (which has been disconcertingly prevalent in the recent past)—poses a great challenge for artistic representation or treatment. This challenge does not disappear—it may even increase—when the extreme or exceptional appears in the everyday as a distorted "normality" that subverts normativity.

One important question here is the role of empathy or compassion in understanding, including historical understanding, and its complex relations to objectivity and transference. Objectivity is indeed a goal of professional historiography, related to the attempt to represent the past as accurately as possible. One may reformulate and defend this goal in postpositivistic terms by *both* questioning the idea of a fully transparent, unproblematic, neutral representation of the way things in the past "really were" *and* recognizing the need to come to terms with one's transferential and affect-laden implication in the object of study by critically mediating perhaps inevitable projective or incorporative identifications, undertaking meticulous research,

[39] I would note that confronting traumatic anxiety but remaining self-possessed is constitutive of authenticity (*Eigentlichkeit*) in Heidegger. Moreover, what I have elsewhere termed the Nazi sublime was distinctive in combining the perpetration of extreme, traumatizing, radically transgressive acts with hardness that foreclosed traumatization of the perpetrator.

and being open to the way one's findings may bring into question or even contradict one's initial hypotheses. Study and research may change one's judgments and even affect one's identity, especially in the case of emotionally charged, value-related issues.

While the question of objectivity has continued to preoccupy commentators, empathy has by and large been eliminated from discussions of historiography in the recent past both by historians and by philosophers of history. This is the case despite the widespread turn to the question of experience, including memory, among historians. By and large, the turn to experience has not as yet renewed interest in the role of empathy or even affect in general in historical understanding. One problem is the tendency to disown empathy (as does Inge Clendinnen in *Reading the Holocaust*) after conflating it with intuition or with projective identification.[40] (Something similar happens in the discussion of AIDS by Douglas Crimp and others in the book *Trauma*, edited by Cathy Caruth.) Empathy may also be seen as a self-sufficient psychological response that obviates or obscures the need for sociopolitical understanding, critique, and action. Indeed a prevalent move in recent thought is both to conflate empathy with identification and to oppose it to "compassion fatigue" or numbing, which is presumably caused by the excess of media images or representations of violence and trauma.[41] Aside from its impressionistic nature, such a move is implicitly implicated in the traumatic process of dissociation in that it separates out and hypostatizes one dissociated symptom of secondary traumatization—numbing—and inadequately accounts for its complement in uncontrolled affective overload. It also translates what should be cultural and political critique into unmediated psychological terms and thereby encrypts, obscures, or buries normative judgment. What typically accompanies such analyses is the

[40] Inga Clendinnen, *Reading the Holocaust* (New York: Cambridge University Press, 1999), 90.
[41] There have been discussions of empathy, typically conflated with identification, in certain quarters, notably popular, psychologically oriented writing where the recent past is seen in terms of a voyeuristic fascination with spectacle and atrocity related to the public's numbing inundation with media images and the attendant erosion of empathy or condition of "compassion fatigue." Such analyses at times have the interest and the limitations of impressionistic, theoretically underdeveloped commentary. See, for example, the varying but, in terms of the understanding of the recent past, convergent approaches in Susan Moeller, *Compassion Fatigue* (New York: Routledge, 1999); Stanley Cohen, *States of Denial: Knowing about Atrocities and Suffering*

idea that the media appeal to voyeurism or even pornography in the exploitation of the suffering of others. But this idea, which may be at least partially valid, is not accompanied by explicit normative judgment and critique subject to argument. Psychology, especially popular psychology, takes the place of argument and conceals an unargued crypto-normativism. And empathy, conflated with identification and seen as exhausted or eroded, is not rethought.

In the form I am proposing, empathy is not self-sufficient and does not mean unmediated identification, although the latter does tend to occur. Empathy is bound up with a transferential relation to the past, and it is arguably an affective aspect of understanding that both limits objectification and exposes the self to involvement or implication in the past, its actors, and victims. An empathic response requires the recognition of others as other than mere objects of research unable to question one or place one in question. And it does not substitute for, but on the contrary must be articulated with, normative judgment and sociopolitical response. Desirable empathy, I would suggest, involves not self-sufficient, projective or incorporative identification but what might be termed empathic unsettlement in the face of traumatic limit events, their perpetrators, and their victims. It might also conceivably be understood in terms of the oxymoronic notion of heteropathic identification. And it involves virtual not vicarious experience—that is to say, experience in which one puts oneself in the other's position without taking the place of—or speaking for—the other or becoming a surrogate victim who appropriates the victim's voice or suffering. Instead affective involvement in, and response to, the other comes with respect for the otherness of the other, which is obliterated in identification that may be attended by appropriative or extremely intrusive behavior (for example, at times in the questions and camera work of those making testimonial videos, where the telos may even be the shot of traumatic breakdown dubiously conflated, at least for the viewer, with *jouissance*). Affective involvement, I am suggesting,

(Oxford: Polity Press, in association with Blackwell Publishers, 2001); and Karl F. Morrison, *"I Am You": The Hermeneutics of Empathy in Western Literature, Theology, and Art* (Princeton: Princeton University Press, 1988). Carolyn Dean is currently engaged in a historical study of developments in perceptions of empathy and dignity in the recent past.

takes (or should take) the form of empathic unsettlement—or rather various forms of empathic unsettlement that differ with respect to victims, perpetrators, and the multiple ambiguous figures in Primo Levi's gray zone.[42]

Empathic unsettlement may and even should affect the mode of representation or signification in different, nonlegislated ways—ways that differ by discipline or field—but still in a fashion that places a great stress on writing or representation that addresses traumatic experience and limit events. Such unsettlement varies by object of inquiry and understanding, notably with respect to perpetrators, victims, hybrid perpetrator-victims, bystanders, so-called rescuers, and others within the complex network of relations that are particularly difficult to decipher and address in the case of the traumatic and extreme. But one might contend that in all cases it inhibits or prevents unmodulated, neopositivistic objectification, unmediated identification, and harmonizing narratives. Moreover, empathic unsettlement is related to the performative dimension of an account, and the problem of performative engagement with unsettling phenomena is insistent in an exchange with the past (of course in different, contestable ways in different genres). One's own unsettled response to another's unsettlement disturbs disciplinary protocols of representation and raises problems bound up with one's implication in, or transferential relation to, charged, value-related events and those caught up in them. Hence one may argue that there is something inappropriate about signifying practices—histories, films, or novels, for example—that in their very style or manner of address tend to overly objectify, smooth over, or obliterate the nature and impact of the traumatic events they treat—what is at times mistakenly seen as working

---

[42] One of the dubious bases for the extreme generalization of the gray zone is the belief that the alleged passivity of victims (going "like sheep to the slaughter") itself constitutes a mode of complicity and hence entry into the gray zone. This view may well be based on a misunderstanding of the helplessness, extreme oppression, and effects of traumatization in the case of certain victims, and it may even involve an unfortunate tendency to blame the victim. One finds such a view even in Raul Hilberg's important *Destruction of the European Jews* (New York: Harper & Row, 1961), and its prevalence in Israel during a certain period is evidenced by its appearance in "why-did-you-not-resist"-type questions posed to survivors during the Eichmann trial in 1961 (despite Chief Prosecutor Gideon Hausner's evident sympathy for victims and his insistence on making a place for their testimonies at the trial). One of the beneficial effects of the trial was to help make such a view seem misplaced and insensitive.

through the past (or, in historiography, as repesentation in terms of a dubiously homogenizing notion of *beau style*). Here one may raise questions about the second part of Benigni's film *Life Is Beautiful* (situated in a camp and at times approximating a wishful realization of a posthypnotic suggestion), the penultimate scene of the yellowbrick graveside ritual in *Schindler's List*, (usually remembered as the ending), or the various uses of the Anne Frank story for one's spiritual uplift or as a demonstration of one's human dignity.[43] But one need not simply dissociate affect or empathy from intellectual, cognitive, and stylistic or rhetorical concerns, and one may ask whether empathy is on some level necessary for even limited understanding. One may even contend that there can be no durable ethical and political change without the reeducation of affect in its relation to normative judgment (what one might see as a call for a revisionary understanding of moral sentiments). Such reeducation would have to take place on multiple levels and in multidimensional ways, and it would pose the question of the relation between ethical judgment and sociopolitical critique.

In literature and art, one may observe the role of a practice that is especially pronounced in the recent past but may also be found earlier, notably in testimonial art, to wit, experimental, gripping, and risky symbolic emulation of trauma in what might be called traumatized or posttraumatic writing or signification. This markedly performative writing may be a means of bearing witness to, enacting, and, to some extent, working over and through trauma, whether personally experienced, transmitted from intimates, or sensed in one's larger social and cultural setting. Indeed such writing, with significant variations, has been prevalent in various figures since the end of the nineteenth century. One crucial form it takes—notably in demanding figures such as Blanchot, Kafka, Celan, and Beckett—is what might be seen as a writing of terrorized disempowerment as close as possible to the experience of abject or traumatized victims without presuming to be identical to it. At times this writing involves the attempt at precise, exact, painstakingly literal and detailed rendering or repetition of opaque, incomprehensible events or experiences. In the paradoxically precise or literal rendering of the opaque, one remains at times within

---

[43] See the discussions of Spielberg in my *History and Memory after Auschwitz*, 61, and of Frank in my *Writing History, Writing Trauma*, 42 n.

the compelling symptom that is conveyed in something close to its unmitigated unsettlement. And this procedure in certain ways resonates, as I noted earlier, with Cathy Caruth's construction of trauma in terms of literality as precise, detailed incomprehensibility. Such a procedure might be seen as a form of compulsive discursive repetition of happenings with an undecidable relation to their ritualization or incantatory enunciation. Paradoxically, it is also uncannily close to the method of "literal," minimalist representation that the philosopher Berel Lang has advocated as the only one appropriate for the Holocaust in that it reduces (or seems to reduce) to the vanishing point any interpretation or imaginative intervention by the historian. Hans Kellner has termed Lang's approach "a sort of postmodern literalism, a self-critical (or self-deconstructing, if you will) literalism that points querulously to its own impossibilty."[44] Kellner's characterization brings out both the interest and the problematic nature of Lang's view.

In certain forms of experimental writing or performance, one may even more or less cautiously inhabit, or be inhabited by, the "voices" of others, including the dead, whom one evokes. This type of explicit simulation may be distinguished from unmediated forms of "speaking for" others, which tend to preempt their voices and reinstate oppressive or colonial relations. The validity and rhetorical success of simulation would depend on the specific way it is enacted, and its role in different fields or genres would be open to debate. Those "possessed" by the voices of others may write or enact a variant of the captivity narrative marked by multiple inflections of compulsive repetition and reworking or working through the past. One at times sees the complex movements of a captivity narrative in the writing of Charlotte Delbo, for example, or, in a different register, in dimensions of Alain Resnais's film (scripted by Marguerite Duras), *Hiroshima, mon amour*, which takes the form of an at times noncommunicating interplay of captivity narratives.[45]

In the case of Celan, what might in one sense be read as a form of posttraumatic writing was exacerbated by the way he was dispos-

[44] See Kellner's "'Never Again' Is Now," in *History and Theory: Contemporary Readings*, ed. Brian Fay, Philip Pomper, and Richard T. Vann (Malden, Mass.: Blackwell Publishers, 1998), 235.
[45] On *Hiroshima, mon amour*, see the informative discussion in Nancy Wood, *Vectors of Memory*, chap. 8.

sessed of language. German, his "mother" tongue, had been expropriated and abused to an extreme point by the Nazis, and he was forced to write poetry, or some remnant of it, in what was for him in effect a dead language. Those writing in other languages did not, I think, experience the same extreme of alienation or dispossession with respect to language. Primo Levi retained a love for Italian, and the culture it conveyed was a source of sustenance for him in the camps and after. Here Italian fascism was not as great a linguistic force as Nazism proved to be. Levi even marked his distance from Celan in perhaps too pronounced a way:

> The darkness that grows from page to page until the last inarticulate babble fills one with consternation like the gasps of a dying man; indeed, it is just that. It enthralls us as whirlpools enthrall us, but at the same time it robs us of what was supposed to be said but was not said, thus frustrating and distancing us. I think that Celan the poet must be considered and mourned rather than imitated. If his is a message, it is lost in the "background noise." It is not communication; it is not a language, or at most it is a dark and maimed language, precisely that of someone who is about to die and is alone, as we will all be at the moment of death.[46]

Like the Italians, the French did not undergo extreme linguistic alienation as a consequence of Vichy propaganda or language policy. Blanchot's writing can be uncanny but this is not primarily because of the estrangement or extreme distortion of the French language itself through its political uses and abuses (to some extent including Blanchot's own use of it in his prewar journalism). Even Beckett's linguistic exile and nomadic movement between English and French was to a significant extent self-imposed and involved an adoptive French as an uneasy refuge from an English that had been made in certain ways uninhabitable for the Irish by English rule but not corrupted in the manner in which the Third Reich had transformed German, particularly for Jews. (Here Victor Klemperer's diaries and his book on the language of the Third Reich are pertinent reference

[46] Quoted in Giorgio Agamben, *Remnants of Auschwitz: The Archive and the Witness*, 37.

points.)[47] Celan's residual love of German, the only language in which he felt he could write, was largely unrequited and desperate. Yet his poetic task (*Aufgabe*, or restrained "messianic" hope against hope) was performatively to bear repeated witness—to re-petition in an anguished attempt to (re)open this all-but-dead language not only to other languages but to the other (notably the murdered, spectral Jewish other) in itself.

In historiography bearing witness to, simulating, or even "emulating" trauma in an extremely exposed and experimental style would be a questionable gesture to the extent that it overwhelmed the demands of accurate reconstruction and critical analysis instead of tensely interacting with and perforce raising questions for those demands. I would in general argue that in history there is a crucial role for empathic unsettlement as an aspect of understanding that stylistically upsets the narrative voice and counteracts harmonizing narration or unqualified objectification yet allows for a tense interplay between critical, necessarily objectifying (even self-protectingly "numbing") reconstruction and affective response to certain problems, people, and texts. I would even entertain the possibility of carefully framed movements in which the historian attempts more risk-laden, experimental overtures in an effort to come to terms with

[47] Victor Klemperer, *The Language of the Third Reich: LTI, Lingua Tertii Imperii: A Philologist's Notebook*, trans. Martin Brady (1947; London: Athlone Press, 2000); *I Will Bear Witness: A Diary of the Nazi Years 1933–1941* and *1942–45*, 2 vols., trans. Martin Chalmers (1995; New York, Random House, 1998–99). One may note that Heinrich Himmler makes a suspect appeal to experience in his famous or infamous 1943 Posen speech to upper-level SS officers: " 'The Jewish people is going to be annihilated,' says every party member. 'Sure, it's in our program, elimination of the Jews, annihilation— we'll take care of it.' And then they all come trudging, 80 million worthy Germans, and each of them has his one decent Jew. Sure, the others are swine, but this one is an A-1 Jew. Of all those who talk this way, not one has seen it happen, not one has been through it [or "not one has had the experience"—*keiner hat es durchgestanden*]. Most of you must know what it means to see a hundred corpses lie side by side, or five hundred, or a thousand. To have stuck this out and—excepting cases of human weakness—to have kept our integrity [or decency—*anständig geblieben zu sein*], that is what has made us hard. In our history this is an unwritten and never-to-be-written page of glory" (Lucy Dawidowicz, ed., *A Holocaust Reader*, [West Orange, N. J.: Behrman House, 1976], 133). In this passage Himmler, in a disconcerting use of free-indirect style, is bearing witness to the "authentic" experience of perpetrators, initiated to (or "in the know" about) what he represents as the glory or "sublimity" of mass murder, and contrasting it to the attitude of ordinary party members and then ordinary Germans in general who simply mouth words or even give false testimony in misguidedly seeking the exception, which is excluded by fanatical commitment and devotion to the sovereign will and "sacred" orders of the *Führer*.

limit events. Foucault's *Histoire de la folie* poses the problems I have touched on in an accentuated form in that Foucault at his most disconcerting as writer does not objectively analyze or even quote the voices of the other or of unreason but allows them to infiltrate, agitate, and fracture his own voice in a variant of free indirect style or middle voice.[48] In Michel de Certeau's *The Possession at Loudun* the historian-narrator moves subtly from objective narration to varied relations of proximity and distance to the voices and perspectives of those he discusses. He is closest to Father Jean-Joseph Surin, both quoting the exorcist and at times engaging in (being possessed by?) a kind of free indirect discourse with respect to him.[49]

I would note that the use of a generalized free indirect discourse or style is rather prevalent in recent literary and philosophical criticism that has an emulative or performative relation to its object. Although I think there is a stylistic role for effects of empathic unsettlement in historical understanding, there may be good reasons to resist extreme, generalized forms of *mitsingen* or what might be called sing-along writing—more precisely and less pejoratively, participatory and performative emulation of the object, in which performativity may at times be conflated with identificatory enactment or even acting-out. On these complex issues, there may well be differences of judgment, and where one comes down—or attempts to strike some balance, however tense or uneasy—with respect to them may be related to one's view of the importance of historical truth claims in relation to participatory, performative orientations at times involving projective or incorporative identification and relying on a generalized free indirect style.

The larger question is whether there is a need to stress the significance of a complex, self-questioning understanding of working through the past in which the alternatives are not reduced to a justifiably criticized idea of total transcendence of problems, full ego

[48] See my analysis in *History and Reading: Tocqueville, Foucault, French Studies* (Toronto: University of Toronto Press, 2000), chap. 3.

[49] *The Possession at Loudun*, trans. Michael B. Smith (1970; Chicago: Univesity of Chicago Press, 1990). Here, for example, is a passage describing the "dialogue" between Surin and the possessed nun, Jeanne des Anges: "A strange dialogue begins, and goes on for hours, days, weeks. He begins praying before her. In the presence of a witness who is not an interlocutor, he gives voice to spiritual flights he never allowed himself, or was never able, to express. Little by little, she lets herself be won over by a passion of which, shrewd little girl that she was, she had never suspected the existence. But also, in this face-to-face encounter that is not one, he immerses

identity, totalizing meaning, mastery, or complacent cure on the one hand, and an insufficiently qualified valorization of trauma, the traumatic sublime, symptomatic acting-out, melancholia, the repetition compulsion, and endless aporias on the other. Still, the dubiousness of identification and identificatory acting-out should not eliminate recognition of the importance of transferential implication, empathic response, and the problem of how to come to terms with them in cognitively and ethicopolitically responsible ways. Moreover, it is important to stress that the experiences of victims and survivors of extreme events indicate telling differences between them and those born later, including so-called secondary witnesses—those who were not there but nonetheless problematically try to bear witness to (not for) the witness. These differences are obscured if not obliterated in acts of identification through which one becomes a surrogate victim and appropriates the victim's suffering and voice. The result of such identification may well be the restriction of ethics and politics to the horizon of the disempowered witness to abjection, however much charged with pathos and transfigured into the vehicle of the revelatory sublime—a horizon that, in contexts other than that of the survivor, amounts to a drastic curtailment of possible ethical and political action. Moreover, identification may become projective and conceal the ways survivors are not simply victims but may themselves become effective political and ethical agents, indeed the ways such activity may for them be part of the process of working through the past. The act of transfiguring the experience of the victim, whether or not accompanied by identification, is especially dubious when undertaken by the nonsurvivor or secondary witness who converts another's suffering into the occasion for his or her own entry into a discourse of the sublime. As applied to those born later, the attempt to recognize and work through the aftermath of historical trauma is not a marker of identificatory, surrogate victimage, a purely psychological and therapeutic exercise, or a pretext for an ecstatic or effervescent rhetoric of the sublime. It is rather a self-critical process bound up with critical thought and practice having social and political

---

himself; he is elated; he wears himself out; in one movement, he pursues the logic of redemption to its conclusion, which entails that the doctor must take the illness upon himself to cure it; he sympathizes with the affliction of the hysteric and denies himself the means of resisting it" (206).

import.[50] Working-through in this sense is a process that cannot be confined to clinical categories or one-on-one relations, however much it may draw from them. It raises both professional and cross-disciplinary issues that are themselves open to contestation and require continual rethinking and renegotiation, especially with respect to the question of the relation between thought and practice.

---

[50] Such issues were crucial to Theodor Adorno in his "What Does Coming to Terms with the Past Mean?" (included in *Bitburg in Moral and Political Perspective*, ed. Geoffrey Hartman). In discussing Germany's relation to the Holocaust and its contemporary social and political bearing, he rejects the notion of "coming to terms [*ausarbeitung*] with the past" as a slogan that "does not imply a serious working through of the past, the breaking of its spell through an act of clear consciousness"—a slogan that "suggests, rather, a wishing to turn the page and, if possible, wiping it from memory" (115). Adorno, however, goes on to indicate a complicated relation between acting-out and working-through even as they bear on controversial and complex public issues.

CHAPTER FOUR

Approaching Limit Events:
Siting Agamben

At issue in many approaches to the Holocaust and other extreme or limit events and experiences are two perspectives with problematic relations to each other. One affirms a notion of redemption as absolute recovery with no essential loss, even with respect to so traumatic a past as the Shoah. The second involves the denial or absolute negation of such redemption and a view of redemption in general as unavailable, absent, or repeatedly and aporetically in question. An initial way to see these perspectives is as formulations of working-through and acting-out—working-through construed as redemption of meaning in life and transcendence of problems toward mental health and ego identity; acting-out as often melancholic, compulsive repetition in which any notion of redemption or full recovery is out of the question and problems reappear in disguised or distorted form. If there is any hope of recovery in this second perspective, it is through radical negation of hope in redeeming the past or making sense of it in the present. Instead one affirms a decisive disjunction vis-à-vis the past, pure utopian possibility, creation ex nihilo, and a (post)apocalyptic leap into an unknown future or state of being. One may even apprehend a glimmer of a totally other form of life—a redemptive *Augenblick* or radiant act of bearing witness—in the shadow cast by radically negative critique itself. What tends to be excluded from both perspectives (neither of which I agree with) is a view of working-through not as full redemption, total recovery, or unmitigated caesura but as a recurrent process that, with respect to extreme trauma or limit events, may never totally transcend acting-out or compulsive repetition but that does provide a measure of critical distance on problems and the possibility of significant transformation, including desirable change in civic life with its responsibilities and obligations.

In changing registers in a manner that does not imply total discontinuity with the previous considerations, I would observe that another way to view these two perspectives is as approaches to the sacred or to the sublime. I would like briefly to explore this other way (if only because I have discussed more thoroughly the earlier one—that in terms of acting-out and working-through—in my writings).[1] Here I am suggesting that the sublime and the sacred can be seen as displacements of each other—one in a secular, the other in a religious key—or at least that, in discussions of the sacred and the sublime, there may be a comparable role for the distinction between the immanent and the transcendent. Indeed, in discussions of limit events or situations that invariably seem to bring up (if only to resist) issues typically related to the sublime, one may often be moving in the difficult and somewhat uncomfortable area of secular or displaced theology even when one denies such displacement or attempts to give it the name—perhaps the misleading name—of ethics, of literature as an ethics of writing, or even (as in certain discussions of Claude Lanzmann's film *Shoah*) of autonomous art.

In the first (stereotypically "Hegelian") perspective (involving full redemption or recovery), we have a modality of the immanent (or this-worldly) sublime, and in the second perspective (denying the very possibility of such redemption or recovery—even seeing it as taboo, sacrilegious, or "barbaric"), a modality of the radically transcendent sublime that at the limit (with the "death of God") may be erased or repeatedly held in abeyance (for example, in the form of a messianism without a Messiah or messianism as a structure of expectation that intrinsically requires continual deferral). Yet both perspectives intimately relate trauma and the sublime. The sublime involves a transvaluation or transfiguration of trauma with more or less destabilizing effects for any conventional or harmonizing notion of sublimity (for example, certain nationalistic variants) and perhaps for any

[1] See *Representing the Holocaust: History, Theory, Trauma* (Ithaca: Cornell University Press, 1994), *History and Memory after Auschwitz* (Ithaca: Cornell University Press, 1998), and *Writing History, Writing Trauma* (Baltimore: Johns Hopkins University Press, 2001).

normative conception of ethics or politics whatsoever. The sublime is related to excess or, conversely, lacuna or lack—that which is disconcertingly, perhaps ecstatically other and aporetically beyond (or beneath) any ability to name or to know. It may also be related to radical transgression. It may even approximate disaster and be approached only in a self-effacing writing of disaster marked by a repeated recourse to the paradox, double bind, and *mise en abîme*.

I would note that the immanent sublime finds one of its most unsettling manifestations in what might be termed the Nazi sublime (something Agamben does not—or refuses to—see). This variant can be detected in the words and actions of at least certain perpetrators during the Shoah. Indeed I think that the primary locus of the sublime during the Nazi genocide itself was in this group of perpetrators. A much-discussed document in which it is active is Himmler's 1943 Posen speech, and one finds traces of it in the endlessly repeated, at times elated or even carnivalesque dimensions of killing and torture in the *Einsatzgruppen* and their affiliates. One also finds it in certain forms of activity in the camps or the forced marches at the end of the war. Such "sublimity" involved a fascination with excess or unheard-of transgression, endlessly repeated yet adamantly endured traumatic scenes, a code of silence (or unsayability), and a quasi-sacrificial quest involving regeneration or redemption through violence and purification for the self and the community through the elimination of "contaminating," phobic, even ritually repulsive presences. Here I shall cite some relevant passages from Himmler's Posen speech given to upper-level SS officers (hence intended for the initiated and not as propaganda for the general public—one reason it is such an important document):

I also want to make reference before you here, in complete frankness, to a really grave matter. Among ourselves, this once, it shall be uttered quite frankly; but in public we will never speak of it. Just as we did not hesitate on June 30, 1934 [the purge of Ernst Röhm and his SA leadership], to do our duty as ordered, to stand up against the wall comrades who had transgressed, and shoot them, also we have never talked about this and never will. It was the tact which I am glad to say is a matter of course to us that made us never discuss it among ourselves, never talk about it. Each of us shuddered, and yet each one

knew that he would do it again if it were ordered and if it were
necessary.

I am referring to the evacuation of the Jews, the annihilation of the
Jewish people. . . . Most of you know what it means to see a hundred
corpses lie side by side, or five hundred, or a thousand. To have stuck
this out [or endured this: *durchstehen*], and—excepting cases of human
weakness—to have kept our integrity [or decency: *anständig geblieben zu
sein*], that is what has made us hard. In our history this is an unwritten,
never-to-be-written page of glory.[2]

Paradoxically one may also find another variant of the immanent
sublime in the belated reactions of certain survivors or commentators
who attempt to provide a redemptive, awe-inspiring, at times even
sacralizing account of the Shoah itself and to convert it into a founding trauma that furnishes an affirmative identity for self and community. This gesture cannot be assimilated to, or viewed as simply
"contaminated" by, the Nazi sublime; it is complex. In one sense it is
an attempt to take back the Shoah from the perpetrators and make it
serve the victims (perhaps figured as martyrs) or their descendants.
In significant ways, however, the gesture—whether with respect to
the Holocaust or to other extreme events such as the atomic bombing
of Hiroshima and Nagasaki—often remains within a certain logic of
redemption and has many dubious dimensions, especially in the case
of nonsurvivors who find sublimity through a transfiguration of the
suffering of others.[3] The transfiguration of trauma into a founding
experience or occasion for redemptive sublimity may have a political
and ethical role in justifying policies or practices that are open to question—from Holocaust memorialization in the United States and
certain Israeli figurations of the redemptive nation to martyrological
conceptions of self-destructive acts that kill, wound, and traumatize
noncombatants (for example, suicide bombings).

The transcendent sublime, which may be hesitantly intimated or
under erasure, has the appeal of counteracting the lure of the imma-

[2] Lucy Dawidowicz, ed., *A Holocaust Reader* (West Orange, N.J.: Behrman House,
1976), 132–33.
[3] See, for example, Georges Bataille, "Residents of Hiroshima," in *Trauma: Explorations in Memory*, ed. Cathy Caruth (Baltimore: Johns Hopkins University Press,
1995), where the bombing of Hiroshima attests to the "sovereignty" of *dépense* (excessive expenditure) and "a boundless suffering that is joy, or a joy that is infinite
suffering" (232).

nent sublime, which may include regeneration through violence and a quasi-sacrificial or totalizing logic. Indeed the transcendent sublime would seem to serve as a bar to any mode of sacrifice but at the cost of eliminating all forms of the immanent sacred, including the limits it sets on human assertion and its protective function for nature or human and other than human beings. There is also a sense in which the transcendent sublime remains within an all-or-(almost)-nothing "logic" of the absolute and a displaced theological frame of reference. It too stresses excess or what is (perhaps transgressively) beyond the limits of representation, naming, and normativity. The supplementary stress is on lacuna, lack, or loss and what is beneath representation. Such an orientation may be accompanied by a bracketing or even denigration of knowledge (except for learned ignorance, in which knowledge aporetically returns time and again to its own limits and forms of undoing); it may have a dismissive, demeaning, or begrudging view of this-worldly activity (*divertissement*) in general—or at least it seems to provide little viable space in which to develop such knowledge and activity. In a sense an orientation to the transcendent sublime remains fixated on the absolute in its very elusiveness, unavailability, or unpresentability. Jean-François Lyotard, at least in certain aspects of his thought, would perhaps be a paradigmatic figure here, but he is not alone.[4]

[4] Lyotard's most dubious discussion of the Holocaust probably occurs in parts of *Heidegger and "the jews,"* trans. Andreas Michel and Mark S. Roberts (1988; Minneapolis: University of Minnesota Press, 1990), which I discuss in *Representing the Holocaust*, 96–99. But see also *The Differend: Phrases in Dispute*, trans. George Van Den Abbeele (1983; Minneapolis: University of Minnesota Press, 1988). In the latter book, the discussion of Auschwitz comes relatively early, and the discussion of the sublime primarily, but not exclusively, in the later parts where, via Kant, the French Revolution becomes the primary "sign of history" that Lyotard discusses with respect to the sublime. But the treatment of the "sign of history" that dominates the earlier part of the book carries over for the reader into the later discussion of the sublime, and there are discursive links between parts of the book despite its disjointed structure. Auschwitz emerges as a kind of negative sublime that is incommensurable with or excessive to any attempt to represent or "phrase" it. Lyotard refers disparagingly to thinkers who, in discussing Auschwitz, "claim to have found some sense to this shit" (98). In Lyotard, shit, if not itself sublime, is, as a mark of abjection, intimately related to sublimity as a remainder that "traumatizes" the speculative dialectic by not being integratable into its progressive movement of *Aufhebung* or *relève*. ("With the notion of the sublime . . . Kant will always get the better of Hegel. The *Erhabene* persists, not over and beyond, but right in the heart of the *Aufgehobenen*" [77].) Whatever else one may think of Lyotard's view, it makes use of the historical phenomenon in a manner that provides little understanding of its specificity and instead uses it in a rather instrumental manner to make a philosophical point that could readily have been

It may be debatable whether Maurice Blanchot's writings can be seen as engaging considerations associated with the sublime.[5] Still, in Blanchot a simultaneous attenuation and intensification of the contemplative life and a hesitant, allusive intimation of what might seem to be an effaced or erased transcendent sublime are related to endless waiting, patience, and an ascesis of style (or a self-effacing ethic of writing), even a harrowing isolation in the wake of disaster. Blanchot's writings, insofar as they pertain to the Shoah, may be defensible as a personal, anguished response—a modality of impossible mourning undecidably close to (or sharing a threshold of indistinction with) endless melancholy and (im)personal bereavement. In a sense they may be read as based on extreme, posttraumatic, empathic response to the abject plight of victims, even to the point of self-erasure. But one may doubt whether they should be taken as exemplary, or whether their import for the response to limit events should be generalized. It is unclear whether they become exemplary in Derrida's reinscription of them. In any case, the understanding of ethics in the complex constellation of thought that includes Blanchot and Derrida (for example, in the latter's "Force of Law: The 'Mystical' Foundation of Authority" or *The Gift of Death*) tends in significant ways to be linked to the sublime—ethics in terms of excess or what is beyond the limit of normativity that articulates relations of people in groups or institutional settings such as the family, the school, the workplace, or the polity.[6]

---

made otherwise. (There is a very similar movement in Agamben's analysis.) How Auschwitz as "shit" counters negationism is difficult to see unless one argues that negationists like Faurisson deny the Holocaust because they deny or foreclose the recognition of impediments to speculative dialectics and its uplifting ability to reveal the essential structure of the progressive history of the West. If it is not carefully qualified and further specified, the latter idea (which is defensible within limits) may go to extremes and slide toward overgeneralization that undermines distinctions by making everyone (at least in "the West"), even victims, comparably complicit in the "logic" of the Holocaust insofar as everyone participates in the tendency of "Western metaphysics" to repress or deny "nondialecticizable" residues and remainders. The paradoxical result would be that Faurisson (emerging as the inverted mirror image of the *Muselmann* in Agamben) is also everyman.

[5] See, for example, *L'entretien infini* (Paris: Gallimard, 1969) and *The Writing of the Disaster*, trans. Ann Smock (1980; Lincoln: University of Nebraska Press, 1986).

[6] Jacques Derrida, "The Force of Law: The 'Mystical' Foundation of Authority," *Cardozo Law Review* 11 (1990), 920–1045, and my response to it in the same volume. See also Jacques Derrida, *The Gift of Death*, trans. David Wells (1992; Chicago: University of Chicago Press, 1995).

Here what was traditionally seen as the supererogatory virtue—that which is above and beyond the call of duty or ordinary obligation—seems at times to lessen or even obliterate the significance of the latter or to cast it at best as a necessity, a pragmatic concession made in order to carry on in the world (just as human rights or the subject may be radically criticized in principle but conceded as a necessity for contemporary forms of political and social action).[7] Civic life may even become ghostly or virtual—a spectral hope with at best a virtual agent or bearer, a question of an unavowable or coming community, or, in Derrida's recent formulation (in *Specters of Marx*), of endless longing, a seemingly blank utopianism that denies its own utopian status, a messianism without a Messiah.[8] The relation to every other may even be figured on the model of the radically asymmetrical or nonreciprocal relation (or nonrelation) between the agonized individual (or singularity) and the radically transcendent divinity. This relation involves absolute respect for the Other in others, yet this respect in the seeming register of sublimity provides little sense of how to relate to others in terms of daily commitments, obligations, and mutual rights and duties. It provides a sense of justice not in terms of measure or limits but as an invariably supererogatory virtue that seems to take relations out of institutional settings and even make them transcend or systematically exceed institutions. Justice here is closer to grace or the excessive gift—the *acte gratuit* or the potlatch—than to norms and judgment related to a network of normative limits. The sense of normativity I am invoking should not be conflated with positive law, construed as amenable to programmability and rigid codification, or collapsed into normalization (or the taking of the statistical average or the dominant for the normative). Rather it would relate to articulatory practices that would be open to challenge and

---

[7] For example, Lyotard writes: "We are asked to settle the injustices that abound in the world. We do it. But the anguish that I am talking about is of a different caliber than worrying about civics. It resists the Republic and the system: it is more archaic than either; it both protects and flees from the inhuman stranger that is in us, the 'rapture and the terror,' as Baudelaire said." "Terror on the Run," trans. Philip R. Wood and Graham Harris, in *Terror and Consensus: Vicissitudes of French Thought*, ed. Jean-Joseph Goux and Philip R. Wood (Stanford: Stanford University Press, 1998), 35. What I find dubious in this statement is not Lyotard's affirmation of the "rapture and terror" taken up in anguished isolation by the writer but his assumption that this affirmation requires a hierarchy of values that subordinates, and even situates in a derogatory manner, civic life and its other than sublime requirements.

[8] *Specters of Marx*, trans. Peggy Kamuf (New York: Routledge, 1994).

even at times radical transgression but would nonetheless set limits to personal and group assertion that ideally would be affirmed and could be argumentatively defended as legitimate.

I think there is greater appeal in the second (transcendent) perspective on the sublime than in the first. But the problem that is occluded or at least insufficiently addressed in the second perspective is that of the transitional "space" or mediating and mitigating (but nontotalizable) links (or compromise formations) between absolutes or sublimities, that is, the sublunar or subastral space of ethical and political life. This is the space in which the primary question is the variable relation between limits and excess, including transgression and the limit event or situation, in various institutional settings and sociopolitical forms of activity. It is the space in which the opposition between the human and the nonhuman (which invariably serves invidious functions that often underwrite victimization of the other) may be radically problematized but may not become a deceptive, self-defeating object of fixation—a space in which such problematization is related not only to a notion of the split or disjunctive subject but also to social responsibility and to a notion of the human animal or being as a compromise formation of complex, interacting forces. It is also the space for developing forms of knowledge and understanding (involving affect, notably in the form of empathy) that do not pretend to be identical with things themselves but that do provide some orientation in behavior and have a bearing on ethical judgment. (Hence empathy or compassion in the sense I am using the term involves not full identification but emotional response involving respect for the other as other even when one's response is, in relation to the traumatic, itself unsettled and to some extent uncontrolled.) In this civic space, the other, while recognized as different from the self, is not totally other or a stand-in for the transcendent, Hidden God. And the ethical is not fully calculable or a matter of accounting, but it does involve the mutual ability to count on others in terms of one's fallible knowledge of how they have behaved in the past and may be expected to behave in the future.

Such knowledge is not fully redemptive, but it may confront the problem of transmitting trauma (or rather unsettlement) in a mitigated way that both indicates empathy with victims and—at least with respect to the Shoah—questions (without peremptorily dismissing) a "logic" of the sublime that transfigures trauma. (One may also raise the question of whether the quest for the sublime, especially when related to trauma—however symbolic, is more justified in areas such as religion and art than in politics or everyday ethics.) Constitutively limited knowledge may also help create the readiness to feel anxiety in the face of the unexpected or the uncanny in a fashion that does not assure nonrepetition of the past but that may provide some basis for a nonparanoid response to its displaced repetitions or reconfigurations. Moreover, I do not see the possibility of an ethics of daily life—an ethics with a critical distance on theology—that is not based on a sense of legitimate limits, however much such a sense may be problematic, tested by forms of excess, or open to continual questioning and supplementation (for example, by altogether necessary economic and political concerns). It is in terms of ethics in this nonsublime or subastral sense—a social and civic sense that is remedial but not fully redemptive, that one may ask for an explicit acknowledgment of one's past, for example, in the (different) cases of de Man, Heidegger, or Blanchot. I think ethics is misconstrued as, or even sacrificed to, sublimity when Derrida, in what would seem to be an unguardedly transferential act of projective identification, writes these startling words: "Perhaps Heidegger thought: I can only voice a condemnation of National Socialism if it is possible for me to do so in a language not only at the peak of what I have already said, but also at the peak of what has happened here. He was incapable of doing this. And perhaps his silence is an honest form of admitting he was incapable of it."[9] Here it seems that Heidegger remained silent about Auschwitz perhaps because he was incapable of achieving effects of sublimity, moving from peak to peak, in addressing it— although silence itself is often taken as the appropriate, awe-struck response to the sublime.

Without denying one's own implication in the ambivalent "logic" of the sublime and even recognizing its almost compulsive appeal, one may still insist on the need to develop thought and practice in the transitional civic "space" or modality that at times seems reduced to a vanishing point in an emphasis on either an immanent or a radically transcendent sublimity. Or to put the point in deceptively simple

[9] "Heidegger's Silence," in *Martin Heidegger and National Socialism: Questions and Answers*, ed. Gunther Neske and Emil Kettering, trans. Lisa Harries (New York: Paragon House, 1990), 148. See also my "Heidegger's Nazi Turn," in *Representing the Holocaust: History, Theory, Trauma*, chap. 5.

nominal terms: after a generation devoted to exploring what was gained in the paradoxical mode of pure waste or excessive expenditure [*dépense*], it may now be time to ask whether something important was obscured or lost yet may still be recoverable (or "redeemable" in a more modest sense) in readings of Bataille, notably with respect to his response to Durkheim, to wit, a sense of legitimate limits not only or even predominantly as a pretext for, but rather as a strong countervailing force to, excess and the allure of transgression.[10] (Of course the challenge would be to articulate such limits, not

[10] For two important readings of Bataille, which were crucial in setting the tone of poststructural approaches to him, see Jacques Derrida, "From a Restricted to a General Economy," in *Writing and Difference*, trans. (1967; Chicago: University of Chicago Press, 1978), 251–77, and Michel Foucault, "A Preface to Transgression," in *Language, Counter-Memory, Practice*, ed. Donald F. Bouchard, trans. Donald F. Bouchard and Sherry Simon (1963; Ithaca: Cornell University Press, 1973), 29–52. Within this line of thought, Michèle Richman, in *Sacred Revolutions: Durkheim and the Collège de Sociologie* (Minneapolis: University of Minnesota Press, 2002), makes a commendable, well-researched attempt to trace the relations between Durkheim's sociology and the "sacred sociology" of Bataille and the College of Sociology as well as the events of May 1968 in France (viewed as an uncanny return of repressed, sacralizing collective effervescence). Her account has the virtue of highlighting the thought-provoking dimensions of Bataille's approach and of stressing the importance of affect in collective life, including its role as "collective effervescence" in Durkheim's understanding of the sacred and its displacements in secular life. (She also provides an extensive analysis of the radical ambivalence of the sacred that may be contrasted to Agamben's views.) But her analysis of Durkheim's thought and related problems is too restricted, focused preponderantly on *The Elementary Forms of the Religious Life* (scant attention is given to Durkheim's classic *Suicide*, in which many of his basic views were elaborated), and undertaken for the most part from an uncritical, participatory Bataillian perspective that emphasizes excess and *dépense* (useless expenditure). In brief, Durkheim is read only through Bataille's "pineal eye" and is almost converted ideologically into Georges Sorel. As a consequence, Richman glosses over the tensions between Durkheim and Bataille in analyzing and evaluating the interaction between normative limits (not reducible to a "restricted economy" of production or instrumental rationality) and what transgressively exceeds them. More generally, Richman does not account for the shift in culture and the social imaginary (for example, with respect to the prevalence of sacrificial notions of regeneration through violence) that occurred between Durkheim and Bataille in part because of the depradations of World War I and its turbulent aftermath. Nor does she attempt to situate explictly and critically her own interpretive emphases and selectivity in a context she seems to apprehend as socioculturally depleted and disenchanted if not postapocalyptic. Richman repeatedly invokes and valorizes collective effervescence in overly general terms without providing a sustained, differential, critical analysis of it or its concomitants. One issue is the complex manner in which "effervescence" may be related to, or distinguished from, an aesthetic or, more generally, a "logic" of the sublime, including its elation or transport, insofar as the sublime itself may be seen as one possible displacement of the sacred. And she does not address the problem of victimization in sacrifice or in "violent" eroticism patterned on it; she views the victim only as a necessary intermediary between the collectivity and sacred

forces (168). Without centering his conception of the sacred on sacrifice in the manner of Bataille (or René Girard, who is surprisingly absent from Richman's discussion), Durkheim did see anomic as well as institutionalized excess as necessary components of social life that were valuable in tense interaction with limits. But unlike Bataille he did not throw caution to the wind and construe normative limits or prohibitions predominantly as a pretext for, or preface to, their transgression in extreme, often eroticized and violent, excesses. Moreover, from Durkheim's perspective, periods of revolutionary turmoil marked by rampant excess and anomie (a concept not discussed by Richman) would, in the best of circumstances, give rise to more stable (not static or rigid) institutions viably realizing revolutionary goals and values (his aim for his own Third Republic with respect to the French Revolution and its aftermath). Most significantly, Durkheim's larger project in the modern context was to displace the less bound "effervescence" of revolution in institutionalized (hence limited) collective rituals or festivities that reinvigorated shared values within a larger democratic, republican, peace-loving, cosmopolitan framework. Bataille often had a less qualified tendency to validate and even celebrate *"dépense,* where expenditure, loss, sacrifice, eroticism, and violence [Richman elsewhere adds death to the list] provide the basis for communication" (156), and he was also fascinated by the *dépense* in a phenomenon such as the bombing of Hiroshima (something I think would be unimaginable in Durkheim). One may agree with Richman's refusal to present Bataille in terms of a "left fascism" but nonetheless see her approach to Bataille's interest in fascism as inadequate and ameliorative. It does not include a sustained analysis of Bataille's ideas and orientation over time in comparison to those of fascist or *fascisant* thinkers and ideologues. She thus does not do enough to indicate the appeal of fascism for radical critics of "bourgeois" morality or civilization and places insufficient stress on Bataille's own attempt to retrospectively engage in self-critique or indicate dangers in views he espoused in insufficiently qualified or unrestrained, ecstatic terms. Moreover, in attempting to contrast fascism to the views of Bataille, she does not recognize that certain fascists and Nazis—including in certain respects Hitler, Himmler, and Rosenberg—did not simply uphold "institutions sustained by official ideology and political hierarchy" (122) or draw back from "sustaining negativity" in favor of a "recuperative strategy" directed toward "conservation, accumulation, and profit" (129). While making an ideological appeal to tradition and traditional institutions (such as the family), they defended not institutional stability but movement (*Bewegung*) and refused to allow considerations of profit, utility, or instrumental rationality to impede their often "effervescent" movement, notably in the attempt to eliminate Jews figured as heterogeneous others or as impure sacrificial victims. Despite ways in which Bataille's *épater-le-bourgeois,* extremist orientation was at times open to question, a more pertinent point of contrast with fascists and Nazis is that he insistently affirmed the value of heterogeneity and valorized sacrifice only insofar as it did not have a specific set of scapegoated, abject victims but instead could fall to one's own lot. One might nonetheless argue, against the grain of Richman's analysis, that the very idea that communication or opening to the other requires excessive expenditure, wounds, violence, and transgression is itself symptomatic of individualistic assumptions of a monadic if not autistic cast that can be broken through only via some form of extreme rending of the self. (Without drawing pertinent implications for her analysis, Richman herself notes at one point that "central to Bataille's analysis of eroticism is a concept of the self as closed being" [178].) Richman's overall approach may itself be contrasted with the significantly different approaches in Peter Starr's *Logics of Failed Revolt: French Theory after May '68* (Stanford: Stanford University Press, 1995), Jeffrey Herf's *Reactionary Modernism: Technology, Culture, and Politics in Weimar and the Third Reich* (New York: Cambridge University Press, 1984), or my own *Emile Durkheim: Sociologist and Philosopher* (1972; rev. ed. Aurora, Colorado: The Davies Group, 2001) .

in the abstract but in specific, variable, contestable situations.)[11] And the question I would raise is whether and to what extent, with respect to the Shoah and perhaps to other limit events, one should, in one's own voice, resist a "logic" of the sublime and, more generally, whether one should engage in a careful, differentiated critique of an aesthetic of sublimity, particularly when it is deployed to transfigure the suffering of others and when the Shoah becomes the cypher for the sublime. One may raise this question without subscribing to an indiscriminate hostility to the sublime, especially when its role— notably in art and religion—is explored in its tense, mutually questioning relations to an affirmation of legitimate limits (including ethical and political limits).

I would like now to consider the work of Giorgio Agamben, particularly his recent *Remnants of Auschwitz*, in light of the problems I have evoked.[12] Agamben has recently risen to prominence in the

[11] An altogether cogent argument made by Judith Butler is that the identification of the Lacanian traumatic real with castration anxiety in the context of the Oedipal complex, which is particularly forceful in the work of Slavoj Žižek, hypostatizes or substantializes what I term a transhistorical notion of trauma, drains the specificity from historical phenomena, and imposes an illegitimate limit on sexual relations in general and women in particular. (See *Bodies That Matter: On the Discursive Limits of "Sex"* [New York: Routledge, 1993], chap. 7.) The subsequent issue is what would constitute a legitimate normativity with its limits and even its constitutive exclusions. I would argue that one crucial feature of such a normativity would be the "exclusion" not of particular sets of "abjectified" victims but of abjectifying practices of victimization and with them the entire grid of victimization involving the subject positions of perpetrator, bystander, rescuer, and so forth. Such an "exclusion" would require a significant transformation in the articulation of social relations and institutions whereby displaced sacrificialism and victimization would no longer play an important role.
[12] *Remnants of Auschwitz: The Witness and the Archive*, trans. David Heller-Roazen (New York: Zone Books, 1999). Any larger study of Agamben would have to include an extensive discussion of at least his *Homo Sacer: Sovereign Power and Bare Life*, trans. David Heller-Roazen (1995; Stanford University Press, 1998) and *Means Without End: Notes on Politics*, trans. Vicenzo Binetti and Cesare Casarino (1996; Minneapolis: University of Minnesota Press, 2000). Agamben conceives of these works, along with the more recent *Remnants of Auschwitz*, as composing a series. One may note that *la nuda vita* is translated as "bare life" by Heller-Roazen and as "naked life" by Binetti and Casarino. Moreover, the *Muselmann* in *Remnants of Auschwitz* is conceived as the extreme form or instance of the *homo sacer*, who is interpreted by Agamben as the bearer of *la nuda vita* and is reduced to this condition by sovereign power. It is open to debate whether and to what extent the notions of bare or naked life and *homo sacer* as Agamben understands them provide an adequate account of the sacred or even of the status of the Jew as victim under the Nazis. I would argue that this view accounts only for one dimension of the complex figure of the Jew for Nazis—the dimension related to the Jew figured as pest or vermin fit only for extermination. It does not, I

field of critical theory, and there is a sense in which he seems constrained to raise the stakes or "up the ante" (which is already astronomically high) in theoretically daring, jarringly disconcerting claims if he is to make a significant mark as a major theorist. This seemingly inevitable process of vying with, or even trying to outdo, predecessors is one of the more problematic aspects of the movement from high theory to sky-high theory (or theoreticism) in the recent past, an inclination that becomes increasingly tempting to the extent that atheoretical or even antitheoretical tendencies, including a resurgent belletrism and a born-again positivism, displace critical theory, and the latter, both in general and in its significant variations, is subjected to impatient dismissals or misinformed understandings.[13] (This context makes it all the more important to try to develop informed and nuanced—albeit at times forceful—defenses and critiques of specific understandings and articulations of theory.) In Agamben, moreover, a sustained intricacy of formulation and an insistently paratactic or "poetic" style in philosophy make it difficult to understand him in a way that enables critical exchange and also make it possible for a sympathetic (or perhaps extremely generous) reader (or overwriter) to gloss questionable passages in a quasi-theological manner that always displaces attention to other, less dubious passages, even if they are to be found in another work. The fact that Agamben is a writer who seems to elicit this response in some readers (even to generate a discipleship) is itself of interest, but it shall in general not characterize

---

think, account for the more ambiguous dimensions of the Jew (which Agamben rejects in the sacred itself at least as it is conceived in Roman law) whereby the Jew was also an object of quasi-ritual or phobic repulsion and was invested with world-historical, conspiratorial powers of evil and made an object of quasi-sacrificial scapegoating and victimization. One of the difficulties in understanding Nazi ideology and practice involves the role of the shifting registers of pest control and quasi-sacrificial response with respect to the Jew. However, I shall later suggest a sense in which Agamben's view may itself be symptomatic of an exhaustion or depletion of the sacred and sacrificial in the recent past, which I would see as beneficial insofar as it counteracts victimization as a crucial dimension in the appeal of sacrifice. Agamben does not see how the banalized use of the term "Holocaust" may be in part defended as itself symptom and performative force in the erosion or active depletion of the sacrificial and its attraction.

[13] For a discussion of belletristic tendencies in recent literary and cultural criticism, see Jeffrey Williams, "The New Belletrism," *Style* 33 (1999): 414–42. For indications of neopositivism, especially in historiography, see Lynn Hunt, "Where Have All the Theories Gone?" in *Perspectives* 40 (2002): 5–7.

the approach I take. Rather I assume that through critical analysis and exchange at least some aspects of Agamben's thought will be disclosed that might otherwise escape attention.

Agamben adamantly rejects the first perspective on limit events, which seeks redemptive meaning, and he often seems to move toward the second perspective. But there are at least intimations of a transitional "space" or nonbinary network of possibilities—a "threshold of indistinction"—that cannot be reduced to the options allowed by my two perspectives or even conceived in spatial terms. (A closer analysis would disclose comparable dimensions in the thought of Blanchot or Derrida.) In *Means without End* such a threshold of indistinction seems related, however problematically, to the form of life involving open possibilities that Agamben defends and opposes to the nexus of sovereign power and bare or naked life. The allusive status of this dimension in *Remnants of Auschwitz*, where, if anything, it should have been elaborated further with respect to Agamben's notion of ethics, is unfortunate. Moreover, Agamben in the latter book also refers to a state of exception (also invoked in his earlier works) and to a gray zone (a move made with reference to Primo Levi's *The Drowned and the Saved*) whose relations to the threshold of indistinction and to each other are not explicitly thematized and explored as a problem.[14] The larger question that arises is how the transitional "space" or "threshold of indistinction" (close to Derrida's notion of undecidability) operates historically and transhistorically as well as empirically and ideally (or normatively); how it problematizes, or even undoes, existing concepts or norms—indeed entire conceptual and normative orders, perhaps even the very concept of normativity; and how it may possibly help to generate newer conceptual and normative articulations explicitly recognized as problematic but nonetheless in important ways affirmed as legitimate.

Agamben clearly (and, I think, rightly) rejects the idea of any full recovery, redemption, or use of the Holocaust (a term he rejects for etymological reasons) for spiritual uplift or as proof of the essential dignity of the human being and the ability of the human spirit to endure all hardship and emerge on a higher level of spirituality.[15]

[14] *The Drowned and the Saved* (1986; New York: Random House, 1989).

[15] Agamben does not comment critically but only in etymological and semantic respects on a term that is crucial to his account: *Muselmann* or Muslim (44–46). This prejudicial appellation was camp slang for the absolutely exhausted and beaten down

Indeed he even sees Auschwitz (a metonym he employs and apparently finds unproblematic) as radically undermining or delegitimating all preexisting ethics and all postwar discourses relying on traditional notions of ethics as well as any and every ethics related to dignity and conformity to a norm.[16] In his approach, Auschwitz gives rise to an aftermath that is decidedly postapocalyptic.

> Auschwitz marks the end and the ruin of every ethics of dignity and conformity to a norm. The bare life to which human beings were reduced neither demands nor conforms to anything. It is itself the only norm; it is absolutely immanent. And "the ultimate sentiment of belonging to the species" cannot in any sense be a kind of dignity. . . .

------

who had given up hope in life and led a living death. Agamben notes the disagreement concerning the etymology of the term. He thinks "the most likely explanation of the term can be found in the literal meaning of the Arabic word Muslim: the one who submits unconditionally to the will of God"—a "meaning that lies at the origin of legends concerning Islam's supposed fatalism" (45). He also notes views concerning the "typical attitude" and the "typical movements" of *Muselmänner*, notably the "swaying motions of the upper part of the body, with Islamic prayer rituals" (quoted ibid.). He does not observe that these characterizations or stereotypes have also been applied to Jews, that Jews and Arabs have been understood as enemy brothers, and that the characterizations have more the nature of rationalizations than of explanations. He also does not indicate the way the anxiety generated by the *Muselmann* as the image of the camp inmate's own possible if not probable future is related to the possible projection of this anxiety onto a scapegoated "other" distanced from oneself by the very name applied to him or her. Indeed the use of such a term would seem to illustrate the tendency of the oppressed and abject to locate invidiously, as their constitutive "other" or exclusion, a presumably even more abject group, and the history of strained relations between Jews and Arab Muslims renders particularly dubious the choice of "*Muselmann*" as the term of distancing and denigration.

[16] In his discussion of Ruth Klüger, Michael Rothberg brings out the dubiousness of "Auschwitz" or any unifying metonym to name the concentration and death camps. See Michael Rothberg, "Between the Extreme and the Everyday: Ruth Klüger's Traumatic Realism," in *Extremities: Trauma, Testimony, and Community*, ed. Nancy K. Miller and Jason Tougaw (Urbana: University of Illinois Press, 2002), 55–70. Klüger writes: "The disinclination of most people . . . to note the names of smaller camps perhaps is attributable to the fact that one would like to keep the camps as unified as possible and under the large labels of the concentration camps that have become famous. That is less tiring for the mind and emotions than coming to terms with differentiations. I insist on these differentiations . . . in order to break through the curtain of barbed wire that the post-war world has hung before the camps. There is a separation between then and now, us and them, which doesn't serve truth, but rather laziness" (quoted 58). Rothberg comments: "In her insistence on differentiation and her critique of separation, Klüger provides tools for thinking beyond the dominant tendencies within Holocaust studies, which often homogenize the camps either through a hyperbolic discourse of extremity or through their banalization. . . .

The atrocious news that the survivors carry from the camp to the land of human beings is precisely that it is possible to lose dignity and decency beyond imagination, that there is still life in the most extreme degradation. And this new knowledge now becomes the touchstone by which to judge and measure all morality and all dignity. The *Muselmann*, who is its most extreme expression is the guard on the threshold of a new ethics, an ethics of a form of life that begins where dignity ends. And Levi, who bears witness to the drowned, speaking in their stead, is the cartographer of this new *terra ethica*, the implacable land-surveyor of *Muselmannland*. (69)

In a sense the provocation and promise of, as well as the problems involved in, Agamben's approach are condensed in this passage (including the confusing, dissonant use of "guard"—a seeming lapsus that implies a collapse of the distinction between perpetrator and victim that becomes explicit in Agamben's understanding of the gray zone). It signals the way Agamben offers what might be seen as a powerful but questionable conception of the relation between the post-Auschwitz and the poststructural (or perhaps the postmodern) that is of world-historical and fundamental philosophical importance. I shall begin with the issue of the relation of the historical to the transhistorical. Often Agamben seems to subsume Auschwitz as a complex historical phenomenon in a theoreticist or high-altitude dis- course that eliminates its specificity, and he uses it to make points (for example, concerning the role of paradox and aporia) that might have been made without it. In any case his understanding of the relation between history and theory does not set up a sustained, mutually interrogative relation in which questions are posed in both directions without the hope of a final synthesis or reduction of one term to the other. In another sense, however, Agamben attributes uniqueness to Auschwitz that goes beyond any notion of specificity or distinctive- ness and is related to the world-historical, even apocalyptic signifi- cance he attributes to it, both in placing in question and even

---

Breaking through the barbed wire means learning to differentiate between differen- tiation and separation. Unlike separation, which marks out clear boundaries, differ- entiation can be seen as a non-totalizing process of distinction whereby differences are held together, while simultaneously a 'displacement of the clear borderlines of thought' also takes place" (58).

eliminating the relevance of all preexisting or conventional ethics (whose nature he does not really investigate) and in posing the problem of rethinking ethics from the ground up, indeed from an indistinct point of virtuality that undercuts any conceivable ground.

Here I would mention a number of other features of Agamben's thought that one may accept, reject, or have mixed reactions to on the basis of one's own (often unexamined) assumptions. Indeed how one describes these features or tendencies depends on how one reacts to them (my own reactions are mixed). Agamben has a sense of the apocalyptic and a penchant for the all-or-nothing response that help to induce the figuration of Auschwitz as a radical rupture or caesura in history that leads to the construction of the post-Auschwitz world in postapocalyptic terms.[17] This radically new state of affairs, signaled

---

[17] In *The Coming Community* (trans. Michael Hardt, 1990; Minneapolis: University of Minnesota Press, 1993), Agamben contrasts an ethics of pure possibility and openness (which in certain ways seems close to the early Sartre's notion of pure, evacuated *disponibilité*) to a conception of morality. "Morality" is castigated and would seem to include any normativity including repentance, responsibility, and guilt—perhaps any normativity at all. The correlate of Agamben's "ethics" is an apocalyptic politics of the coming community of totally open and substitutable "whatever" singularities. The nature of this putative ethics is elaborated via an analogy to the cabala in a fully apocalyptic-messianic manner reminiscent of aspects of the thought of Walter Benjamin:

> In the society of the spectacle [i.e., contemporary society], in fact, the isolation of the Shekinah [the word of God] reaches its final phase, where language is not only constituted in an autonomous sphere, but also no longer even reveals anything—or better, it reveals the nothingness of all things. There is nothing of God, of the world, or of the revealed in language. In this extreme nullifying unveiling, however, language (the linguistic nature of humans) remains once again hidden and separated, and thus, one last time, in its unspoken power, it dooms humans to a historical era and a State: the era of the spectacle, or of accomplished nihilism. . . .
>
> The era in which we live is also that in which for the first time it is possible for humans to experience their own linguistic being—not this or that content of language, but language *itself*, not this or that proposition, but the very fact that one speaks. Contemporary politics is this devastating *experimentum linguae* that all over the planet unhinges and empties traditions and beliefs, ideologies and religions, identities and communities.
>
> Only those who succeed in carrying it to completion—without allowing what it reveals to remain veiled in the nothingness that reveals, but bringing language itself to language—will be the first citizens of a community with neither presuppositions nor a State, where the nullifying and determining power of what is common will be pacified and where the Shekinah will have stopped sucking the evil milk of its own separation.
>
> Like Rabbi Akiba, they will enter into the paradise of language and leave unharmed. (*The Coming Community*, 82–83)

by the advent of the *Muselmann*, creates a sense of urgency and extreme insistence that might also be described as lending itself to a rhetoric of histrionic hyperbole that contrasts significantly with the general tone of understatement, broken only at times by emotional upset and stylistic hyperbole in Primo Levi, who has a privileged place in Agamben's study of the remnants of Auschwitz. The privileged position is, however, somewhat equivocal, in that Levi is both taken as a paradigm and employed as an object of projective identification whom Agamben ventriloquizes, just as he sees Levi ventriloquizing or speaking for the *Muselmann*. In the former respect, Agamben can write: "Primo Levi is a perfect example of the witness" (16). In the latter respect, Levi serves Agamben as a prosthetic device (not to say a dummy-figure) in a covert process of identifying with, and speaking for, the ultimate victim and instance of abjection, the *Muselmann*.

Agamben is justifiably concerned not with delimited historical research that uncovers new facts about Auschwitz but with its "remnants" or remainders construed in terms of the problem of the possibilities and limits of understanding it—"the ethical and political significance of the extermination" and "a human understanding of what happened there—that is, . . . its contemporary relevance" (11). One question, however, is whether certain forms of specificity are eliminated by the overly homogeneous view of Auschwitz as a *unicum* that marks a radical break in history or at least in the history of the ethical and political. For example, Agamben insists quite rightly on the need for a sustained inquiry into the *Muselmann* that has not as yet been undertaken. He relates and contrasts the *Muselmann* and the witness. The *Muselmann* is one who cannot bear witness for him- or herself and hence needs to be supplemented by the witness, who nonetheless is paradoxically forced to bear witness to the (*Muselmann*'s) impossibility of witnessing. And the *Muselmann* is Primo Levi's drowned victim, the only true witness, the bereft witness unable to give testimony or bear witness. He or she is also the Gorgon whom others could not bear to behold but on whom Agamben gazes and enjoins us all to gaze. The Gorgon is the *antiprosopon*, the prohibited face that does not give itself to be seen (53). And "the Gorgon designates the impossibility of seeing that belongs to the camp inhabitant, the one who has 'touched bottom' in the camp and has become a non-human" (54). (Here one broaches the question of the turn to a discourse of the sublime in the attempt to account for the most extreme form of abjection and victimization—a *coincidentia oppositorum*, or meeting of extremes.) Yet there are a number of dubious dimensions in Agamben's ambitious and admirable attempt to affirm the importance of, and somehow come to terms with, the *Muselmann*.

Agamben takes the *Muselmann* in isolation from his or her context—the historical conditions of emergence, which cannot be seen only in terms of a homogeneous idea of Auschwitz or a few restricted references to the SS. (This diremption or decontextualization may be necessary for the figuration of the *Muselmann* as a sublime object.) Indeed Agamben almost seems to come upon the *Muselmann* as one might discover a creature in the wild or on another planet—planet *Auschwitz* as it has sometimes been called, to distinguish it from anything we have hitherto known on planet Earth. And in Agamben the planets collide and interpenetrate to the point of indistinction. One difficulty in treating the *Muselmann* as an *objet trouvé* is that Agamben offers no sustained inquiry into the ideology and practice of perpetrators in the creation of the historical state of affairs that brought the *Muselmann* into being. One gets almost no sense of the perpetrator-victim dynamic, which was crucial in the emergence of, or the erosive process leading to, the *Muselmann*. One would think that the perpetrators and their role in the genesis of the *Muselmann* would also be among the remnants of Auschwitz that are deserving of contemporary understanding and relevance. Indeed Agamben's use of the historical for transhistorical purposes postulates the *Muselmann* as the prototype of the split subject, and in the process Auschwitz itself tends to become a paradoxically abstract counter or philosophical *Lehrstück*.

Agamben has a general conception of the modern age as one tending toward or even embodying the combination of sovereignty and mere, bare, or naked life—of unlimited power and the reduction of the human being to a being denuded of possibilities and in a condition of ultimate abjection. (One might compare naked life to Heidegger's conception of the *Gestell*, or reduction of all things to a standing stock or reserve of raw material, perhaps even to Marx's notion of abstract exchange value.) Auschwitz and the *Muselmann* are the fullest realization to date of this extreme or excessive state of affairs, which Agamben both severely criticizes and at times seems to approximate or even replicate, at least in part, in his own all-or-nothing, insistently evacuating, postapocalyptic assumptions or assertions. Indeed in Agamben the immanent sacred is denuded of all traditional dimensions of the sacred (its ambivalence, its attraction-repulsion, its elation or ecstasy, its limit-setting and limit-transgressing power).[18] It is reduced to bare or naked life. Instead of seeing this reduction as one important effect of recent history (related to developments within religion and to modes of secularization, including capitalism and positivism)—an effect nonetheless countered by other significant forces, he at times seems to postulate it as a general theory of the sacred in transhistorical terms. Insofar as this postulation occurs, he discloses, apparently as a belated, posttraumatic effect of Auschwitz, what putatively was the case all along: the sacred presumably always already was bare or naked life.[19] The begged ques-

[18] For an account of the sacred that focuses on these features, see Julia Kristeva, *The Powers of Horror*, trans. Leon S. Roudiez, (1980; New York: Columbia University Press, 1982). Kristeva does not apply her analysis of the sacred to the Nazi genocide, in part because, in her sometimes apologetic understanding of Céline's antisemitism and sympathy for fascism, she focuses in an analytically isolating manner on aesthetic issues and even construes Céline's antisemitism in the narrowly biographical terms of a personal need for identity. And, at least in this book, Kristeva is at times close to Agamben in bringing together the abject and the sublime (with the sublime functioning as a secular displacement of the sacred). Kristeva's recent work often goes in other directions, including a notion of working-through that is not tantamount to total redemption or healing. See, for example, her "Forgiveness: An Interview" (with Alison Rice), in *PMLA* 117 (2002): 278–95.

[19] In *Homo Sacer* Agamben argues that neither Foucault nor Arendt, whose insights he presumably combines and raises to a higher level, saw that biopolitics is the politics of bare or naked life that allows total domination and is realized in the camps. Indeed "only because politics in our age had been entirely transformed into biopolitics was it possible for politics to be constituted as totalitarian politics to a degree hitherto unknown" (120). Moreover, "only because biological life and its needs had become the *politically* decisive fact, is it possible to understand the otherwise incomprehensible rapidity with which twentieth-century parliamentary democracies were able to turn into totalitarian states and with which this century's totalitarian states were able to be converted, almost without interruption, into parliamentary democracies. . . . Once their fundamental referent becomes bare life, traditional political distinctions (such as those between Right and Left, liberalism and totalitarianism, private and public) lose their clarity and intelligibility and enter into a zone of indistinction. . . . From this perspective the camp—as the pure, absolute, and impassable biopolitical space (insofar as it is founded solely on the state of exception)—will appear as the hidden paradigm of the political space of modernity, whose metamorphoses and disguises we will have to learn to recognize" (122–23). Instead of providing critical perspective on certain tendencies in "modernity," Agamben's own indiscriminate, postapocalyptic perspective leads him here to make short shrift of complex historical, analytic, and political issues, which he merges to the point of fusion and confusion.

tion is whether, to what extent, and in what specific ways, this is the case even now.[20]

Elaborating this theory is a basic project in *Homo Sacer*, where Pompeius Festus's *On the Significance of Words* becomes the basis of a conception of the "sacred man" as a victim or outsider, subject to being killed at will by anyone but not to being sacrificed (in any traditional sense) or murdered (in any criminal or legal sense of homocide).[21] The result in that book is a rather reduced understanding of the Holocaust in terms of biology, medicalization, and eugenics, related to a Foucauldian notion of biopower and biopolitics. This line of argument continues in *Remnants of Auschwitz* (see, for example, 82–86), and, as in the earlier book, it leads to an excessively one-sided or analytically reduced understanding of the victim as mere or naked life. Hence the camps are "the site of the production of the *Muselmann*, the final biopolitical substance to be isolated in the biological continuum. Beyond the *Muselmann* lies only the gas chamber" (85). Agamben's

[20] Another way to put the point is to argue that Agamben, in a dubious metalepsis, sees bare life as an exclusion at the origin rather than a result of an analytic reduction that is always unstable and problematic. For example, in a Heideggerian gloss on Aristotle and Foucault, he writes: "In Western politics, bare life has the peculiar privilege of being that whose exclusion founds the city of man" (*Homo Sacer*, 7).
[21] A generally favorable reading of Agamben, focusing on *Homo Sacer*, is offered by Andrew Norris, "Giorgio Agamben and the Politics of the Living Dead," *Diacritics* 30 (2000): 38–58. (This issue actually appeared in September 2002, after the present study was virtually completed.) For Norris Agamben elaborates a radically original theory of sacrifice as a negation of naked life or the mere body and a metaphysical-political quest for absolute transcendence of it. On this conception, sacrifice is understood reductively as tantamount to a radicalized version of Hegelian *Aufhebung* (sublation or transcendence). The univocal, transhistorical, universalizing theory of sacrifice that results construes it in terms that not only strip it of all ambivalence (contra Bataille and others) but also might be more critically analyzed as a projection from a specific frame of reference partially pertinent to the recent past. A different, more complex view would pose the problem of the relation between sacrifice and *Aufhebung* in terms of variable displacements of each other related as well to forms of narrative and figurations of the sublime. The difficulties of a theory of sacrifice as negation and transcendence of naked life are multiple, although, as I intimate, such a theory might help account for aspects of certain phenomena (for example, Norris gives the case of "neomorts," and I refer to the construction of the Jew as pest or vermin). Still, the theory fails to account for: 1) the way religions of radical transcendence either come to oppose and attempt to prohibit sacrifice or transfigure it into a symbolic form not involving the repeated, actual killing of victims; 2) the role of the immanent in sacrifice that is maintained and reaffirmed, for example, in this-worldly or bodily modes of elation, ecstasy, or sublimity and the regeneration of the self or the group through violence, including the bloodbath; 3) the way victims are ambivalently or equivocally valorized and cathected sources of anxiety with the possible

notion of mere, bare, or naked life may in important ways apply to the reduced state of the *Muselmann* and to one dimension of other victims insofar as they were considered mere raw material or stock, treated as vermin, or hunted as "mere" game by perpetrators and bystanders. (It may also apply to recent conceptions of the other-than-human animal, for example, in the mass production of foodstuff.)[22] But, as I shall try to indicate, it eliminates or ignores other aspects of Nazi ideology and practice with regard to victimization. Agamben himself, moreover, sees the *Muselmann* not as mere life but as a threshold figure: he or she "marks the threshold between the human and the inhuman" (55). How the notions of *Muselmann* as naked life and as marker of a threshold relate to each other is not clear, but in any case, for Agamben, "the sight of *Muselmänner* is an absolute new phenomenon, unbearable to human eyes" (51). In the *Muselmann* we presumably behold and bear witness to the absolutely, blindingly, even apocalyptically new. And in our relation to Auschwitz and the *Muselmann*, we are decidedly within a postapocalyptic condition of existence, a condition of remnants or perhaps of ruins.[23]

---

reduction to naked life as one possibility in a variegated constellation of forces; 4) the way victims are not merely random "bodies" but are selected, however prejudicially, in historically specific contexts that cannot simply be subsumed by a transhistorical, universalistic theory. Norris writes: "Sacrifice is the performance of the metaphysical assertion of the human: the Jew, the Gypsy, and the gay man die that the German may affirm his transcendence of his bodily, animal life." (47) Nazis glorified certain body types as beautiful or even sublime and did not try to achieve radical transcendence. Indeed their alliance with "pagan" mythologies and their critique of Christianity had the affirmation of certain body types and the negation of other types as a central feature. And one cannot so readily amalgamate the Jew, the Gypsy, and the gay man, who each had different roles in Nazi ideology and practice, although the dynamic of victimization, having quasi-sacrificial dimensions, might at times lead to their approximation. But why were Jews "sacrificed" and not, say, oxen or poultry? Of course problems can be explained away as facets of a false consciousness as seen through and explained by a univocal, reductive, transhistorical "theory."

[22] On the latter issue, see Eric Schlosser, *Fast Food Nation: The Dark Side of the All-American Meal* (Boston: Houghton Mifflin, 2001).

[23] For an extensive, critical yet sympathetic account of the postapocalyptic mode, see James Berger, *After the End: Representations of Post-apocalypse* (Minneapolis: University of Minnesota Press, 1999). In certain important respects, Agamben's sensibility and approach to problems may be compared to that of Bill Readings in *The University in Ruins* (Cambridge: Harvard University Press, 1997). See my discussion in "The University in Ruins?" *Critical Inquiry* 25 (1998): 32–55 (a revised version appears as chapter 5 of this book) as well as Nicolas Royle, "Yes, Yes, the University in Ruins," *Critical Inquiry* 26 (1999) and my rejoinder ("Yes, Yes, Yes,

Here one may mention the importance for Agamben of Carl Schmitt's notion of the state of exception.[24] He does not examine to any significant extent Schmitt's ideas on secularization as the displacement of the religious to the secular which, I think, might in certain ways inform a treatment of the sublime, including unthematized dimensions of Agamben's own thought, for example, its insistence, if not fixation, on the dubious human/nonhuman opposition and its relation to the sublimely apocalyptic and postapocalyptic. In the runaway state of exception (which seems close to Schmitt's state of emergency), the exception becomes the rule (hence the distinction between rule and exception becomes blurred or breaks down), and preexisting normative and legal orders are suspended. The sovereign is one who declares and decides on the state of exception. Agamben sees this condition as generalized or rampant in the post-Auschwitz world, and this allows him to assert that the camp is the prototype of modern life and that Auschwitz is now everywhere. As he puts the point in one of his more resounding declamations: "Behind the powerlessness of God peeps the powerlessness of men, who continue to cry 'May that never happen again!' when it is clear that 'that' [Auschwitz] is, by now, everywhere." The postapocalyptic Auschwitz-now-everywhere hyperbole is one insistently repeated and variously reformulated feature of Agamben's account that lends itself to an elated, seemingly radical, breathlessly ecstatic discourse of the sublime. Hence in his chapter "The Witness," after putting forth a pathos-charged, participatory evocation of Levi's discussion of the wordless child Hurbinek (who utters an "obstinately secret" word whose meaning is undecidable—the word *mass-klo* or *matisklo*, which Agamben approximates to "the secret word that Levi discerned in the 'background noise' of Celan's poetry" [38]), he ends with these intricately straining (unsayable?) words (reminiscent of certain passages in Foucault's *Histoire de la folie*): "The trace of that to which no one has borne witness, which language believes itself to transcribe, is not the speech of language. The speech of language is born where language is no longer in the beginning, where language falls away from it

---

Yes . . . Well Maybe") in the same issue. See also Royle's postapocalyptic *After Derrida* (Manchester: Manchester University Press, 1995).

[24] See Carl Schmitt, *Political Theology: Four Chapters on the Concept of Sovereignty*, trans. George Schwab (1922, 1934; Cambridge: MIT Press, 1985).

simply to bear witness: 'It was not light, but was sent to bear witness to the light'" (39).[25]

One might, however, also argue that the hyperbole (even the cryptic prophetic mode) allows for a justifiable sense of urgency and indicates the limitations of ethics or politics as usual or indeed of any useful, easy, or even immediately accessible approach to problems. Indeed if one agrees with Agamben, he is not being hyperbolic but lucid in the arresting manner of the child who sees that the emperor has no clothes—that the post-Auschwitz world is itself utterly bereft or bankrupt, irremediably ruined and in dire need of some inconceivably new politics and ethics. In any event, one (or at least I) would like to know more than Agamben provides about the usual or conventional state of ethics and its relation to traditions. One result of his procedure is that he offers little room for immanent critique or deconstruction based on a careful analysis of the past and the "unredeemed" possibilities it may offer for action in the present and future (the possibilities that interested Walter Benjamin in his historical and critical dimension—Benjamin's more decidedly apocalyptic-messianic moments are the ones that captivate Agamben). One may well argue that Auschwitz itself provided no such possibilities either in itself or in its aftermath, and this would seem to be Agamben's view. But one may contest this view without going to the other extreme of

[25] Compare the sober words of Levi, which, despite their own dubious aspects (for example, the facile invocation of pathology or the decisive opposition between humans and other animals with a limited idea of language serving as an invidiously differentiating criterion), may raise the question of the unexplored relations between certain forms of existentialism and of poststructuralism: "According to a theory fashionable during those years [the 1970s], which to me seems frivolous and irritating, 'incommunicability' supposedly was an inevitable ingredient, a life sentence inherent to the human condition, particularly the life style of industrial society: we are monads, incapable of reciprocal messages, or capable only of truncated messages, false at their departure, misunderstood on their arrival. Discourse is fictitious, pure noise, a painted veil that conceals existential silence; we are alone, even (or especially) if we live in pairs. It seems to me that this lament originates in a dangerous vicious circle. Except for cases of pathological incapacity, one can and must communicate, and thereby contribute in a useful and easy way to the peace of others and oneself, because silence, the absence of signals, is itself a signal, but an ambiguous one, and ambiguity generates anxiety and suspicion. To say that it is impossible to communicate is false; one always can. To refuse to communicate is a failing; we are biologically and socially predisposed to communication, and in particular to its highly evolved and noble form, which is language. All members of the human species speak, no nonhuman species knows how to speak" (*The Drowned and the Saved*, 88–89) On Foucault, see my discussion in *History and Reading: Tocqueville, Foucault, French Studies* (Toronto: University of Toronto Press, 2000), chap 3.

spiritual uplift or fixation on the moments of resistance (the Warsaw ghetto uprising, for example) or of mutual aid in the most dire of circumstances (some instances of which Levi recounts and which appear in many survivor testimonies). One may also contest Agamben's view while recognizing the importance of sustained reflection on the *Muselmann* and, more generally, on the question of posttraumatic repetition of the conditions and experience of victimization, including extreme disempowerment and harrowing isolation, even in survivors who have in certain significant respects reconstructed a life "after Auschwitz."[26]

One reason for what might be seen as a deficit of historical understanding and of immanent critique is Agamben's reliance on etymology, which tends to substitute for both historical analysis and argument. Agamben will often provide an etymology, at times lending it greater certainty than it may warrant, or he will cite some authority who has provided such an etymology, and then proceed from the putative etymology to a conclusion, thereby omitting any analysis or argument linking the etymology to the point he wants to assert. This is a feature Agamben shares with Heidegger, the philosopher who has probably had the most formative role in his thought. Etymology, however putative or even fictive, can be thought-provoking when it opens up a line of investigation or reflection. But can it substitute for historical analysis or argument?

I would like to look closely at the way Agamben invokes etymology to dismiss any use of the term "Holocaust." He is not alone in doing so, although he declares his dismissal in peremptory tones that seem to imply an unawareness of the extensive discussion of usage in this matter. But the more important point is that his appeal to etymology not only substitutes for historical analysis and argument but also ignores the way usage over time may deplete or even wash away etymological sediment in the meaning of a term. I think this process has occurred for many people who employ the term "Holocaust" largely because it is the one having currency in their society and culture and not because of any investment in a certain idea of sacrifice.

[26] See Lawrence Langer, *Holocaust Testimonies: The Ruins of Memory* (New Haven: Yale University Press, 1991) and my discussion of the book in *Representing the Holocaust*, 194–200.

Agamben rehearses the well known etymology of "Holocaust" as a burnt sacrificial offering, to which he adds many less known, erudite details. The telos of his account is that the term is "intolerable" and he "will never make use of this term" (31). (The apodictic nature of his statements might suggest that his analysis and critique function subtextually as a ritual of purification with respect to a "contaminated" usage.) The intolerability of the term "Holocaust" derives from its ambiguity as a euphemism and an intimation that the events in question could possibly have sacred meaning. Agamben also makes reference to the use of "Holocaust" as a component of an antisemitic diatribe. One may agree with these excellent reasons for suspicion and still question whether the use of the term necessarily entails them. One may also raise a question about a term Agamben seems to use as if it were unproblematic. "The Jews also use a euphemism to indicate the extermination. They use the term *so'ah*, which means 'devastation, catastrophe' and, in the Bible, often implies the idea of a divine punishment" (ibid.). But what about the term "extermination"? Was this not a term employed by the Nazis—a term that is far from unproblematic? Is it not a component of the discourse of pest control if not bare or naked life? The point I would like to make is that no term is unproblematic for "the events in question." The best (or "good-enough") strategy may be both to recognize that there are no pure or innocent terms (however "purified" by critical analysis) and to avoid fixating on one term as innocent or as taboo. Instead, while being especially careful about unintentional repetitions of Nazi terminology, one might employ a multiplicity of terms (Holocaust, Auschwitz, Shoah, Nazi genocide . . .) in a flexible manner that resists fixation while acknowledging the problem in naming. Moreover, as I intimated earlier, the banalized use of the term "Holocaust" may be beneficial in eroding any sacrificial connotation not only with respect to "Auschwitz" but even more generally—a process Agamben might also see as beneficial (and that could be taken as the desirable, "demystifying," or delegitimating dimension of his own conception of *homo sacer* and bare or naked life). It is also noteworthy that the term "Holocaust" is used not only by antisemites, as Agamben seems to imply, but also by Jews, including survivors, and this could be another reason for its use more generally. (In a comparable way the broader population of those who try to avoid prejudice or even to be "politically correct" tend to follow usage in self-designation within a relevant group, say, of "African Americans" or "Latinos" and "Latinas.") Agamben notes that Levi used the term "Holocaust" reluctantly "to be understood" and that he believed that Elie Wiesel "had coined it, then regretted it and wanted to take it back" (quoted 28). But whether Wiesel "coined" it or not, it came into general currency among survivors, Jews, and the general population with the varied effects I have touched upon.[27]

I have noted that Agamben moves from a rejection of an immanent sublime or a redemptive reading of Auschwitz to a more transcendent sublime that is nonetheless complicated by certain movements in his thinking. Particularly problematic is his use of Primo Levi as privileged witness (or "example") in relation to the *Muselmann*. Agamben at first supplements his rejection of redemptive readings with a critique of the view that Auschwitz is unsayable (32). He also criticizes Shoshana Felman, who is often associated with an extremely sophisticated variant of this view. But his criticisms are, I think, local disagreements within a more general accord. Felman traces a labyrinthine paradox or aporia whereby the witness cannot bear witness from either inside or outside the events of the Shoah but can only at best bear witness to the breakdown of witnessing (a now-familiar topos in discussions of the Holocaust). For Agamben, Felman does not interrogate "the threshold of indistinction between inside and outside" the Shoah, and she aestheticizes testimony in appealing to the song as a performative event that "speaks to us beyond its words, beyond its melody" (quoted 36). But Agamben is in fundamental agreement with the view she elaborates in *Testimony* of the Shoah as an event without witnesses or an event that paradoxically bears witness to the breakdown of witnessing, thereby leading to endless aporias.[28] He also invokes Jean-François Lyotard's *The Differend* in noting that "there is something like an impossibility of bearing witness" (34). And like Felman and Lyotard he stresses the excess and

---

[27] For one chapter in the use of the term, see Gerd Korman, "The Holocaust in American Historical Writing" (1972) in *The Nazi Holocaust*, vol. 1, ed. Michael Marrus (Westport and London: Meckler, 1989), 284–303. For Korman, Wiesel did not coin the term "Holocaust" but with "other gifted writers and speakers" helped to make it "coin of the realm" (294).

[28] See Shosana Felman and Dori Laub, M.D., *Testimony: Crises of Witnessing in Literature, Psychoanalysis, and History* (New York: Routledge, 1992). I discuss Felman's contributions to this book in the three works mentioned in n. 1.

the lacuna at the heart of the limit situation or event. The question here is how his critique of the appeal to unsayability relates to his affirmation of what seems to be very close to it, indeed even within the same "threshold of indistinction": the notion that the Shoah in its excess and its lack (its supplementary uncanniness and disconcerting challenge) bears witness to the impossibility or breakdown of witnessing. In Lyotard and at times in Agamben, this paradoxical view prompts a dual movement: both toward the insistence on the paradox as paradox and in the direction of the necessity of working or playing out new formulations to respond to the excess/lack that continually requires rearticulations that can never reach total closure. (I find this approach to be valuable.) At other times, however, there seems to be a compulsively repetitive return to, or even presupposition of, the paradox or aporia to which one moves like the moth to the flame.

Let us look more closely at these complex movements. While relying on the unexplicated notion of uniqueness, Agamben nonetheless puts forth a relatively rare appeal to caution:

> Those who assert the unsayability of Auschwitz today should be more cautious in their statements. If they mean to say that Auschwitz was a unique event in the face of which the witness must in some way submit his every word to the test of an impossibility of speaking, they are right. But if, joining uniqueness to unsayability, they transform Auschwitz into a reality absolutely separated from language, if they break the tie between an impossibility and a possibility of speaking that, in the *Muselmann*, constitutes testimony, then they unconsciously repeat the Nazis' gesture; they are in secret solidarity with the *arcanum imperii*. (157)[29]

Agamben probably means "survivor" or "witness" rather than "*Muselmann*" in the last sentence. But such slippage aside, he elsewhere restricts the possibility of testimony to bearing witness to the impossibility of witnessing, or speaking "only on the basis of an impossibility of speaking," which, mirabile dictu, presumably will be

---

[29] I indicate ways Agamben himself seems to "unconsciously repeat the Nazis' gesture." This transferential repetition, which is often invoked dubiously as an ultimate "knock-down" argument, confronts all discourses on the topic, and the problem is not whether it threatens to occur but how one comes to terms with it in more or less explicit fashion—to what extent and how one acts it out and works it through.

the ultimate rejoinder to negationism. In light of such "undeniable" testimony, "Auschwitz—that to which it is not possible to bear witness—is absolutely and irrefutably proven" (164). In addition, "the witness attests to the fact that there can be testimony because there is an inseparable division and non-coincidence between the inhuman and the human, the living being and the speaking being, the *Muselmann* and the survivor" (157). What Agamben does not cogently attempt is to relate the threshold of indistinction to an understanding of the human being as a compromise formation between biological life (not reducible to mere life) and political or ethical life—an understanding that allows for a complex, nonabsolute interaction between the two.

At times Agamben formulates problems in a manner that itself seems to eradicate the paradox in paradox and to lead to a pure, all-or-nothing antinomy that eventuates in a stark decision and eliminates any tension between a disjunction, radical difference, or internal alterity within the human and an understanding of the human as a compromise formation:

> When one looks closely, the passage from language to discourse appears as a paradoxical act that simultaneously implies both subjectification and desubjectification. On the one hand, the psychosomatic individual must fully abolish himself and desubjectify himself as a real individual to become the subject of enunciation and to identify himself with the pure shifter "I," which is absolutely without any substantiality and content other than its mere reference to the event of discourse. But, once stripped of all extra-linguistic meaning and constituted as a subject of enunciation, the subject discovers that he has gained access not so much to a possibility of speaking as to an impossibility of speaking—or, rather, that he has gained access to being always already anticipated by a glossalalic potentiality over which he has neither control nor mastery. . . . He is expropriated of all referential reality, letting himself be defined solely through the pure and empty relation to the event of discourse. *The subject of enunciation is composed of discourse and exists in discourse alone. But, for this very reason, once the subject is in discourse, he can say nothing; he cannot speak.* (Ital. in original; 116–17)

Such a formulation deprives one of an ability to ascribe responsibility and agency. It vastly oversimplifies the problem of language in use. And it amounts to a philosophical analogue of both the political idea of a postwar *Stunde Null*, or point zero, and the theological concept of creation ex nihilo. It also indicates Agamben's proximity to a variant of existentialism as well as a variant of structuralism.[30] One finds a comparable formulation in *Means without End* (141), where options are restricted to the poles of the antinomy between the view of humanity as having one, fully unified identity, telos, essence, or ergon and its construction in Agamben himself as pure possibility related to the absolute bankruptcy of the past and the irrelevance of every preexisting value (an enumeration of these values gives "freedom, progress, democracy, human rights, constitutional state" [124]). Such an antinomic and antinomian formulation eliminates the mediations provided by history in its relation to theory.

In *Remnants of Auschwitz*, via the universalization of the *Muselmann* and his or her identification with the divided subject, Agamben goes on to assert that "the living being and the speaking being, the inhuman and the human—or any terms of a historical process . . . have not an *end*, but a *remnant*. There is no foundation in or beneath them; rather, at their center lies an irreducible disjunction in which each term, stepping forth in the place of a remnant, can bear witness. What is truly historical is not what redeems time in the direction of the future or even the past; it is, rather, what fulfills time in the excess of a medium. The messianic Kingdom is neither the future (the millennium) nor the past (the golden age); it is, instead, a *remaining time*" (159). One may agree with Agamben's criticisms of teleology, foundationalism, and modes of redemption as fulfillment at the beginning or end of time but still raise questions about what he affirms (insofar as it is understandable) as a fulfilled time (in the key of excess) or perhaps an always already available remnant. Indeed he seems to redefine the "truly historical" in terms of transhistorical, theoreticist notions of an "irreducible disjunction" (for some others this would be trauma) and a paradoxical time-fulfilling excess that entail a construction of all history as a postapocalyptic remnant whose terms

[30] The variant of existentialism to which I refer is pronounced in one important dimension of Sartre's *Being and Nothingness* wherein the for-itself has a "nihilating" relation of disjunction and transcendence to the in-itself, a relation that aligns the for-itself with pure possibility or *disponibilité* and with the imaginary. A variant of structuralism, while it may downplay or deny the freedom and agency of a "for-itself," nonetheless stresses a relation of radical disjunction or epistemological break between structures.

both bear witness to the apocalypse and hold out a saving grace in the form of an ever present *Jetztzeit* or "remaining time."[31] Agamben's conception of the "truly historical" may even be residually indebted to a sacrificial logic involving substitution, in which the part that remains (the remnant) somehow saves or redeems the whole in however paradoxical or aporetic a manner.

Other movements in Agamben's account would seem to invalidate any notion of redemption or salvation.[32] The witness (Levi, for "example") bears witness to the *Muselmann*, hence to the most extreme or abject impossibility or breakdown of witnessing. (Is the difference between the unsayability Agamben criticizes and such paradoxical witnessing one of reflexivity: one now repeatedly says that there is unsayability rather than just saying the event is unsayable? Is Agamben's approach different from one, which I would accept, that does not begin with, or become fixated on, breakdown or aporia but is open and alert to such breakdown or aporia when it occurs in the witness's attempt to recount traumatic experience and perhaps in the commentator's empathic attempt to render such an attempt?) Such paradoxical or aporetic saying or witnessing, as Agamben discusses it, often seems close to a discourse of the sublime, which Lyotard has elaborated, and Felman enacted, in more explicit terms. Except for the sacrificial form the analysis at times seems to take, the sublime here is radically transcendent in that one can bear witness to it only indirectly or paratactically by indicating time and again, and in various repetitive formulations, the impossibility of acceding to it through representation. And it is now radically disjoined from any positive or

[31] For a different articulation of the relations between the transhistorical and the historical, which does not collapse them or evacuate historical specificity by deriving the historical from the transhistorical, see my "Trauma, Absence, Loss," *Critical Inquiry* 25 (1999): 696–727, a version of which is chapter 2 of *Writing History, Writing Trauma*.

[32] The background noise in the following passage might seem to drown out any meaning, but the passage in its reference to the "non-coincidence of the whole and the part" might conceivably be read as countering a sacrificial logic: "In the concept of remnant, the aporia of testimony coincides with the aporia of messianism. Just as the remnant of Israel signifies neither the whole people nor a part of the people but, rather, the non-coincidence of the whole and the part, and just as messianic time is neither historical time nor eternity but, rather, the disjunction that divides them, so the remnants of Auschwitz—the witnesses—are neither the dead nor the survivors, neither the drowned nor the saved. They are what remains between them" (163–64). Is the philosopher, in Agamben's vision of him as one who sees the world from an extreme situation that has become the rule, one of these remnants?

affirmative senses of the sacred, from any intimation of the martyro-logical, or from any unspoken promise of parousia in the mode of neg-ative theology. Yet the lowest of the low, the *Muselmann* as the limit of abjection, seems to evoke a discourse that, in its own excess and its insistent, at times intolerant, struggle with the aporetic limits of thought, seems at least like a specter of the sublime. If one may refer to sublimity at all (and one may conceivably argue against this move), it now seems like the horizonless pale shadow of a god that has not died but has been recognized as absent, perhaps endlessly.

Still, there are times in Agamben when the *Muselmann* him- or herself becomes sublime in effulgent yet chiaroscuro terms that outdo, while recalling, passages in Kant:

> This is language of the "dark shadows" that Levi heard growing in Celan's poetry, like a "background noise"; this is Hurbinek's non-language (*mass-klo, matisklo*) that has no place in the libraries of what has been said or in the archive of statements. Just as in the starry sky that we see at night, the stars shine surrounded by a total darkness that, according to cosmologists, is nothing other than the testimony of a time in which the stars did not yet shine, so the speech of the witness bears witness to a time in which human beings did not yet speak; and so the testimony of human beings attests to a time in which they were not yet human. Or, to take up an analogous hypothesis, just as in the expanding universe, the farthest galaxies move away from us at a speed greater than that of their light, which cannot reach us, such that the darkness we see in the sky is nothing but the invisibility of the light of unknown stars, so the complete witness, according to Levi's paradox, is the one we cannot see: the *Muselmann*. (162)

Even aside from the question of whether the *Muselmann* can or should serve as the occasion for a dark-winged lyrical flight into sub-limity, one may ask whether there is a crucial dimension of bearing witness and giving testimony that Agamben occludes. He discusses the *Muselmann* as the ultimate victim, the one who died or was com-pletely crushed, and yet who is also the true witness, the sublime witness whose testimony would be truly valuable, but who cannot bear witness. He also discusses the survivor-witness as ultimately bearing witness to the *Muselmann*. What he does not investigate with care is the arduous process whereby bearing witness and giving testimony are themselves crucial aspects of the movement (however incomplete and subject to remission) from the victim—indeed the potential *Muselmann*—to the survivor and agent. Agamben concludes his book with a series of quotations from former *Muselmänner*, and one may ask how it is even possible to refer to oneself as a *Muselmann* in the past tense, given the utterly abject, disempowered position from which one has to emerge, at least to some extent or momentarily, to make this usage possible. Indeed one might argue that part of the process Agamben elides is crucial in understanding the witness who performatively is not only a victim but a survivor who lives on in part precisely by giving testimony or bearing witness. (When the ability or the inclination to bear witness ends, the life may also end.)

This process is obscured, perhaps even devalorized (whether intentionally or not), by the relentless insistence on the aporias and paradoxes of bearing witness to the impossibility of witnessing—aporias and paradoxes that may indeed arise but should not be presupposed or converted into a vehicle for a repetition compulsion. In Agamben one often has the sense that he begins with the presupposition of the aporia or paradox, which itself may at times lose its force and its insistence in that it does not come about through the breakdown or experienced impasse in speaking, writing, or trying to communicate but instead seems to be postulated at the outset. In other words, a prepackaged form seems to seek its somewhat arbitrary content. And the paradox and the aporia become predictable components of a fixated methodology. Indeed the terms in which the aporia as assumed, self-negating telos are sometimes (not always) formulated can be rather unconvincing. For example, near the beginning of the book, he writes:

> What is at issue here is not, of course, the difficulty we face whenever we try to communicate our most intimate experiences to others. The discrepancy in question concerns the very structure of testimony. On the one hand, what happened in the camps appears to the survivors as the only true thing and, as such, absolutely unforgettable; on the other hand, this truth is to the same degree unimaginable, that is, irreducible to the real elements that constitute it. Facts so real that, by comparison, nothing is truer; a reality that necessarily exceeds its factual elements— such is the aporia of Auschwitz. (12)

This formulation may give one an indistinct sense of a problem, but the indistinction is more vague than indicative of one's implication in a threshold of indeterminacy or undecidability. "The only true thing," "irreducible to the real elements that constitute it," "facts so real," "a reality that necessarily exceeds its factual elements"—these formulations gesture off-handedly without evoking an aporia. Or, if the aporia is evoked, it is in rather routinized terms with reference to an excess in the limit event that others (notably Lyotard and Saul Friedlander) have discussed extensively.[33]

One may nonetheless argue that Agamben's concluding paradoxical gesture of ending the book with a series of quotations from former *Muselmänner*, who in principle should not be able to speak or bear witness, is subject to multiple readings. It gives the final word to a spiraling, self-consuming paradox or aporetic *mise en abîme*. It also gives a privileged place to these quoted words as sacred text that can only be defiled by commentary. It seems to imply that these words speak for themselves or even speak in many tongues, which the reader must decipher or simply behold with awe. And it may suggest a reading of Agamben against the grain whereby he is, intentionally or not, caught up in a bitter irony, performatively self-deconstructing by bearing witness to his inability to bear witness and, paradoxically, supporting his abject identification with the *Muselmann* who paradoxically states: "I was a *Muselmann*."

In any event, the relations between and among the threshold of indistinction, the gray zone, and the state of emergency are not elucidated in *Remnants of Auschwitz*—indeed the three seem at times to be conflated, at least "after Auschwitz."[34] The lack of elucidation may be abetted by postapocalyptic assumptions, the acting-out of post-traumatic symptoms, and the fragmented, paratactical nature of Agamben's approach. (Reminiscent of Wittgenstein in the *Tractatus* and the *Philosophical Investigations* or Lyotard in *The Differend*, he

[33] Along with Lyotard's *Differend*, see especially Friedlander, *Memory, History, and the Extermination of the Jews of Europe* (Bloomington: University of Indiana Press, 1993).
[34] In *Homo Sacer* Agamben explicitly links the state of exception and the threshold of indistinction: "The situation created in the exception has the peculiar characteristic that it cannot be defined either as a situation of fact or as a situation of right, but instead institutes a paradoxical threshold of indistinction between the two" (18). The question is whether the converse is also the case and whether the threshold of indistinction always creates a state of exception. The more important question is whether, in modernity and especially "after Auschwitz", the exception becomes increasingly the fundamental political structure and ultimately the rule.

employs numbered paragraphs.) I would suggest that the "threshold of indistinction" is a transhistorical concept that is evoked in variable ways by historical phenomena or "cases," while the gray zone and the state of exception as rule refer to more historically determinate situations that may nonetheless become a basis for transhistorical reflection, just as the historical figure of the *Muselmann* may become a basis for a general or transhistorical reflection on abjection. I would also suggest that the threshold of indistinction has an affirmative or at least an undecidable valence that both problematizes norms and may help in the generation of newer normative articulations. When approximated to or conflated with the state of exception, it is generalized and given a political and juridical inflection. As such it may be related to a condition of normative dislocation, which the sovereign through a decisionist gesture is supposed to determine and resolve. One may of course argue that one goal of social, political, and civic life is to avoid the rampant state of exception or to see it at best as an extreme condition in an intolerable state of affairs that may be a prelude to revolution. Hence one might even want to bring about something at least close to a state of exception in oppressive regimes, but the judgment concerning which regime falls into this "category," and whether collapse, panic, and disarray are more likely than revolution in any desirable sense, is debatable. The postapocalyptic Auschwitz-now-everywhere hyperbole obviates this problem in judgment by generalizing the state of exception along with the gray zone and the threshold of indistinction. Hence the routine yet surrealistic soccer match in Auschwitz between the SS and Jewish members of the *Sonderkommando* "repeats itself in every match in our stadiums, in every television broadcast, in the normalcy of everyday life. If we do not succeed in understanding that match, in stopping it, there will never be hope" (26). How would one go about stopping that match, and, if one accepts the limited value of the afterimage of unsettlement projected forward by the match at Auschwitz but objects to the shrill yet leveling logic in Agamben's exclamation, is one condemned to hopeless complacency and business as usual?

One might also contend that the gray zone in its historical sense (as used by Primo Levi) is not so much a threshold of indistinction or even a state of exception as it is a condition of extreme equivocation that is created largely through the practices of perpetrators and imposed on victims, typically in the form of double binds or impossible situations. Moreover, as a historical condition, the gray zone need not be generalized (as it may tend to be in a state of exception or in extremely equivocal conflicts) but at least at times may exist as an intermediary zone between relatively clear-cut cases or groups of perpetrators and victims (as Levi believed to be the case in the Holocaust). Indeed one may argue that the gray zone and, in different ways, the rampant state of exception, may obviate confrontation with the threshold of indistinction as it exists and poses problems for everyone. This is because the gray zone and the state of exception, particularly when it gives way to an anomic state of emergency, typically involve, or devolve into, a binary opposition between self and other (perpetrator and victim, friend and enemy, us and them) in which anxiety may be projected from the (oppressing) self onto the (oppressed) other as well as localized invidiously in those placed in equivocal or double-bind situations (particularly perpetrator-victims or collaborators). Moreover, the generally applicable threshold of indistinction creates anxiety that normative orders may mitigate but never entirely eliminate. It relates to the manner in which decisions, especially extremely difficult decisions, are never entirely predetermined by norms, although norms may indeed guide decisions in many cases and to some extent in all but the most difficult and problematic cases. In addition, one may defend as desirable a condition of society in which the threshold of indistinction exerts pressure on everyone but is not generalized as a state in which the exception becomes the rule—a state that is of direct political consequence. The legitimate normative articulation of life in common would be such that one could in general distinguish between the exception and the rule and not expect everyone to live according to the extreme or excessive demands placed upon the exception (something that may be argued to occur in the state of exception). Within any concrete situation, one would of course have to further articulate these general considerations, for example, with reference to questions of equality and hierarchy involving specific economic, political, and social issues. The considerations on which I have touched all too briefly seem to have little role in Agamben's discussion, in *Remnants of Auschwitz*, of the gray zone, the threshold of indistinction, and the state of exception.[35]

[35] For a careful, thought-provoking discussion of related issues, see Etienne Balibar, *Masses, Classes, Ideas: Studies on Politics and Philosophy before and after Marx*, trans. James Swenson (New York: Routledge, 1994), esp. part 3.

Agamben not only sees Primo Levi as speaking for the *Muselmann* but he generalizes the gray zone in a manner that threatens to undo significant distinctions and to eventuate in a view of all existence in terms of the limit event or situation as a state of exception, if not emergency or crisis, in which the exception becomes the rule. I have noted that, from Agamben's postapocalyptic perspective, "Auschwitz marks the end and the ruin of every ethics of dignity and conformity to a norm" and "Levi, who bears witness to the drowned, speaking in their stead, is the cartographer of this new *terra ethica*, the implacable land-surveyor of *Muselmannland*" (69). Of Levi, Agamben also writes: "He is the only one who consciously sets out to bear witness in place of the *Muselmänner*, the drowned, those who were demolished and touched bottom" (59). The problem here is not the argument that Auschwitz, or the *Muselmann* in particular, poses distinctive problems for ethics or that it is dubious to impute essential dignity to the *Muselmann*, especially for self-serving reasons. What is problematic pertains to the synecdochic *use* of the *Muselmann* as a theoretical cypher to disprove human dignity and to discredit all preexisting (perhaps all presently conceivable) forms of ethics. What remains of ethics (if it still can be called ethics) in Agamben is dissociated from law and voided of all forms of normativity (including responsibility and guilt). It seems to eventuate in an empty utopianism and a form of political romanticism ("as Spinoza knew, the doctrine of the happy life" [24]). In any case, Agamben takes a potential in humanity and, rather than examining closely its historical role in Auschwitz and comparing it carefully to other situations and possibilities, actualizes it in universal terms by generalizing the *Muselmann* as the prototype or exemplar of humanity. This *condition humaine*, as "life in its most extreme degradation," becomes "the touchstone by which to judge and measure all morality and dignity" (ibid.).[36] The result is an unsituated, extreme mode of victimology or identification with the abject and utterly disempowered—something that, despite its transhistorical cast, might most generously be seen as a radical reversal of, or perhaps an overcompensation for, extreme victimization under the Nazis.

[36] See also Slavoj Žižek, *Did Somebody Say Totalitarianism?* (London: Verso, 2001), chap. 2. One difficulty with Agamben's generalization of the gray zone is that it allows an illegitimate metaleptic slippage from the defensible view that there is an important sense in which everyone is a potential *Muselmann* (or, for that matter, perpetrator) to the dubious view that the *Muselmann* is everyman.

In his brief but trenchant reflections on ethics, Agamben apparently takes Auschwitz as an apocalyptic divide between past and present that delegitimates all uses in the present of past ethical assumptions or discourses. He even attributes such a view to Levi: "The *Muselmann*, as Levi describes him, is the site of an experiment in which morality and humanity themselves are called into question" (63). Moreover:

> The unprecedented discovery made by Levi at Auschwitz concerns an area that is independent of every establishment of responsibility, an area in which Levi succeeded in isolating something like a new ethical element. Levi calls it the "gray zone." It is the zone in which the "long chain of conjunction between victim and executioner" comes loose, where the oppressed becomes oppressor and the executioner in turn appears as victim. A gray, incessant alchemy in which good and evil and, along with them, all the metals of traditional ethics reach their point of fusion. (21)

There are many contestable features in these statements to which I shall return. Here I would point out the dubiousness of seeing total ethical meltdown in Levi, who drew from traditional culture and ethics both to provide him with sustenance in the camps and, in a manner that was, if anything, perhaps insufficiently informed by the concerns that preoccupy Agamben, to inform his postwar reflections on his experience.

If one recalls the quotation from Himmler's Posen speech, one may well sympathize with Agamben when he asserts of the *Muselmänner*: "To speak of dignity and decency in their case would not be decent." Sympathy wavers when he adds, in his prevalent turn to a kind of free indirect style or middle voice: "The survivors [including Levi as Agamben speaks with(in) and for him] are not only 'worse' in comparison with the best ones—those whose strength rendered them less fit in the camp—they are also 'worse' in comparison with the anonymous mass of the drowned, those whose death cannot be called death. This is the specific ethical aporia of Auschwitz: it is the site in which it is not decent to remain decent, in which those who believed themselves to preserve their dignity and self-respect experience shame with respect to those who did not" (60). Auschwitz epitomizes the absolute impossibility of "death with dignity" in the modern world, the way in which death gives way to the manufacture of corpses.

"This means that in Auschwitz it is no longer possible to distinguish between death and mere decease, between dying and 'being liquidated'" (76).[37] More generally, in the modern world one's unease about dying is related to its privatization, deritualization, and concealment from public view.

Agamben is touching on important issues here—issues that should not be obliterated by any reservations about his approach. Still, Agamben is so concerned with the problem of death that he pays scant attention to processes of killing among the Nazis and their relations to specific objects of victimization. In the relatively few references to the SS, even they undergo, rather than activate, processes and are often framed in the passive voice or in something approximating a bystander position or a position that almost seems to place them (as in the soccer game) on a gray on gray, level playing field with victims. "The SS could not see the *Muselmann*, let alone bear witness to him" (78). Or again: "Both the survivor's discomfort and testimony concern not merely what was done or suffered, but what *could* have been done or suffered. It is this *capacity*, this almost infinite potentiality to suffer that is inhuman—not the facts, actions, or omissions. And it is precisely this *capacity* that is denied to the SS" (77).

There may be a worthwhile shock or scandal induced by accusing the SS of an incapacity to be inhuman—a shock relating to an attempt to rethink the threshold between the human and the inhuman or nonhuman and to reposition ethics as other than purely humanistic. Agamben does not make explicit and explore the implications of this unsettling, seemingly paradoxical idea, for example, concerning the "rights" or claims of other-than-human animals. (Indeed, one danger of Agamben's sharp binary between the human and the inhuman or nonhuman, which he maps onto the opposition between the speaking being and mere or naked life, is the exclusion or even scapegoat-

[37] Certain things Heidegger said or wrote may be recalled here, some of them very equivocal. For example, in a 1949 lecture comment at Bremen, Heidegger is reported to have said: "Agriculture is now a motorized food industry: in its essence it is the same thing as the manufacture of corpses in gas chambers, the same thing as blockades and the reduction of a region to hunger, the same as the manufacture of hydrogen bombs"; cited by Wolfgang Schirmacher, *Technik und Gelassenheit* (Freiburg: Alber, 1983), 25. Heidegger elsewhere insists that the same is not the identical, but his comment warrants a careful exegesis in terms of similarities and differences among the phenomena to which he referred. At least evoked in his comment is the problem of the treatment of animals in factory farms and the mass manufacture of food products.

ing of nonhuman animals who, by implication, seem reduced to mere life or raw material.) Moreover, *pace* Agamben and whatever may be the case concerning almost infinite potentiality, the capacity to suffer is something humans share with other animals, and it is related to empathy, which the SS did not have for victims. But this capacity (or Agamben's postulated incapacity, for that matter) was not simply denied the SS as passive recipients. It was actively countered, blocked, or eliminated through ideological and related practical forces as well as through the dynamic of victimization that brought victims to the abject state Nazi ideology, in circular and self-fulfilling fashion, attributed to them. A particularly questionable feature of Agamben's orientation is that the deficit of the SS, in terms of a lack of inhumanity, is itself construed in terms of an almost infinite (quasi-divine?) capacity or potentiality for suffering. No known being, human or otherwise, has this infinite capacity. Beyond a certain threshold of suffering, one blacks out, and it would seem that Agamben strives to write from, or even from beyond, that threshold. Once again we seem to be in the vicinity of ethics understood in paradoxical terms as supraethical, supererogatory excess rather than in more socially and politically viable terms. Does empathy for both human and other-than-human beings require an infinite capacity for suffering, or does the latter radically transcend empathy into an ecstatically indistinct realm of sublimity that would itself seem, in any social or political terms, to be isolating? (Almost involuntarily, I think of the unimaginably suffering but transfigured Christ ascending into heaven.)

Agamben's related understanding of the meaning of Himmler's Posen speech is curious at best. He sees it in line with his idea of the SS as not having the inhuman, almost infinite capacity to suffer. He relates the latter to another passive position with a paradoxical twist: the *Befehlnotstand*. "The executioners unanimously continue to repeat that they *could* not do other than as they did, that, in other words, they simply *could* not; they had to, and that is all. In German, to act without being capable of acting is called *Befehlnotstand*, having to obey an order" (77–78). Agamben then relates the perpetrator's claim to submit to orders that one must obey, thereby acting without really acting, to the passage from Himmler's Posen speech (which I earlier quoted in a somewhat different translation): "Most of you know what it means when 100 corpses lie there, or when 500 corpses lie there, or when 1,000 corpses lie there. To have gone through this and—apart from a few exceptions caused by human weakness—to have remained decent, that has made us great. That is a page of glory in our history which has never been written and which will never be written" (quoted 78).

Himmler himself shows a preference for passive or indeterminate constructions that veil somewhat the fact that those whom he addresses not only have beheld a scene but are responsible for having brought it about. One may analyze the functions of such a construction but one ought not simply to repeat it transferentially in one's own analysis. Moreover, Himmler in this passage is not altogether like Eichmann on trial appealing to a distorted Kantian sense of duty in doing one's job and obeying orders; he does not simply appeal to a *Befehlnotstand* or the inability to do otherwise. There are in his words an appeal to the sublime (notably a mathematical sublime in the geometrically increasing expanse of corpses), to the fascination with excess and radical transgression in the form of unheard-of mass destruction, to the glory that the uninitiated will never understand, to the quasi-sacrificial allure of victimization in the absolute injunction to kill all Jews without exception (by definition there is no such thing as a good Jew), and to the superhuman ability to become hard (interestingly mistranslated in the above quotation as "great"— "absolute greatness" characterized the sublime for Kant) by enduring (*durchstehen*) the aporia or combining in oneself the antinomic features of decency and radical transgression.[38] In other words, for Himmler,

---

[38] The Eichmann who is more like Himmler in his Posen speech is evoked by Saul Friedlander: "Could one of the components of 'Rausch' be the effect of a growing elation stemming from repetition, from the ever-larger numbers of killed others: 'Most of you know what it means when 100 corpses are lying side by side, when 500 lie there or 1000.' This repetition (and here indeed we are back, in part, at Freud's interpretation) adds to the sense of *Unheimlichkeit*, at least for the outside observer; there, the perpetrators do not appear anymore as bureaucratic automata, but rather as beings seized by a compelling lust for killing on an immense scale, driven by some kind of extraordinary elation in repeating the killing of ever-huger masses of people (notwithstanding Himmler's words about the difficulty of this duty). Suffice it to remember the pride of numbers sensed in the Einsatzgruppen reports, the pride of numbers in Rudolf Höss's autobiography; suffice it to remember Eichmann's interview with Sassen: he would jump with glee into his grave knowing that over five million Jews had been exterminated; elation created by the staggering dimension of the killing, by the endless rows of victims. The elation created by the staggering number of victims ties in with the mystical Führer-Bond: the greater the number of the Jews exterminated, the better the Führer's will has been fulfilled." *Memory, History, and the Extermination of the Jews of Europe*, 110–11. Friedlander also observes that "for further analysis, we would need a new category equivalent to Kant's cate-

Nazis did look the Gorgon directly in the face, and this "sublime," petrifying gaze made them hard in a sense they desired. What is interesting is Agamben's inability to detect these aspects of the Posen speech and to focus instead on what would seem unaccentuated in, if not projectively inserted into, it.[39]

There is also a problem with respect to what might be termed, for lack of a better word, subject positions. For Levi as survivor to say that not he but the *Muselmann* is the true witness is, I think, an acceptable hyperbole. For Agamben to identify with Levi and hence speak for (or in the stead of) Levi and hence for the *Muselmann* (as he believes Levi does) may be hyperbolic in an objectionable sense.[40] Moreover, the idea that Auschwitz radically delegitimates all preexisting ethics and all present appeals to them, including all notions of decency and dignity, paradoxically runs the risk of granting a posthumous (postapocalyptic?) victory to the Nazis. In any event it obviates a careful inquiry into the uses of such concepts by victims and survivors themselves as well as their attempts to preserve some sense of dignity and decency in impossible situations (for example, by washing themselves with filthy water). It also risks handing the concept of decency over to Himmler as his heritage rather than to struggle for and to rethink it (for example, by criticizing any invidious use of it to distinguish the human from the other-than-human, including the animal, which should not itself be reduced to bare or naked life or be understood in neo-Heideggerian terms as not having a world or a form of life).

---

gory of the sublime, but specifically meant to capture inexpressible horror" (115). The question of course is precisely how one invokes this category, including how one addresses the role of critical precautions, concerning the possibility of transferential repetitions, particularly when an appeal to some aspect of the discourse of the sublime is undertaken in one's own "voice."

[39] Agamben goes on to argue that Auschwitz "calls into question the very possibility of authentic decision [particularly with respect to death] and thus threatens the very ground of Heidegger's ethics" (75). The apparent implication is that one must have an ethics that goes beyond even Heidegger in its fundamental radicality and break with the past—an ethics Agamben seeks.

[40] If there were textual evidence that Agamben were, through his study of them or in some other fashion (for example, friendship with former *Muselmänner* or their intimates), possessed by *Muselmänner* and hence in that sense "speaking for" them or in their voices, one would have to treat his text in a very different manner that might suspend criticism. One might then see Agamben as a medium for the voices of the most abject of victims. But I find little basis in the text for this kind of reading, which might well be pertinent in other cases. (See, for example, the approach of Michel de

One important feature of Agamben's notion of ethics is its radical disjunction from law—with responsibility and guilt placed squarely on the side of law. I would agree that ethics may not be identified with or reduced to law (or vice versa) and that protesters are evasive if they claim moral but not legal responsiblity for their actions (22). But this does not imply a total disjunction between ethics and law or a relegation of responsibility and guilt to law and their elimination from ethics. Responsibility and guilt are concepts that are differentially shared by ethics and law, and Agamben does not provide any idea of a form of social life in which ethics would not involve these concepts. Nor need responsibility as answerability be reduced to a rigidly codified, quasi-legal formula, as Agamben seems to imply in his etymological analysis of *sponsa* and *obligatio* as well as in a pseudo-historical just-so story that at most would apply to a restricted idea of the subject and subjectivity. ("Responsibility and guilt thus express simply two aspects of legal imputability; only later were they interiorized and moved outside the law" [22].) The unstated horizon of his view would seem to be an ecstatic, anarchistic utopia that remains terra incognita and whose relevance to present problems or commitments is left utterly blank. Indeed not only is it dubious to make Auschwitz the bomb that explodes the status quo; the sublime negativity and the hope against hope that combine to inspire such a gesture may all too readily become a license for evasiveness with respect to responsibilities and commitments in the present. Moreover, in Agamben's approach one loses sight of the tense, mutually engaging relation between the "law" or the strength of norms and what it fails to encompass—what indeed remains both as remnants and as possibly valuable irritants that indicate the limits of the law and areas demanding change. And generalizing the ecstatic, including the ecstatically transgressive, threatens to dissipate or neutralize it, eliminating the very force of its challenge. As I have intimated, one may recognize a tendency in modernity, perhaps accentuated in the recent

---

Certeau in *The Possession at Loudun*, trans. Michael B. Smith [1970; Chicago: University of Chicago Press, 1996]. Laura E. Donaldson is currently engaged in a study of nineteenth-century Shaker mediums who, she argues, were "possessed" conduits for the voices of oppressed Native American women in a manner that publicized the genocidal and misogynist violence of white society.) I find Agamben's modality of "speaking for" to be rhetorical in a restricted sense and to appropriate the voice of the other rather than being appropriated or possessed by it. Still, one should keep in mind the complexities of identification and the fallible nature of one's own readings.

past, for the sublimely ecstatic and the transgressive to be generalized and banalized but while not repeating and aggravating it to the point of hyperbole in one's own voice.

I have indicated that it is indeed important to reflect in a sustained manner on the phenomenon of the *Muselmann*, the living dead or hopeless being on the verge of extinction who was the object of disdain and avoidance among camp inmates themselves. But here one could maintain that the *Muselmann* should not be directly identified with, universalized, or spoken for—something that Primo Levi, despite a reference Agamben quotes ("we speak in their stead, by proxy," 34), at times resists doing, even as he presents the *Muselmann* as the true witness. (As Levi, in markedly nonsacrificial terms, puts it in *The Drowned and the Saved*, "one is never in another's place" [60].) Rather one might argue that the *Muselmann*, an actuality in Auschwitz, represents a potential that may become a real possibility for anyone in certain conditions, and the possibility may be related (as Agamben indicates) to split subjectivity and the "real" as analyzed by Lacan. This may be why the *Muselmann* provoked anxiety and avoidance, not simply indifference or curiosity, in the camps. One might also see Samuel Beckett as having had the daring to stage, in an incredible series of radically disempowered beings, the—or at least something close to the—*Muselmann*'s experience of disempowerment and living death—a view that would give a different perspective on Adorno's paradoxical attempt to present Beckett as more politically relevant and radical in his seemingly autonomous art than was Sartre in his defense of committed literature. Here something Žižek writes of the *Muselmann*, as one who is paradoxically beneath or beyond tragedy and comedy, is apposite: "Although the Muslim is in a way 'comic,' although he acts in a way that is usually the stuff of comedy and laughter (his automatic, mindless, repetitive gestures, his impassive pursuit of food), the utter misery of his condition thwarts any attempt to present and/or perceive him as a 'comic character'—again, if we try to present him as comic, the effect will be precisely *tragic*."[41]

One should certainly acknowledge the importance of Levi's gray zone and recognize that it often presents the most difficult cases for analysis and understanding. But (following Levi rather than Agamben) one need not construe it as all-encompassing even in the camps, much less in present societies figured as the covert, postapoc-

[41] *Did Somebody Say Totalitarianism?* 85.

alyptic embodiment of the concentrationary universe. Although one may mention still other cases without utterly blurring the distinction between perpetrator and victim, Levi restricts his discussion of the gray zone to the *Sonderkommando* and the Jewish Council, notably the case of Chaim Rumkowski of the Lodz ghetto. The "Auschwitz-now-everywhere" hyperbole is itself provocative only as a prelude to a differential analysis of how and to what extent, in Benjamin's phrase, "the exception is the rule" in contemporary societies—an analysis Agamben does not provide. While Levi certainly did, in trying circumstances, get carried away and returned at least verbal blows in a manner that brought him close to his sometime adversary, Jean Améry,[42] I have noted that the gap between Levi and Agamben is marked by the distance between typically careful reserve or even cautious understatement and prevalent, at times histrionic, hyperbole. There is even a paradoxical sense in which the Auschwitz-now-everywhere hyperbole eventuates in a banalizing rhetoric (or a rhetoric of banalizing hyperbole in which almost every sentence seems to be followed by a virtual exclamation point) bizarrely reminiscent of Ernst Nolte's normalization of the Holocaust, during the 1986 *Historikerstreit*, through an appeal to the prevalence of genocide in modern times.[43] Indeed one finds the Auschwitz-now-everywhere hyperbole in surprising quarters. It is, for example, invoked by radical antiabortionists in the self-styled Army of God, which even contains a "White Rose" faction. For those in the "Army of God," abortion is tantamount to the Holocaust, and they are resisters and rescuers for whom violence, including the murder of supposedly SS-like doctors practicing abortion, is justified. Of course Agamben would not seem to mean "that," but what he means—and how one stops the putatively omnipresent soccer match—is often unclear.

I would simply note in passing that the fact that perpetrators may be traumatized by what they do does not make them victims in the

---

[42] See the discussion in Nancy Wood, *Vectors of Memory: Legacies of Trauma in Postwar Europe* (Oxford: Berg, 1999), chap. 3. See also the contributions to the special issue edited by Karyn Ball of *Cultural Critique* 46 (2000) on "Trauma and Its Cultural Aftereffects."

[43] Ernst Nolte, "Vergangenheit die nicht vergehen will," *Frankfurter Allgemeine Zeitung*, June 6, 1986; trans. as "The Past That Will Not Pass" in *Forever in the Shadow of Hitler: Original Documents of the Historikerstreit, the Controversy Concerning the Singularity of the Holocaust*, ed. James Knowlton and Truett Cates (Atlantic Highlands, N. J.: Humanities Press, 1993). See also my discussions in *Representing the Holocaust: History, Theory, Trauma*, chap. 2, and *History and Memory after Auschwitz*, chap. 2.

relevant sense. The very term "trauma victim" may invite confusion, and there is still much to be done in perpetrator history and theory. Hence Primo Levi's gray zone should not be made into an oil slick or radically deregulated and generalized threshold of indistinction that covers everyone indiscriminately. It is inaccurate and perhaps projective to write of Levi, as Agamben does: "The only thing that interests him is what makes judgment impossible: the gray zone in which victims become executioners and executioners victims" (70). With respect to the Shoah, the gray zone for Levi exists in between relatively clear-cut "zones" of perpetrators and victims, and as Levi himself writes in his chapter "The Gray Zone" itself:

> I do not know, and it does not much interest me to know, whether in my depths there lurks a murderer, but I do know that I was a guiltless victim and I was not a murderer. I know that the murderers existed, not only in Germany, and still exist, retired or on active duty, and that to confuse them with their victims is a moral disease or an aesthetic affectation or a sinister sign of complicity; above all, it is precious service rendered (intentionally or not) to the negators of truth. I know that in the Lager, and more generally on the human stage, everything happens, and that therefore the single example proves little. (*The Drowned and the Saved*, 48–9)

Levi goes on to qualify but not to retract these emphatic comments made with some degree of exasperation.

Without fully agreeing with all of its aspects, one may also quote another passage from Levi that Agamben himself quotes without engaging its critical implications for aspects of his own approach. It concerns the poetry of Celan:

> This darkness that grows from page to page until the last inarticulate babble fills one with consternation like the gasps of a dying man; indeed, it is just that. It enthralls us as whirlpools enthrall us, but at the same time it robs us of what was supposed to be said but was not said, thus frustrating and distancing us. I think that Celan the poet must be considered and mourned rather than imitated. If his is a message, it is lost in the "background noise." It is not communication; it is not a language, or at most it is a dark and maimed language, precisely that of someone who is about to die and is alone, as we will all be at the moment of death. (quoted 37)

A crucial reason Agamben believes the *Muselmann* invalidates all previous ethics and notions of dignity and decency is that the latter prove not to be universal since they do not apply to the *Muselmann*. He is also at points alert to the danger that his own views may approximate those of the SS, although he does not seem effectively to counter or perhaps even mitigate that possibility. He even asserts that "the SS were right to call the corpses *Figuren*" (70). He also writes: "Simply to deny the *Muselmann*'s humanity would be to accept the verdict of the SS and to repeat their gesture. The *Muselmann* has, instead, moved into a zone of the human where not only help but also dignity and self-respect have become useless. But if there is a zone of the human in which these concepts make no sense, then they are not genuine ethical concepts, for no ethics can claim to exclude a part of humanity, no matter how unpleasant or difficult that humanity is to see" (63–4).

The logic of this paragraph is specious. One does not counteract the danger of transferential repetition with respect to the SS by claiming that it is the *Muselmann* him- or herself that "moved into a zone of the human where not only help but also dignity and self-respect have become useless." Indeed this view would seem once again to avoid the role of the perpetrators as agents (not simply spectators, commentators, gesticulators, or judges) in creating the conditions Agamben tries to understand. It might seem to involve blaming the victim in a manner not that different from "gestures" of the SS. The *Muselmänner* did not simply "move" into a zone of abjection; they were kicked, whipped, and beaten into it. And the SS and their affiliates were the ones who conducted the "experiment" that Agamben seeks to replicate in his own way.

Moreover, one may claim that certain values are general or even universal in their relevance while nonetheless maintaining that in certain extreme situations, such as that of the *Muselmann* as well as other inmates of concentration and death camps, they are not applicable. Being placed in such a genuinely paradoxical position with respect to relevant, at times pressingly insistent, but inapplicable values or norms may be a reason why survivors felt "shame"—a reason Agamben does not entertain. Instead the dominant note he strikes in his chapter on shame is the largely asocial idea that shame is ontological and constitutive of subjectivity. Shame is presumably the way, according to Heidegger, "we find ourselves exposed in the face of Being" (106) or, in a quotation from Levinas, "what is shameful is our intimacy, that is, our presence to ourselves" (105). However one may respond to this understanding of shame as Agamben employs it (I think it diverts attention from social interaction and ethicopolitical issues), one may insist that the nonapplicability of values or norms to the *Muselmann* would be primarily the responsibility of the perpetrators, and it is only from a questionably skewed perspective that the *Muselmann* could be invoked to invalidate them.

The nature of this perspective is indirectly illuminated by a comment Agamben makes about philosophy and the state of exception: "Philosophy can be defined as the world seen from an extreme situation that has become the rule (according to some philosophers, the name of this extreme situation is 'God')" (50).[44] Here philosophy itself becomes a postapocalyptic, post-Auschwitz perspective of conceptual and ethical meltdown, or radical blurring of distinctions, wherein the threshold of indistinction, the gray zone, and the rampant state of exception seem fully to meld. And, in Agamben's understanding, this perspective, at least "according to some philosophers," is a God's-eye view—a god (or sovereign) who is decidedly astigmatic if not cockeyed. But does anyone have the right to speak on behalf of, or as proxy for, this god?

Put in less polemical terms, one might say that writing from within the limit situation or the state of exception in which the *Muselmann* is everyman, Auschwitz is now everywhere, and the exception becomes the rule, is in a sense to write in extremis as if each moment were the moment of death. One question is how general this exceptional writing should be and whether it should function to provide the perspective from which all else is approached "after Auschwitz." In what I would see as its most general form of pertinence, Agamben's threshold of indistinction might be related to transference and one's transferential implication in the object of study, with the tendency to repeat symptomatically the forces active in it and, as well, to react to the formulations of others in a highly "cathected" or charged manner. My own response to Agamben has not escaped this pattern. As Agamben

---

[44] In *The Coming Community*, Agamben formulates what might be read as a view of the sacred as radically transcendent: "What is properly divine is that the world does not reveal God" (91). Paradoxically, he also has a notion of what could be termed transcendence from below: "The world—insofar as it is absolutely, irreparably profane—is God" (90).

himself at times intimates, the challenge is not how to escape it but how to come to terms with it—how to work it through and acquire some critical perspective on it and some enlarged sense of possibility without ever entirely transcending its at times compulsive force. A question Agamben leaves one with is how to understand the historical and transhistorical, as well as the empirical and normative, relations between and among the threshold of indistinction, the gray zone, and the state of exception (and emergency), as well as the possibilities of a rethought (but not entirely new or sublimely postapocalyptic) ethics and politics. Another crucial question is whether utter abjection can be construed as both the end of all previous ethics and the beginning of a radically new ethics ecstatically linked to the sublime. I have tried to argue that utter abjection is the end point of ethics in that ethical norms do not apply to the behavior of the utterly abject and disempowered but, paradoxically, still remain relevant to it. I have also argued that the sublime does not suspend, or configure a radically new, ethics for sublunar beings such as humans, for whom the specific conditions of possibility for ethics are not ontological but instead concrete social, economic, and political conditions. And I have resisted the attempt to conjoin abjection with, or transfigure it into, sublimity, particularly on the part of those who have not experienced the abjection in question, those who "were not there," except perhaps in their imagination and in their rhetoric.

One may be in a better position to come to terms critically with Agamben's own perspective on these questions, as well as my response to it, if I gather together and make explicit what I have represented as basic aspects of his orientation or framework that I find both problematic and worthy of further thought. (The issues raised are of course not restricted to Agamben.)

 1. Modernity, especially after Auschwitz, is bereft, bankrupt, and within the age of accomplished nihilism.

2. Thought is to push this putative condition to the limit and make its vacuousness evident. In other words, thought is to engage in unyielding, radical critique of the present in its relation to the past. Hence the key role for aporia, paradox, and hyperbole as "in-your-face" strategies of provocation. (Indeed a postapocalyptic orientation is inherently paradoxical in that you somehow live on after the end.)

3. Especially in the present, one has only two real choices: a mystified view of full identity, rights, essence, and telos or an authentic,

postapocalyptic, neo-Heideggerian vision of the human (or posthuman) as pure potentiality related to the bankruptcy of the past and all preexisting values along with the reduction of life to naked, bare, or mere life. (One implication is that Auschwitz, which Heidegger tended to avoid except for a few at best equivocal remarks, can now be addressed by Agamben in a manner that mirabile dictu reveals the basic truth of Heidegger's philosophy—although at times even Heidegger is not radical enough for Agamben.)[45]

4. The consequence of Agamben's choice of the latter postapocalyptic option is an elimination or downplaying of a view of the human being as a compromise formation (in a sense even a "threshold of indistinction") between body (not reducible to naked or mere life) and signifying practices that are social, political, and ethical in various ways.

5. The further consequence is the unavailability of an immanent critique of the past or the present. Rather one is in a position of *Stunde Null*, or point zero, requiring creation ex nihilo. Moreover, the idea that the limit situation or experience is especially revelatory or disclosive is collapsed into the idea that, at least after Auschwitz, every situation or experience is a limit event and that a state of emergency is generalized, with the exception becoming the rule. (Expressed in other terms, the transhistorical idea that existence is in some basic way traumatic—an idea that in a qualified manner I would accept—is collapsed into the idea that history in general, at least after Auschwitz, is traumatic or posttraumatic.)

6. In the post-Auschwitz context, the only true "ethics"—in contrast to a derided "morality" of responsibility, guilt, repentance, and perhaps normativity and normative limits in general—is an ethics of pure potentiality, openness, and exposure.

7. The only true "politics" is a form of blank utopian, messianic postapocalypticism that combines Heidegger and a certain Benjamin.

In this intellectual context, the ultimate in traumatized abjection, the *Muselmann* becomes both the model of everyman and a figure of sublimity, and Auschwitz emerges as a transhistorical exemplum or *leçon de philosophie*. The formula here—whether paradox or one of the oldest of Christian doxa—seems to be that only by descending to the

---

[45] On the question of Heidegger's relation to the Nazis and the Holocaust, see my *Representing the Holocaust*, chap. 5.

depths can one ascend to the paradisiac heights of revelatory language. But a basic question I am raising is: can one enter this heaven on the back of the *Muselmann* employed as the vehicle for a postapocalyptic sublime?[46]

[46] Debarati Sanyal's partially convergent analysis of Agamben came to my attention after the completion of this book. See *Representations* 79 (2002): 1–27, esp. 5–10. Sanyal focuses her critique on complicity or identification with a rashly generalized conception of the gray zone, a process that erases historical specificity and blurs distinctions between various subject positions, including victims and perpetrators—a critique that is prominent in my discussion of Agamben and elsewhere in my work. However, Sanyal misreads certain of my earlier analyses or arguments, perhaps for the sake of creating marginal differentiations between our approaches. I have insisted that the relation between acting-out and working-through does not constitute a simple binary, and I would take issue with the assertion that "almost all the works examined in [my] books are criticized for 'acting out' rather than 'working through' their transferential relationship to trauma, even those that most thoughtfully reflect on the ethics of their representational choices" (26). Curiously, Sanyal selects my analysis of Art Spiegelman's *Maus* in *History and Memory after Auschwitz* to illustrate the point despite the fact that I manifestly analyze this work as a relatively successful combination of acting-out and working-through. (I doubt if there is ever a totally successful case of "working-through" trauma although this doubt in no sense eliminates the value of the analytic distinction or the problem of seeing how it—as well as the subtle modulations between its terms—relates to particular instances or artifacts.) The misreading may be due to Sanyal's belief that I "complain that Art Spiegelman insufficiently scrutinizes his own subject-position vis-à-vis his material" (26)—a point I make about Artie in *Maus* whom I distinguish from Spiegelman at this point in my analysis (see *History and Memory after Auschwitz*, 177–79). Moreover, Sanyal oversimplifies my analysis of Camus's *The Fall*. I do not "end up substituting Algeria for the Holocaust as the novel's central (albeit repressed) trauma" (25). I criticize any narrowly historicized or overly contextualized reading that denies a text's critical and transformative potentials, but, in addition to providing an extensive analysis of the workings of the text, suggest in tentative terms (see especially 73 and 89) that the emphasis on the earlier "trauma" of the Holocaust (whose significance in *The Fall* I in no sense deny) may function to displace attention from the later trauma of the Algerian war that preoccupied Camus in nonfictional writing contemporaneous with *The Fall* and to which there is at least a veiled allusion in the text of *The Fall* itself. My general approach to *The Fall* is closely bound up with a critique of the generalization of the gray zone or the blurring of all distinctions with an attendant loss of historical specificity. But Sanyal's attempt to present Camus's text *only* as an unambiguous "proleptic critique" (17) of present-day tendencies is to reprocess it projectively, obscure its historical specificity through excessive decontextualization, and undercut its complexity, including its rhetorical mode of inducing complicity with Clamence and of placing in question Camus's own public persona as a secular saint. I would also note that, while I certainly recognize the importance of trauma as well as its relation to extreme or limit events, I do not "privilege" it (26). I provide an extensive critique of certain fixations on and transfigurations of trauma as well as of the conflation of trauma with history, and I stress the role of historical processes that counteract traumatization, notably processes of working-through and institutions or practices that may limit or avert the incidence of traumatizing events. Still, these divergences are relatively minor in light of the large areas of agreement between Sanyal's analyses and my own.

CHAPTER FIVE

The University in Ruins?

The apocalyptic "event" giving rise to a postapocalyptic sensibility, which has been remarkably prevalent in the recent past, is often left opaque or vague, but at times it is named or at least some phenomenon is seen as crucial in its genesis.[1] In Giorgio Agamben the decisive "event" (or series of events) is Auschwitz. In Bill Readings, it is global capitalism.[2] And the specific object of postapocalyptic disarray that concerns Readings is the university.

The status and role of the university in society have long been objects of reflection for many scholars who have assumed the position of public intellectuals. Such scholars may not share a pronounced apocalyptic or postapocalyptic bent, but in the modern period the crisis metaphor, or some variant of it, has been widespread. The views of three significantly different "critical" thinkers, at three different

---

[1] See James Berger, *After the End: Visions of Post-apocalypse* (Minneapolis: University of Minnesota Press, 1999).

[2] Capitalism and Auschwitz have of course been brought together in various ways that are addressed by neither Agamben nor Readings. Especially by Marxists, capitalism has been seen as a direct or indirect cause of the Holocaust or at least as key to its functioning. Such views may range from the extreme of seeing Nazism and all it produced as the "last stage" of capitalism (a view prevalent among Marxists between the two world wars) to the more subtle argument of Arno Mayer that anti-semitism in German policy was a "graft or parasite" on anti-Bolshevism and the eastern campaign against Russia. See *Why Did the Heavens Not Darken?: The "Final Solution" in History* (New York: Pantheon, 1988), 270. Some on the far left have also persisted, however implausibly, in seeing concentration and death camps as functionally and economically rational organizations of labor. See the critical discussion

moments in modern history, can provide some perspective on Readings's views. The first is Emile Durkheim, toward the end of the nineteenth century, facing the challenge of both quelling the turbulent aftermath of the French Revolution and inaugurating the first long-lived democratic republic in French history, which, for him, was dedicated to institutionalizing ideals enunciated in the great revolution. Crucial to this broad, idealistic political mission was the role of the university in elaborating and disseminating an ethically and politically self-conscious understanding of society: "Our society must restore the consciousness of its organic unity. . . . No doubt these ideas will become truly efficacious only if they spread out into the depths of society, but for that it is first necessary that we elaborate them scientifically in the university. To contribute to this end to the extent of my powers will be my principal concern, and I shall have no greater happiness than if I succeed in it a little."[3]

This is Durkheim near the beginning of his career, "founding" sociology in France with a conception of its scientific and ethicopolitical mission, and seeing its challenge as to bring legitimate order to society within the context of republican democracy. Durkheim's conception of desirable social solidarity in modernity was different both from desires for communal oneness (or *Volksgemeinschaft*) and from certain postmodern notions of pronounced difference, if not differends, as constitutive of a sociality without unity or common ground. Indeed Durkheim's project was to combine a tolerant, nontotalitarian solidarity, based on a shared *conscience collective* that centrally included institutionalized and at times sanctioned norms and values, with an articulated social differentiation and division of labor required by the complexity of modern society.

Next we turn to Martin Heidegger, rector of the University of Freiburg, at a different "founding" moment—the institution of the

---

of such tendencies, for example, in Pierre Guillaume and the journal *La Vieille Taupe*, in Pierre Vidal-Naquet, *The Assassins of Memory: Essays on the Denial of the Holocaust*, trans. Jeffrey Mehlman (1987; New York: Columbia University Press, 1992), esp. 10–13. For most historians, the instabilities of interwar capitalism, notably including the Great Depression, may have been contributing factors in the development and success of fascism and the Nazis but not full "causes" or explanations of all their significant features.

[3] "Cours de science sociale," *Revue Internationale de L'enseignement* 14 (1888): 48–49. See also my *Emile Durkheim: Sociologist and Philosopher* (1972; revised edition, Aurora, Colorado: The Davies Group, 2001).

Nazi regime in Germany with its ideological and deceptive quest for a robust if not ecstatic *Volksgemeinschaft* in a society that would be based on *Gleichschaltung* (full coordination or synchronization—in a sense, marching in step):

> Assuming the rectorship means committing oneself to leading this university *spiritually and intellectually*. The teachers and students who constitute the rector's following [*Gefolgschaft der Lehrer und Schüler*] will awaken and gain strength only through being truly and collectively rooted in the essence of the German university. This essence will attain clarity, rank, and power, however, only when the leaders are, first and foremost and at all times, themselves led by the inexorability of that spiritual mission which impresses onto the fate of the German Volk the stamp of their history. . . .
>
> If we will the essence of science in the sense of *the questioning, unsheltered standing firm in the midst of the uncertainty of the totality of being*, then *this* will to essence will create for our Volk a world of the innermost and most extreme danger, i.e., a truly *spiritual* world. For "spirit" is neither empty acumen nor the noncommittal play of wit nor the busy practice of never-ending rational analysis nor even world reason; rather, spirit is the determined resolve to the essence of Being, a resolve that is attuned to origins and knowing. And the *spiritual world* of a Volk is not its cultural superstructure, just as little as it is its arsenal of useful knowledge [*Kentnisse*] and values; rather, it is the power that comes from preserving at the most profound level the forces that are rooted in the soil and blood of a Volk, the power to arouse most inwardly and to shake most extensively the Volk's existence. A spiritual world alone will guarantee our Volk greatness.[4]

There are some significant continuities between Durkheim and Heidegger with respect to the "idea" of a university, owing in good part to their common involvement in a philosophical tradition for which spirit was essential, the university its institutional home, and society the larger order or lifeworld that the university was to render more spiritual. But the meaning of these broad values or goals also reveals

---

[4] "The Self-Assertion of the German University," in *The Heidegger Controversy: A Critical Reader* ed. Richard Wolin (New York: Columbia University Press, 1991), 29, 33–34. See also my "Heidegger's Nazi Turn," in *Representing the Holocaust: History, Theory, Trauma* (Ithaca: Cornell University Press, 1994), chap. 5.

drastic differences as one moves from Durkheim to Heidegger. In Durkheim spirit or the object of idealist philosophy was in modernity to be translated into the medium of a democratic society that would be based on a sense of legitimate limits and would strive for justice domestically while restricting and channeling national assertion in the interest of international cooperation. When he wrote the above passage Heidegger saw the determined *volkish* resolve and sublime spiritual mission of the university in terms that would coordinate it with the will of Hitler as supreme leader under whose direction other leaders, such as himself as rector, would bring about the overcoming of the presumably ruinous collapse not only of the university but of the Western world itself. Heidegger is a noteworthy instance of the appeal of fascism to intellectuals in the interwar period as a "third way" bringing about a "spiritual" revolution that would transcend not only bourgeois society but also the materialism of both capitalism and communism.[5] And Germany was for Heidegger the special if not unique modern bearer of spirit. Its enemies were undermining the lofty, heroic ideals of true culture in the interest of a leveling idea of civilization for which democracy itself was a primary conduit. Indeed in the sociocultural context in which Heidegger wrote, the scapegoated bearers of "empty acumen," "the noncommittal play of wit," and "the busy practice of never-ending rational analysis," even a suspect "world reason" itself, were the Jews and the French, and Durkheim, a French Jew, might well, from the Heideggerian perspective on authenticity adumbrated in the above paragraph, be their abject epitome.

No one has been a more steadfast, at times adamantly insistent, adversary of Heidegger than Jürgen Habermas, and one of his goals, in elaborating a critical theory of society in the tradition of the Frankfurt school, has been to provide a radically different understanding of the place and mission of the university in a democratic society— one that selectively assimilates and places in another frame of reference the contributions of Durkheim and other major social theorists. Habermas has not offered a shattering critique of technical or instrumental rationality or related it to the putative nihilism of Western

[5] One finds a development of this theme that, despite its overemphasis on the ideological slippage from the far left to the far right, is broad-ranging and thought-provoking, in Zeev Sternhell, *Neither Right nor Left: Fascist Ideology in France* (1983; Berkeley: University of California Press, 1986).

metaphysics in the manner of Heidegger, who could at least initially see the Nazis as the force for overcoming this nihilism and then, after the war, intimate that their regime was itself the enactment of an accomplished nihilism—an enactment that, while prevalent in the modern West, was nonetheless characterized by an "inner truth and greatness" in the Nazi case.[6] Rather Habermas would, if anything, have a phobic reaction to Heidegger and those who looked, with whatever critical reservations, to his philosophy (including Derrida). Habermas's own daunting project has been to coordinate a necessary technical rationality with practical (or ethicopolitical) and emancipatory interests as the triangulated axes of knowledge. Here is Habermas on the eve of the tumultuous, indeed, for some, near-apocalyptic events of 1968, in which he would see both promise and threat with respect to his conception of the university and society:

> Universities must transmit technically exploitable knowledge. That is, they must meet an industrial society's need for qualified new generations and at the same time be concerned with the expanded reproduction of education itself. . . . Thus, through instruction and research the university is immediately connected with functions of the economic process. In addition, however, it assumes at least three further responsibilities.
>
> First, the university has the responsibility of ensuring that its graduates are equipped, no matter how indirectly, with a minimum of qualifications in the area of extrafunctional abilities. In this connection extrafunctional refers to all those attributes and attitudes relevant to the pursuit of a professional career that are not contained per se in professional knowledge and skills. . . . [7]

---

[6] In his 1953 republication of the *Introduction to Metaphysics*, initially a lecture course given in 1935, Heidegger retained the following statement: "What today, finally, is being passed around as the philosophy of National Socialism, but has not the least to do with the inner truth and greatness of the movement (namely the encounter of planetarily determined technology and modern man) goes fishing in these murky waters of 'values and wholes'" (*Einführing in die Metaphysik* [Tübingen: Niemeyer, 1953], 152. There is a debate about whether the specification contained in the parenthesis was added in 1953 or appeared in the earlier version.

[7] This is the area Durkehim discussed in terms of professional ethics and civic morals—an area whose problematic relation to capitalistic enterprise has been brought home once again by accounting scandals and shady bankruptcies of huge corporations such as Enron and WorldCom.

Second, it belongs to the tasks of the university to transmit, interpret, and develop the cultural tradition of the society. . . .

Third, the university has always fulfilled a task that is not easy to define; today we should say that it forms the political consciousness of its students. For too long, the consciousness that took shape at German universities was apolitical. It was a singular mixture of inwardness, deriving from the culture of humanism, and of loyalty to state authority. This consciousness was less a source of immediate political attitudes, than of a mentality that had significant political consequences.[8]

Habermas is well aware of the fact that a seemingly apolitical, inward, state-conservative posture would incapacitate, or reduce to a pathetic bystander's position, groups in society, including those in the academy, when they confronted a more activist political movement, including one that had among its various legitimations Heidegger's conception of spirit. In one dimension of Habermas's own thought, the indebtedness to the idealist tradition has always seemed to involve a notion of theory as a desired (but invariably hobbled or "dangerously supplemented") "emancipation" from, or transcendence of, the body and affect into a realm of pure cognition and normative or practical "interests."[9] And the later Habermas, in his quest for a universal pragmatics, went in abstract, universalistic directions with a questionable relation to the critical-theoretical and political promise of his early thought. Such a quest put him in an even less favorable position to relate his concerns to the more excessive, opaque, and "noncommunicative" dimensions of language and affect that were of prominent, even at times obsessive, concern to poststructuralists. But my more general point is that the references to Durkheim, Heidegger, and Habermas indicate that a sense of the university in crisis has been a recurrent topos of modern thought, especially among intellectuals, and it has been invoked in very different contexts and in significantly different ways.[10] This fact alone should

[8] Jürgen Habermas, "The University in a Democracy—Democratization of the University," in *Toward a Rational Society*, trans. Jeremy J. Shapiro (1968; Boston: Beacon Press, 1970), 1–3.

[9] For a discussion of this dimension of Habermas's thought, see my "Habermas and the Grounding of Critical Theory," in *Rethinking Intellectual History: Texts, Contexts, Language* (Ithaca: Cornell University Press, 1983), esp. 172–74.

[10] Many of the problems being discussed recently, including those of concern to Bill Readings, were addressed a generation ago in *The University Crisis Reader: The*

make one especially careful in its invocation and use, particularly when it assumes an extremely heightened tonality and is conveyed in a rhetoric of relatively unqualified hyperbole. In Readings's *University in Ruins*, a book he finished writing just before his untimely death in a plane accident, the sense of crisis at times attains postapocalyptic heights or depths.[11]

One might justifiably argue that there is a limited sense in which the university—or at the very least the humanities and interpretive social sciences—are and should always be in crisis, in that debate in them bears on essential questions, including the very identity or boundaries of disciplines and the types of questions that are legitimately raised in them.[12] But just as this point may induce banalization and the complacencies of crisis management, so the crisis metaphor readily lends itself to abuse, particularly when it is indiscriminately inflated and generalized. One may even question whether it is the most pertinent metaphor for important dimensions of the thought of someone like Walter Benjamin, who is evoked through the ruins metaphor and who even

---

Liberal University Under Attack, vol. I, ed. Imanuel Wallerstein and Paul Starr (New York: Random House, 1971). Written during the student movement and protest against the war in Vietnam, the contributions to this important volume are gathered under the headings: The Educational Role of the University; The University as a Firm; The University, the Government, and the War; Racism and the University; University Governance; and The Educational Process. It is disheartening to report that, soon after its publication, I was able to buy what was apparently a remaindered paperback copy of the book for ninety-eight cents.

[11] *The University in Ruins* (Cambridge: Harvard University Press, 1996). Both here and in the preceding chapter, I am not engaging in a general critique of rhetoric or defending the naive and self-defeating idea of a "nonrhetorical" or purely "logical" style. I am, however, affirming the desirability of a modulated rhetoric in which hyperbole has a place but is tested by experience and contested by a sense of legitimate limits as well as by understatement. On the question of rhetoric and historiography, see my *History and Criticism* (Ithaca: Cornell University Press, 1985), chap. 1.

[12] Basic questions may of course also be raised of the natural sciences, concerning their relation to society and politics, as is evident in the approach to these questions in the field of the social studies of science. See, for example, David Bloor, *Knowledge and Social Imagery* (London: Routledge and Kegan Paul, 1976); Bruno Latour, *We Have Never Been Modern*, trans. Catherine Porter (London: Harvester Wheatsheaf, 1993); Michael Lynch, *Scientific Practice and Ordinary Action: Ethnomethodology and Social Studies of Science* (New York: Cambridge University Press, 1993); and Steven Shapin and Simon Schaffer, *Leviathan and the Air Pump* (Princeton: Princeton University Press, 1985). See also Margaret C. Jacob, "Science Studies after Social Construction: The Turn toward the Comparative and the Global," in *Beyond the Cultural Turn*, ed. Victoria E. Bonnell and Lynn Hunt (Berkeley: University of Caifornia Press, 1999), 95–120.

may elicit an other-than-purely-negative response to something in ruins.[13] It might in certain ways be closer to the concerns of Benjamin, as well as to important currents in recent thought, to refer to the university in shock, the university of *Erlebnis* without *Erfahrung*, the university of trends and fashions devoid of narrative coherence or wisdom, the university of aimless wayfarers without an "idea" of the university (in Cardinal Newman's sense), the university that emulates the top-down, efficiency-driven, hard-bitten, corporatized ethos of big business (despite the latter's palpable shortcomings), the traumatized or, better, posttraumatic university—perhaps even (to extend Giorgio Agamben's hyperbole) the post-Auschwitz (or, in another context, postcolonial) university in a recurrent state of emergency at times bordering on panic. These views, as the work of Benjamin itself would indicate, need not induce a narrowly psychological account of issues or divert attention from larger sociopolitical problems to personal pathologies. They may be bound up with the type of political and social analysis that Readings himself desires, and might even add a missing historical and critical dimension to his account. Such views (as at times in Benjamin himself) might nonetheless gravitate into the orbit of the crisis metaphor and a utopian-messianic sense of the apocalyptic or postapocalyptic, and they would need to be specified, qualified, and supplemented in order to get at the question of the more basic difficulties in Readings's approach.

I would begin by noting that, on a more sober level of analysis, the contemporary academy might to some extent be seen as based on a systemic, schizoid division between a "corporatized"

---

[13] Benjamin was not the only one interested in ruins. As Jeffrey Herf points out, "Albert Speer reports listening to Hitler's theory of 'ruin value,' according to which the purpose of Nazi architecture and technological advance should be to create ruins that would last a thousand years and thereby overcome the transience of the market" (*Reactionary Modernism: Technology, Culture, and Politics in Weimar and the Third Reich* (New York: Cambridge University Press, 1984), 194. Here one may note a difference between an apocalyptic and a postapocalyptic orientation, even though the two may in important ways be close, for example, in their extreme utopianism. Especially in its more destructive impetus (which may be intricately bound up with its creative side), an apocalyptic movement anticipates or even looks forward to the genesis of durable, even monumental, ruins, without the often nostalgic tendency to look back on what has already (even always already) been reduced to ruins. In Benjamin, however, the ruin was not monumentalized or sentimentalized but instead was a frequently evanescent index of a past from which certain "weak messianic" possibilities for the future might be "redeemed."

market model and a model of corporate solidarity and collegial responsibility.[14] (The two models are of course ideal-typical schematizations that overlap in part, do not cover all aspects of the university, and may in certain ways be misleading. Still, one or the other model is often invoked in ways that best serve the self-interest of the commentator.) The market model may find its extreme form in the virtual university or franchiselike pseudopod of the university— the e-university (with "e" standing for extension, E-mail, and "excellence" in Readings's sense). This variant, with its correspondence courses or digital forms of distance learning, is tantamount to a fee-for-credit educational service industry that sells "McNuggets" of knowledge. More generally, it is found in the prevalent producer/consumer or business schema in which undergraduates subsidize research as well as graduate education and may not be getting their money's worth, notably at a time when tuition is very high and has been outpacing the general rate of inflation. The market model has also played a significant role in the establishment of criteria for teaching and reward in departments and in the setting of salaries and perquisites for individuals. The idea here is that a department, to be competitive nationally, must conform to national criteria, for example, with respect to the faculty it is trying to recruit. And major increases in an individual's salary or other perquisites have typically depended on the reception of an "outside" offer from a "peer" institution. In the broadest and most pressing terms, a more or less relativized market model is active not only in the conception of a university itself as a corporation but in its status as the complement of private-sector business enterprises, a conception in which the university is based on knowledge as information, and information technology is dominant,

---

[14] Like Readings, I orient my comments primarily to the role of the humanities and the liberal arts. They would have to be differentiated to account for the natural and the social sciences. In the natural sciences, governmental and market pressures are more pronounced or at least more direct than in the humanities. (In professional schools, market considerations and pragmatic concerns are often of immediate significance.) The picture may be more complex and internally fragmented in the social sciences, notably in tendencies toward positivistic research and more interpretive, humanistically inclined orientations. Readings's point is, of course, that market pressures have become increasingly generalized to affect all areas of the university, but he may not pay sufficient attention to the differential impact of such pressures and the reasons for them. For example, diffuseness and even disarray in the humanities may in certain ways be functional in eliminating or defusing effective criticism of social institutions and governmental policies.

from the primacy of the "hard" sciences to the restructuring and "digitization" of the library, even to the point of continual technical "upgrades" of systems that far exceed (or even counter) the needs of those who use libraries most, the humanists.[15] In terms of resources, disproportionately preponderant allocations and fund-raising efforts are dedicated to the "hard" sciences and allied fields (such as computer science) where equipment and "start-up" costs for faculty are very high, and a comparatively small remainder (at least at research universities) is left for the social sciences and even less for the humanities. Here resource allocation is a zero-sum game, and each area (natural—or "hard" and "big"—sciences, social—or "soft"—sciences, and humanities) as well as each sector within a broad area (biology, physics, chemistry, astrophysics, and so forth) functions as an interest group trying to maximize its allocations and perquisites.

By contrast there is also the belief that the university is a community made up of smaller communities guided by nonmarket-oriented norms and values. On this model, each unit should conceive of its needs in terms of the interests of the university—if not the broader academy—as a whole, and the task of the upper-level administration is to adjudicate claims in the common interest. Moreover, departments and individuals should be bound by the value of dedicated service to the institution independent of market considerations, even if such service is not directly rewarded in material ways. Peer review is paramount in evaluating research that should not be subject to direct government or market control. A faculty or a college may be seen as having at least relative autonomy that requires modes of self-government and resists pressures toward centralized management and top-down control of the university, although the role of the central administration may of course be recognized in coordinating efforts, funding "big" science, and working out certain priorities (notably in maintaining or building on a university's relative strengths and compensating more or less selectively for its weak-

[15] One example of counterproductivity is the trashing of older card catalogs that may have included valuable notations or comments and in any case allowed for the kind of browsing or serendipitous discovery that cannot be matched by computers, whose demands for exactitude to the last period or colon often make locating a title extremely difficult, especially when the system undergoes one of its "upgrades." Of course the Internet brings its compensations in title or topic searches, which should not be discounted. But such evident benefits do not justify the digitizing frenzy that has seized certain librarians, technicians, and administrators.

nesses). The solidaristic-collegial model is particularly prominent in the idea that faculty have a special if not quasi-religious responsibility for the education of the nation's youth (an idea, often spotlighting humanists, that may perhaps be seen as one residue of the early ministerial function of important universities such as Harvard). It is also evident in the attempt to bring the university community together in vigils, collective forms of mourning, and potentially critical practices such as teach-ins in order to respond to extreme, possibly traumatizing events such as the September 11 (2001) suicide bombing of the World Trade Center and the Pentagon. From this point of view, the complaint about tendencies in the academic system may be tantamount to saying that it has become, or at least threatens to become, overly aligned with short-term pragmatism and the more or less modified market mechanisms operative in the rest of the economy and society.

The two models are in turn related to two ideal types of faculty member, what might be called the entrepreneurial globe-trotter and the local hero. The former is administratively adept, always in the process of putting together some new arrangement or academic deal, and continually on the move. She or he is a highly marketable commodity, has had many grants or competitive fellowships, changes positions frequently (or at least has the opportunity to do so), spends at least as much time away from a home university as at it, and has a vita the size of an average telephone book. The hipper kind of globe-trotter seems to exist in the superspace between the Deleuzian nomad and the Reebok executive. By contrast, the local hero, typically existing in a relation of mutual disdain and grumbling denigration vis à vis the globe-trotter, is ensconced within the workings of the institution itself. She or he has a large, even cultlike undergraduate following, serves on numerous committees, faithfully attends faculty meetings, and is a nodal point in on-campus activities as well as in gossip and rumor mills (a "premodern" form of communication still very important in the university or college setting). These ideal types are of course extremes, but they do have their "instantiations"—at times schizoid instantiations—whom most of us can furnish with proper names. Fortunately, they do not exhaust, dominate, or even typify the academic landscape.

It is paradoxical that the demand to make the university conform to an ever-increasing extent to a market or business model seems oblivious to the fact that the U.S. university has probably been the most successful of its type in the world, that students from other countries disproportionately desire to study in it, and that one problem within the university is how to bring all employees and work relations into a system more closely resembling the one applied to faculty and administration. It would be an understatement to say that the rest of the economy in the recent past has not been performing as well as the university. One might even argue that weak business sectors should investigate and emulate the way universities, at their best, work, including mechanisms for resisting the more extreme imbalances of a market system, such as overly centralized managerial control and incredible discrepancies in reward between those at the top and at the bottom of the economic ladder.

It is, moreover, curious that jeremiads about the insufficient attention paid to undergraduate education often come not from local heros, who may actually do much committed teaching and advising, but from neoconservative think-tank affiliates who themselves do little or no teaching and seem quite adept at conforming their own behavior to market criteria (such as charging enormous fees for repetitive, evangelical lectures bemoaning the way the academic market has led to careerism and the decline of undergraduate teaching). And the intemperate quality of recent complaints is often attended by an avoidance of more specific and detailed inquiry into the actual activities of those who are objects of criticism, notably the activities of humanists who typically do more teaching, including undergraduate teaching, than any other group on campus. Jeremiads about the decline of teaching may of course also be coordinated with a beatific vision of the holy family, in which academics—especially humanists—spend most of their time in the classroom nurturing youth with motherly solicitude, while administrators govern like authoritative fathers, and think-tank affiliates have primary responsibility for the production of knowledge and the dissemination of evangelical admonitions.[16]

[16] On these issues see the important article of Ellen Messer-Davidow, "Manufacturing the Attack on Liberalized Higher Education," *Social Text* 36 (1993): 40–80. See also E. Ann Kaplan and George Levine, eds., *The Politics of Research* (New Brunswick: Rutgers University Press, 1997). Richard J. Mahoney, Distinguished Executive in Residence at the Center for the Study of American Business and former chairman and chief executive officer of Monsanto, argues that the academy should be made to

Readings stresses only the way in which the university has become a corporation in the modern, market-oriented sense, and for Readings this market model is hegemonic to the point of creating but one dominant identity for the modern university and its components. There is no significant tension within the university because the market model has won, and what remains is a mop-up operation allowing only for something analogous to guerilla-type resistance and utopian hope on the part of oppositional faculty and students. Indeed his own positive countervision, as we shall see, is close to an idealized version of the scholar (largely if not almost exclusively the humanistic and allied interpretive social-scientific scholar) as agonistic nomad if not conceptual guerilla fighter, who, as a member of evanescent project-oriented groups, moves across disciplinary space with mobile, phantomlike agility in the attempt to elaborate something Readings calls Thought (a view not too far from the later, transdisciplinary,

---

conform more fully to the recently renovated, slim and trim, efficiency-driven corporate model that Readings deplores yet believes actually is already instantiated by the modern university. (" 'Reinventing' the University: Object Lessons from Big Business," *Chronicle of Higher Education*," October 17, 1997, B4–B5.) In a draconian defense of strictly prioritizing tasks, Mahoney even asserts: "What are the core functions and departments of the university? Can you dispose—and I don't use that word lightly—of unproductive programs? What is the primary goal of the institution? If you were absolutely forced to choose research or teaching, which would it be? Although institutions needn't choose just one or the other, they need to be clear about which activity they value more" (B4). In a letter critical of Mahoney's argument, R. Keith Sawyer, assistant professor of education at Washington University and former management consultant for eight years, notes that "the top research universities (those that are the most criticized for their lack of attention to the 'customers,' the students) are exactly those that maintain artificially low prices for their products—lower prices than the market would support." For Sawyer the reason universities do not simply follow the law of supply and demand is "because they are non-profit institutions, committed to education, learning, and knowledge" (*Chronicle of Higher Education*, November 28, 1997, B3) Mahoney also ignores the possibility that teaching and research may be considered of comparable importance and that there may be a fruitful interaction between them. I would further note that there is a need for academics to reclaim the importance of undergraduate teaching in their own voices and that one justification for it, especially for scholars concerned about the role of the public intellectual, is that undergraduate teaching is a force for making difficult theories and methodologies more open to understanding and informed criticism by a general public. It is of course also important to elicit and stress the qualities and justifiable expectations pertinent to the university as a distinctive not-for-profit institution serving educational and public interests that cannot be understood or evaluated according to other models, especially a business-oriented, task-specific, top-down model.

postphilosophical orientation of Heidegger or, more recently, of Agamben). For Readings the older corporate or solidaristic idea is quite simply anachronistic, as is the so-called university of culture, which supposedly was its cognate.[17]

Readings is not unhappy about the end of the university of culture and all that it presumably stood for, but he is far from happy about its market-oriented replacement. Still, he tries to see the opportunities created by the new university modeled on the transnational corporation, and he makes some attempt to place his conception in a larger frame of reference. Given his image of a university in ruins, he asks how best to dwell in the ruins of reason, culture, the centered subject-citizen, nationalism, and a sense of evangelical if not redemptive mission. For what is indeed definitively ruined, in Readings's eyes, is the university of culture that provided citizen-subjects for the nation-state and in which the humanities were the site of liberal education, displaced religiosity, and identity-forming culture. In Readings the ruins of this university are more like the rubble of a collapsed modern skyscraper than like the crumbling but inhabitable, ivy-covered walls of a venerable structure.

I find Readings's argument hyperbolic, and I think his hyperbole would be more effective if it were explicitly framed as hyperbole and if more attention were paid to specific historical contexts and to the uneven developments and countercurrents that he intentionally excludes (166). Hyperbole certainly serves to sound the alarm, but the bell has been ringing in many cacophonous registers for quite some time, and those inclined to take Readings seriously have been attentive to it. The price paid for his one-sided approach with its emphatic exclusions is that his own argument in its excess, lack of nuance, totalizing or globalizing incentive, elimination of irritating countercurrents, and categorical sweep rather unself-consciously replicates some of the most dubious features he imputes to his object of analysis and criticism: the globalizing, bureaucratically administered, transnationally corporate, consumingly co-opting university itself. The fact that Readings's own account manifests these features lends it a degree of transferential or observer-participant credibility, yet its generally

[17] A surrealistic but far-from-inconceivable possibility is that some upper-level administrators may read Readings against the grain not as sounding an alarm but as providing a how-to book for managing—and averting certain resistances in—the contemporary university.

unqualified assertions also raise doubts about its analytic and critical value in understanding and working through specific problems with some sense of discriminating judgment and viable alternatives. He also is at times restricted to a strategy of reversal that does not deliver on the attempt to rethink basic concepts and procedures but instead leads him to go to the opposite but symmetrical extreme with respect to the tendencies he criticizes, for example, when he opposes full transparency, communication, and consensus with aporia, differends, and dissensus.

The credibility of Readings's account is also undermined by the fact that his criticisms, as he partially acknowledges, parallel those of neoconservatives such as Allan Bloom. In fact his account shares more with neoconservatives than he acknowledges. Yet Readings may be successful to the extent he not only informs but motivates others at times to agree and at other times to take issue with him. If we are to believe him, he does not want to convince. As he puts it, "if I have certain principles (more accurately, certain habits or tics of thought), they are not grounded in anything more foundational than my capacity to make them seem interesting to others, which is not the same thing as convincing other people of their 'rightness'" (168). One may assent to the contention that there are no absolute foundations for principles but still find that going to the opposite (in a sense inversely absolutist or excessively relativist) extreme and settling for the capacity to make principles, indeed tics of thought, "interesting" to others is not enough; indeed that capacity can be seen as yet another feature of the exhaustion of culture and ethical thought—a feature of the vacuous university of excellence where "interesting" is the last (often weakly ironic) qualifier one may use without scare quotes, and just about anything may be found interesting. Resisting this tendency, one may instead contend that one must be cautious and self-critical in normative matters yet should try to convince oneself and others in a nondogmatic fashion that brings commitment but does not deny the need to listen attentively to one's critics and possibly to change one's mind, indeed to try to act (not simply act out) on the basis of views and convictions open to debate and revision.

For purposes of closer scrutiny, I think one can usefully distinguish among three dimensions of Readings's important account, all of which should be taken seriously but the first of which I find more convincing than the others. It would be shortsighted to allow one's objections to Readings's hyperbole or to the other limitations of his argument to detract from recognizing the pertinence and importance of certain points he makes, especially in the first dimension of his account. The three dimensions among which I would distinguish are: (1) the understanding of tendencies or strong pressures in the contemporary university; (2) the larger historical and critical picture in which this understanding is inserted; and (3) a conception of alternatives to the modern corporate university that are nonetheless related to its tendencies and in a sense might be seen as positive possibilities in its negative features.

What is Readings's understanding of the strong (for him, dominant) pressures affecting the university today? (Here one must indeed listen to him attentively and acknowledge the force and importance of his argument.) The university is marked by an empty ideal of excellence that is itself determined by market criteria of efficient functioning and is applied indiscriminately to all activities. The tendency is to seek top-down, narrowly technical, operational solutions to all problems. Cultural studies itself, at least in certain of its forms, is, for Readings, not a way to save the university of culture but a symptom of its demise and, in its indiscriminate attention to all forms of "culture," from pornography and Pop Tarts to papal encyclicals and *The Pirates of Penzance*, it is an approach easily co-opted by the university of excellence. Whatever sells without offending a significant constituency (especially donors, trustees, and paying parents) has a place in the curriculum, including Greeks on the half shell and Romans with french fries (a phrase actually used by one of my very "performative" colleagues to describe his popular course on Western civilization). "Excellence" is itself the shibboleth inscribed on the banner that floats misleadingly over the university in ruins—a market-oriented university that treats students as consumers and enables the role of administrators to overshadow that of teachers and scholars. This university models itself on the transnational corporation and insistently seeks corporate-type executives, strategic planning, multicultural marketing, and globalization of its wares. It is characterized by the confusion of accountability with accounting, and one of Readings's strongest arguments—something I would be willing to see as a principle that is more than "interesting"—is that one should not be identified with the other. The reduction of accountability to accounting is part and parcel of a market-oriented, bureaucratically administered university in which the rule of exchange value leads to questionable equations in the attempt to abet efficient functioning. One case of the conflation of accountability with accounting is the use of multiple-choice or fill-in-the-blank evaluation forms that lend themselves to rapid responses and numerical tabulation, rather than the use of critical essays through which students may reflect on the nature of a course or universities may address the state of their own activities and investments.

Agreeing with Leo Bersani and others, Readings argues against the understanding of culture in general and the university in particular as a site of salvation or redemption, a feature prominent in the older idea of a university of culture. But he apparently accepts (as I do) the more limited Benjaminian notion of redeeming aspects of a past or present situation that may be reactivated, transvalued, or refunctioned and inserted into a significantly different context. However, the primary, somewhat spectral and elusive, feature he finds redeemable in the modern university is what he terms dereferentialization, that is, the loss or absence of a specific referent for such concepts as culture or excellence. These concepts become formalistic floating signifiers—word-balloons without words—to be filled with any possible content, however gaseous. Dereferentialization has its downsides (one may also add its downsizing sides, when the dispensed-with "referents" become jettisoned ballast and are cast into the ranks of the unemployed), and Readings is even willing to assert that the university system has become an autonomous, self-regulating, if not self-referential institution, more like the National Basketball Association than a culture-bearing surrogate for the Church. But there is still a blue flower of hope that sublimely appears in the impasses generated by the university's internal workings. As Readings puts it, "the process of dereferentialization is one that opens up new spaces and breaks down existing structures of defense against Thought, even as it seeks to submit Thought to the exclusive rule of exchange value (like all bourgeois revolutions). Exploring such possibilities is not a messianic task, and since such efforts are not structured by a redemptive metanarrative, they require of us the utmost vigilance, flexibility, and wit" (178). The obvious question is whether dereferentialization opens up new spaces in the fashion of a bulldozer that clears obstacles for development by plowing everything under, with the good chance that one will wind up with still another parking lot or a row of cinder-block buildings. The further question is whether vigilance, flexibility, and wit are themselves autonomized and free-floating in a disembodied, or at best stand-up comic, manner that shadows or parallels, rather than interferes with or provides cogent alternatives to, the dereferentialized university of excellence. In any event, this line of thought leads to Readings's own idea of alternatives in terms of evanescent work groups, and the motif of dereferentialization, along with his alternatives, brings Readings close to poststructural figures with whom he explicitly claims affiliation, notably, Jean-François Lyotard, Jacques Derrida, and Jean-Luc Nancy.

In the second, "big-picture" dimension of his account, however, Readings is much closer to Marx, indeed the Marx of economism and determinism, who here returns with an other-than spectral vengeance to provide what may look very much like a grand narrative and a totalizing explanation of the features Readings detects in the modern university. (One may of course also see a more openly "dialectical" and optimistic Marx in the idea that dereferentialization, like capitalism, which destroys older relations, simultaneously opens up new possibilities.) Readings is also close to the Theodor Adorno who envisioned a totally administered modern society in which the faint glimmers of a chastened, nonredemptive, at most weakly messianic utopia appear only in the somber negative spaces of insistently critical thought. A totalizing perspective, perhaps closer to Herbert Marcuse than to Adorno, was also a dimension of radical thought in the 1960s, particularly in the idea of "the system" that was all-powerful and all co-optive. (Without treating this side of '68, Readings offers a largely positive reading of its other, more hopeful dimensions, notably the role of "a thought or study in excess of the subject, which rejects the metanarrative of redemption" [145].)

The ultimate, totalizing cause, indeed what looks suspiciously like the evil demon, in Readings's account, is global capital, and the market model seems to reign supreme with its advent. The all-pervasive movements of GloboCap are themselves not explicated in any detail but are instead insistently and repeatedly invoked to explain why the university is how it is and why the older ideals of culture, *Bildung*, the liberal subject-citizen, and the nation-state are no longer relevant. A seeming counterexample, such as the important practice of individual and institutional gift-giving to universities, is seen as a bizarre anachronism, even an effect of false consciousness in tune with an older idea of ideology that Readings in general finds irrelevant. And the macrolevel references to global capital are related neither to structural analyses of its movements and effects nor to the experiential level of life within the university system, with its responses to the market and its pockets of resistance or countercurrents (including animus against overly entrepreneurial colleagues or even administrators).

I have noted that, in his belief that the liberal university of culture is in ruins, Readings is closer to neoconservatives such as Allan Bloom than to liberal commentators, such as Jaroslav Pelikan, who would like to reassert liberal ideals and save the university of culture. Readings certainly does not believe that one may return to the past and redeem a canon of great texts or resurrect the Arnoldian idea of salvaging "the best that is known and thought" as the basis of a valid liberal arts education or a unified national culture. But Readings is dangerously close to neoconservatives in what appears (despite his protestations to the contrary) to be his dire conception of the existing state of things and his extreme, often all-or-nothing rhetoric, notably his jeremiads against the lingering proponents of liberalism and culture. Less obviously, he is close to neoconservatives in relying on an abstract, decline-and-fall variety of the history of ideas to elaborate his "big picture" based on a contrast between past and present. Indeed Readings's very understanding of institutions is largely conceptual rather than oriented to institutions as historically variable, more or less flexible sets of practices, beliefs, and binding norms relating groups of people. His perspective on the institution and what he considers institutionally relevant thinking thus seems very high-altitude. In this approach to the university of culture and perforce to its contrasting pendant, the university in ruins, Readings does not provide even a schematic intellectual, cultural, and institutional history in a long-term comparative frame of reference that might shed critical light on the modern university, for example, in a comparison between recent forms of corporatization, on the analogy of the profit-making business enterprise, and older forms of corporative organization that have at least a residual role in the contemporary university. Nor does he appeal to sociological and economic studies of the institutional functioning of universities in their relations to the larger society and polity. Instead he offers a decontextualized, largely homogenizing reading of such figures as Kant, Humboldt, Arnold, and Newman. These figures did elaborate paradigms or normative models, at times embodying critical and self-critical elements, and these models may have had a problematic relation to institutional practice and operative norms that varied over time, space, and specific context. But what that relation was, including the differences between model (which often served legitimating rather than formative functions) and practice, is not immediately obvious. In any event, for Readings the model elaborated in their writings corresponded to, or performatively created, a university of reason, then of culture, which in turn created or helped to create a unifed liberal subject committed to the nation-state and somehow consonant with the demands of capital in a preglobalized period of its formation.

Thus, although he is very much committed to the thought of difference and to the importance of tentativeness and uncertainty on a conceptual or discursive level, the difference between the textually elaborated model and institutional practice, including the experience of people in institutional settings, is one difference Readings tends to obscure insofar as he proceeds as if the model defined the reality without allowing for areas of uncertainty and uneven developments in its application or pertinence. He is himself so imprinted by the Idea of the university of culture that he is unable to inquire into the extent to which it was always a phantasm; instead he continues to see everything through its lens or by using it as a standard of comparison. But to the extent that the model of the nation-building, subject-suturing, identity-forming university of culture was itself a phantasm or at best an idealization, made to cover a much more complex and changing constellation of forces that varied by nation, region, and group, the contrast with it that is basic to the very idea of a university in ruins is itself phantasmic. What, for example, was the relevance of the university of culture for women, workers, colonial subjects, and various minorities? What were the variations in its functioning or even in the way it was envisioned with respect to them in contrast to upper-class white males? To what extent did it provide what might be called the uplifting, motivational canon folderol to accompany the use of the lower classes and the colonized as actual cannon fodder in the expansion of capital and colonial power? And to what extent did it allow for critiques of that accommodating service function? Was it countered or even displaced by more pragmatic concerns, including economic and political interests, with the so-called university of culture itself already a site for market-oriented interests and training? What have been the variations in representations of the university over time, notably with the rise of mass media, and in what ways have those variable representations interacted with, even had performative effects on, the workings of the university and the degree of public, governmental, and private support for it or its component parts? One need not expect Readings to be able to answer such questions with the requisite detail, but one might expect a more careful framing of his argument and its bearing on his analysis of the present. Instead his polemical intent induces him to make short shrift of intricate histories and genealogies that might provide more focused critical perspective on contemporary problems and possibilities. And one may suggest that, whether as phantasm or as partial reality, the idealistic university of culture was born in ruins insofar as it was class-based, sexist, and ethnocentric. Even if one brackets historical questions and explicitly understands the university of culture to a significant extent as a critical fiction that rhetorically motivates Readings's argument, one may insist that its problematic status should be made evident and ask whether the nature of the fiction has some uncontrolled, adverse effects.

The application of Readings's big picture to the present raises comparable questions. His analysis has little to say about class and even seems to dismiss the question in favor of a globalizing and homogenizing notion of a worldwide petite bourgeoisie that includes the professoriat, from well-endowed chair-holders to part-time, limited-contract lecturers. Here his analysis is as loose as the forms of cultural studies he criticizes. Indeed one might even suspect in Readings's subject position as analyst (whatever his autobiographical situation may have been) a patrician or quasi-transcendental perspective of one who is not concerned about social mobility or the way the university may serve it, indeed one who simply takes certain things for granted (such as an idea of acquired culture or *Bildung*) and so may radically question them. There is no concern for what the acquisition of such culture might mean for those without access to it. In addition, traditional culture, including disciplines or genres, may be refunctioned and turned in critical directions in the activities of those who do not simply "buy into" the dominant system. (For example, Frantz Fanon is in crucial ways a product of the French educational system, and the role of that system in training oppositional figures, both domestically and in the colonies or former colonies, is legendary. In the United States, the trajectory of, say, Noam Chomsky is unimaginable without the university, including the manner in which "cultural capital" acquired in one field has a carryover effect, enhancing credibility in another.) Moreover, Readings's big picture fits into conventional oppositions between a past-we-have-lost (for good or ill) and a present we find problematic—a picture that may be too simplistic to do the critical work Readings wants it to do.

More specifically, in terms of the present, are culture, ideology, and the nation-state as evacuated or obsolete as Readings believes? With reference to culture, I would make three observations. First, high culture, in its increasingly complex and problematic relations with popular and mass culture, may still, at least at times, noninvidiously be an area in which critical questioning is especially intense, in part because components are less commodified or at least less successful by market criteria than other areas of culture. Readings's own reliance for critical orientation on figures such as Lyotard and Derrida would itself seem to imply as much. Second, Readings devotes little or no attention to such crucial areas as corporate and mass culture, areas that are themselves both globalized and significantly inflected by national differences. Mass culture can be dismissed only on the basis of a massive generalization along the lines of Horkheimer and Adorno's scathing indictment of the culture industry in *Dialectic of Enlightenment*.[18] One would, at the very least, want a more discriminating judgment in this respect. In any case, in daily life and as an object of interest or involvement, mass culture plays an obvious role. Indeed one may ask the degree to which mass culture, in the delimited sense of commodified culture, has incorporated popular culture and whether and to what extent there are still viable areas of popular culture either within or not entirely within mass culture. (Popular culture in this differential sense is culture produced, or at least significantly refunctioned, as well as consumed, by its recipients— indeed culture involved in dialogic exchange in the Bakhtinian sense Readings rightly valorizes, that is, mutually provocative but asymmetrical exchange between people [singularities for Readings] who cannot be reduced to senders and receivers of messages.)

Corporate culture is of course a phenomenon that accompanies the tendencies on which Readings concentrates, and it may both reinforce

---

[18] Max Horkheimer and Theodor W. Adorno, *Dialectic of Enlightenment* (1944; New York: Seabury Press, 1972), 120–67 (chapter on "The Culture Industry: Enlightenment as Mass Deception").

and in certain ways mitigate them. For example, the role of fraternities and other student associations at universities attests to the importance of corporate culture and in fact helps to create it, for relations formed in these institutions may both carry over into later life and establish patterns of culture that will be applied in dealings with future business and professional associates. Moreover, such associations have important experiential functions, whether commendable or dubious. For one thing, they facilitate the transition from high school to college or university life and may even mitigate culture shock, a function that is especially significant in the case of underprivileged groups. The role played by fraternities, program houses, eating clubs, and similar institutions is a crucial reason why attempts to eliminate them tend to fail, especially when those attempts are motivated by high-minded but less substantive ideals such as promoting diversity or disseminating classically liberal or cosmopolitan culture. Moreover, corporate culture to some extent varies along national lines. In the United States, the movement away from a specifically religious or ministerial function for the university was related to the rise of education geared to the occupational market, with its professional and pragmatic needs, and still with us is the issue of the extent to which a liberal education is relevant to these needs and to the formation of the type of person best able to answer them.[19] A parallel question is the central significance of the humanities in a liberal education—or even of a more critically oriented idea of education in accordance with conceptions of critical theory, postcolonial studies, or sociocultural critique. This question becomes especially pointed in light of the actualities of university policy (including vastly disproportionate funding or allocation of resources) with respect to the sciences, especially when one or another of them seems to be in the vanguard of research (formerly physics, currently biology).

With respect to the nation and the role of nationalism as it bears on the university, one may mention a point to which Readings himself alludes in passing. Readings was an Englishman residing and teaching in Quebec, where resurgent nationalism, more or less militantly (however unrealistically or at times strategically) in quest of state

[19] See, for example, Hugh Davis Graham and Nancy Diamond, *The Rise of American Research Universities: Elites and Challenges in the Postwar Era* (Baltimore: Johns Hopkins University Press, 1997); Alexandra Olson and John Voss, eds., *The Organization of Knowledge in Modern America* (Baltimore: Johns Hopkins University

formation, has been pronounced but obviously not shared by someone with his subject position. In his context, the idea that the nation-state with a political and ideological content is largely a thing of the past (47) might seem to be wishful thinking. Had he lived to see the upsurge of patriotic sentiment in the aftermath of the attacks on the World Trade Center and the Pentagon—sentiment that accompanied a complex constellation of heartfelt mutual aid, crass commercialism, militant nationalism, increasingly rote ritualization, and objectionable increases of mistrust if not paranoia, at times paired with the scapegoating of Arabs and Muslims—he might have had second thoughts about the idea that nationalism was clearly on the wane. And however "imagined" the ideological bases of large, non–face-to-face "communities" such as nations may be, the policies and practices undertaken in their name by governments and other groups obviously have other than only imagined effects.[20]

The foregoing comments imply that resurgent nationalism is overdetermined. It is not a univocal sign of the breakdown of the nation-state, and the latter's continued existence or reassertion is not simply subordinated to the demands of a global market. Indeed the nation-state and a global market (as well as coalitions such as NATO or the European Union) are tensely related and not simply incompatible phenomena (or differends). Readings himself almost identifies globalization with Americanization, but he does little to investigate the extent to which globalization serves certain national interests (notably those of economically powerful nations) more than others, when it does not simply mask those interests. For such an inquiry, a closer study than Readings's of the global market and the movements of capital would be required. In it one would have to account for such phenomena as the size of military budgets and the continued importance of national and ethnic conflict in the wake of the end of the Cold War and, more recently, the upsurge of the seemingly interminable, ill-defined, but not altogether dereferentialized "war" against terrorism (for which certain nations

---

Press, 1979); and Laurence Veysey, *The Emergence of the American Research University* (Chicago: University of Chicago Press, 1965).
[20] One should not infer from this statement that small, face-to-face communities without a particular kind of print culture do not have "imagined" bases as well.

and groups serve as anxiety-producing, targeted points of condensation).

A third observation relates to Readings's reformulation of the end-of-ideology thesis. He refuses to see excellence as an ideology since it does not address or interpellate the subject in Althusser's sense or provide a "sutured," centered identity having quasi-religious, redemptive functions. Here I would object that a both/and logic is more applicable than an either/or approach. One may have the more or less contentious coexistence of ideology in the older sense of false consciousness or at least in the sense of displaced or quasi-religious commitments that provide a measure of identity (however problematic) for the subject along with a technocratic perspective that may be seen either as other than ideology (with Readings) or as a specific mode of technology-as-ideology (as Habermas and others have contended). (Readings's own analysis of continued gift-giving to universities would itself, as I indicated earlier, seem to rely implicitly on the continued relevance of ideology in the sense of substantive belief or commitment or even false consciousness.) One may also have "cynical reason" in the sense of Peter Sloterdijk and Slavoj Žižek, in which a subject sees through or recognizes the baselessness of an ideological perspective but affirms or follows its injunctions anyway. And the activity of various "fundamentalist" groups, including those in the United States and other "Western" countries, at least inserts sharp-edged oppositional shards into any generalized idea of the end of ideology. Indeed the staying power of religion and the prevalence of more or less inchoate desires for the "sacred" (or some secular analogue of it, such as the sublime) pose difficult theoretical and practical problems for those who see themselves as critical secular intellectuals.

My three observations bespeak the importance of countercurrents to the currents Readings singles out, sees as dominant, and even construes in totalizing and globalizing terms. Recognizing the role of countercurrents has implications not only for one's analysis of a situation but for one's understanding of possible alternatives: one may then inquire into the complications if not intractable situations they create as well as try to build on certain of them or at least turn them, if at all possible, in relatively desirable directions. Readings's more emphatic, totalizing approach runs the risk of combining a devastating if not leveling critique with a notion of alternatives that, especially in contrast to the awesome magnitude of problems highlighted in the critique, seems particularly weak or ineffective if not hopeless. In any case, Readings's alternatives seem very abstract or conceptual, indeed diaphanous, in the face of the problems he discusses, even with respect to the first dimension of his account, much less the second, more world-historical one.

Before discussing Readings's alternatives, I would make special mention of two further considerations bearing on phenomena that have been eroded but not eliminated by the corporatization of the university—considerations indicating perhaps the most hopeful countercurrents to Readings's emphases. I am referring to the dual status of the university as a nonprofit institution and as a polity. Although the university shares features with other large institutions, including corporations in the sense of business enterprises, its dual status distinguishes it from the latter in limited ways recalling certain older forms of corporative organization.

As a nonprofit institution, the university, in different ways depending on the type of school, serves the public interest and enjoys certain privileges (for example, tax exemptions). While it must be financially sound and fiscally responsible in raising funds and allocating resources, it is not geared to profit maximization, and the bottom line or a narrow conception of efficiency need not be the dominant criterion in evaluating what it does. This situation makes possible certain activities that yield little in the way of immediate returns on investment (for example, classical studies or other forms of research into remote times and places). It is also essential for the general ambience of the university, which furthers noninstrumentalized inquiry and critical thought. One may extend Readings's argument to note that the nonprofit nature of the university has been under severe pressure because of corporatizing forces, and the practice and procedures of profit-making institutions, such as strict cost-benefit evaluations or the maximizing incentive to "grow" the endowment, have made important inroads into the management and functioning of universities and colleges. The question is whether all significant dimensions of a nonprofit institution have been eliminated or rendered irrelevant, whether the university has become in all but name a large corporation. At the very least, one may argue normatively for the nonprofit status of the university and the obligations and possibilities it entails.

One may also do everything possible to prevent the conflation between the university and a for-profit corporation and, conversely, attempt to foster other than profit-making criteria in business enterprises.

As a polity, the university has internal norms, even an unwritten constitution, regulating practices and policies. It is not adequate to understand it as a business enterprise in which the president or provost is a CEO, deans are branch managers, faculty are middle-level management, and students are consumers. For example, a dean is *both* a member of the central administration "team" under the president and provost, often technically subject to top-down appointment and dismissal, *and* the representative of the faculty and chairpersons of a college whose interests he expresses. The latter function is related to the dean's role in a public sphere in which other constituencies (including students) play a role. A dean's situation is thus unlike that of a branch manager, who does not represent constituencies or function in a public sphere. While the dean's two functions (or "two bodies") ideally operate in a harmonious manner, they may in fact enter into tension if not conflict, leading to results that have to be negotiated. Even trustees, who may be prone to see the university on the model of a business enterprise, exercise a public trust in their conduct of financial policy and their oversight of the university.

These considerations may give rise to contestation over decisions or policies (for example, the attempt to eliminate a "nonproductive" department or to dismiss a dean without consulting the faculty). Such contestation may have as its object excessively top-down administration even if one recognizes that certain problems can only be adequately addressed with a very significant role for the central administration (for example, the financing of projects or initiatives in "big" science). Readings, I think, does not give due importance to the dual status of the university as a nonprofit organization and as a polity.

Readings's own alternatives deserve more attention than I shall give them, and, if one sees them as limited regulative ideals and even as elaborated on a relatively abstract conceptual level in good part removed from questions of actual institutional practice or the nature of interactions among people in various roles and subject positions, they are thought-provoking. Readings, however, asserts that his own perspective is one of "institutional pragmatism" (124), and, given his self-understanding, one might either expect more than he is able to deliver or have doubts about his very understanding of how institutions do or may possibly function and what counts as institutionally pragmatic. One might also ask whether the extreme or at least relatively unqualified nature of Readings's advocacy of his alternatives and his seeming belief that they are in some sense either adequate to the situation or all one can expect as a response to it may itself backfire and feed the neoconservative forces that appear to have less formalistic, more substantive, experientially gripping (if not manipulative), and rhetorically powerful answers.

Readings's basic postulate is that dwelling in the university in ruins raises the ethical question in an especially forceful manner. The university becomes not an ideal community in service to the nation but one site among others to raise and explore the question of community or life in common. The community in question is, however, actively recognized not only as exploratory and self-questioning but also as an impossible community. The ethical imperative related to such a community exceeds the subject as it enjoins an incalculable obligation to others *as* others in their irreducible alterity and singularity. Here the alterity of the other is taken to one-sided, even transcendent extremes, and any interaction between respecting or affirming both difference and commonalities seems foreclosed. Moreover, incalculable obligation is perforce excessive. It might even be seen as a symptomatic reversal that nonetheless follows the logic of the profit-making and consumerist excesses of capitalism or, alternatively, verges on the pure gift, which, in the context preoccupying Readings, may be readily appropriated by a neoconservative notion of charity as opposed to forms of social justice and redistribution. Incalculable obligation does not create desirable limiting norms that inform mutual expectations and help articulate possibilities. Nor is it a tie that binds either anxiety within the self or relations between selves, and it sits uneasily with a notion of accountability that enables both trust and an ability to count or rely on others based in part on one's experience with them. Indeed incalculable obligation seems to be the abstract, quasi-transcendental negation of accounting rather than a viable alternative to it. At best it is a supererogatory idea of virtue that must be supplemented and in part countered by specific norms defining determinate obligations and requirements, for example, in establishing floors and ceilings for socially acceptable levels of income and wealth.

The university for Readings also becomes the site for Thought as the endless exploration of differends in Lyotard's sense: Thought as the process of thinking of a community of dissensus rather than consensus, an impossible community of radically different singularities that do not even agree to disagree. "Thought," as Readings puts it, "names a differend" (161). Once again, a logic of reversal seems operative. The dubiousness of perfect consensus or even a conventional pluralism, which often serves ideologically as a legitimation of established interests within a status quo or as a screen for domination or the privileging of an authority or group over others, is replaced by an indiscriminate and unnuanced affirmation of dissensus. (Is one to affirm or even celebrate any difference or differend, indeed magnify it to the quasi-transcendental status of the incommensurable or the totally other?) The affirmation of dissensus, or the postulation of differends, in a context of excessively unequal distribution of power, wealth, income, and status, may serve as little more than an outlet for voices crying in the wilderness. Perhaps with a degree of insensitivity to the echoes of historical voices that may, for certain readers, drown out Kant's, Readings is even willing to formulate the modern analogue of the Kantian categorical imperative as *"Achtung! Ein andere"* (162).

For Readings, the rather grandiose task of the university as the site of impossible community becomes that of "rethinking the categories that have governed intellectual life for over two hundred years" (169), and the university itself emerges as "a shifting disciplinary structure that holds open the question of whether and how thoughts fit together" (191). How Readings's conception of the university applies differentially to the natural sciences, and even to areas of the social sciences, remains sketchy at best, and how his alternatives would apply to these extremely important areas is left to the reader's imagination. It is difficult to see how evanescent work groups in these areas, which may be important for interdisciplinary or even market-oriented research, would serve the critical sociocultural and political functions he seeks. (Here Readings seems to be a humanist who remains within the intramural terms of the "culture wars.") Moreover, it is difficult to discern how his conception of ethics relates to the articulation of rights and duties in an institutional setting or to collective political action. Indeed, like Jean-Luc Nancy and others (including Giorgio Agamben), he goes in the direction of a sublimely ecstatic anarchism with (post)apocalyptic overtones in which the singular self is, in its incommensurable difference, somehow radically open to others.[21] Here what is supererogatory or above and beyond the call of duty threatens to make that call in its specific sites almost inaudible. And an "ethics" of excess, valuable as a supplement or contestatory force, itself becomes excessive and seems to obliterate an ethics based on a normative sense of legitimate limits, including an ethics as well as a politics that might at least help to raise the question of when enough—including enough production or consumption (of published words among other things)—is enough, even if there can be no conclusive or altogether definite answer to such a question.

Readings's alternatives, I think, both go too far and do not go far enough. They go too far in their unqualified nature and their "from-one-extreme-to-another" assumption that the only alternative to the impossible ideals of transparency in communication, total community on the model of the *Volksgemeinschaft*, and absolute grounding of principles in some grand metanarrative or displaced religiosity is an impossible community in which the operative, rather formalistic, "principle" is to have an incalculable obligation toward the other as other and to keep all questions (justice, thought, ethics, teaching) open as differends subject to endless debate. It also goes too far in asserting that the ideals of unity and transparency lead inevitably to terror (184)—a view that too easily amalgamates John Stuart Mill and Hitler and provides too truncated an idea of fascism in general and the Nazi regime in particular. It underestimates the possibility that, in most if not all social contexts, extreme instability, incalculability, self-exposure, and indeterminacy may lead to panic—and panic, to a turn toward an authoritative, possibly fascist, solution. It especially ignores the role in Nazi ideology and practice themselves of the fascination with unheard-of transgression, the allure of a negative sublime, the violent quest for regeneration or redemption requiring the elimination of those (mis)perceived as totally other, and the hyperbolic idea that a civilization—and not only a university—was in ruins.

[21] For a sympathetic but critical discussion of such tendencies, see Peter Starr, *Logics of Failed Revolt: French Theory after May '68* (Stanford: Stanford University Press, 1995).

This example in no sense invalidates radical critique and the ambivalent value of the excessive and the sublime, but it may make one more concerned about specifics, and more discriminating and somewhat tentative in the way one affirms them. It may also induce an attempt, however hesitant and undogmatic, to provide more than a neoformalist understanding of community and possible relations within it, including some idea of social relations not positioned at the extremes of consensus and dissensus, full agreement and nonnegotiable differends, *Volksgemeinschaft* and disseminated singular alterities.

One may agree with the formulation that Readings borrows from Nancy: the desirable community is one wherein there is being in common without common being. But, in thinking that Readings's alternatives do not go far enough, one may see being in common somewhat differently, may consistently raise the question of the relation between normative limits (including considerations of justice) and what goes beyond or transgresses them, and thereby not present the institution and its possibilities only in terms of what exceeds limits and is incalculable, aporetic, or constitutive of a differend. Indeed affirmation of the latter, especially since it offers no specific guides to action, may well in concrete circumstances accompany manipulative, power-hungry behavior in which one advances one's unargued subjective preferences or the interest of one's delimited group or circle of initiates.

At certain points in his account, Readings's approach, although labeled "institutional pragmatism," is decidedly anti-institutional at least insofar as an institution involves a complex relationship between normative limits and what challenges them, for his stress is insistently on excess or what goes beyond limits. Indeed the very interest, for Readings, of a thought of dissensus or of the differend is that it cannot be institutionalized (167). If by this he means that there are no standard operating procedures or bureaucratic mechanisms with which to resolve a differend, one may readily agree. But if one then ignores significant differences in the ways the norms and practices of different institutions may frame, further, or inhibit disagreement and debate, help create community, and inform experience, one easily arrives at an excessively homogenized, rigid, categorical, and uniformly bureaucratized understanding of the institution—one that readily lends itself to the idea or assumption that institutions per se are precipitates of the evil demon and that the only hope lies in subversive, "deterritorialized," or free-form maneuverings in their interstices. One may also note that Readings tends to conflate two senses of the differend: the differend as nonnegotiable difference that marks a total stand-off or an irresolvable aporia and the differend as a difference, residue, or resistance for which there is no metalanguage or higher order normative system but that still allows for imperfect translation between positions in a manner analogous to the process, involving both losses and gains, that takes place between natural languages such as English and French. At least in its bearing on group relations, the former eventuality should, I think, be seen as a limit case rather than generalized and made to obliterate the more diverse possibilities of the latter, including processes of negotiation, partial agreement, and a willingness to get along without claiming to represent a sovereign will.[22]

I have intimated that the incalculability of the ethical relation, which Readings elaborates on the basis of the work of Lyotard, Derrida, and Levinas, may cast ethics itself in too one-sidedly sublime a light whereby ethics is close to (perhaps displaced by) a religious perspective tending to figure every relation on the model of the anguished encounter (or nonencounter) of the singular individual and the radically transcendent, totally other, inscrutable, grace-dispensing (or "excessively" gift-giving), Hidden God. One might indeed want to object to the application to ethics of a model of cal-

---

[22] One may also distinguish here between a compromise formation in a psychoanalytic sense and a compromise in the ordinary sense. A compromise formation may be the condition of possibility for ordinary compromises, including dubious ones. But one collapses the distinction only from an absolutist or all-or-nothing perspective that rejects or denies the role of compromise formations and sees them only in the light of objectionable compromises. I indicated in the last chapter that the human being may be seen as a compromise formation, for example, between "body" and "mind" or "immanence" and "transcendence." One may also argue that institutions are complex compromise formations, for example, between normative demands and pragmatic considerations as well as (in the modern context) between collective duties and individual rights. The university as an institution is also a compromise formation between different instances of authority and different constituencies—presidents, deans, assemblies, department chairs, and so forth, with the different constituencies they represent (trustees, colleges, students, departments). As a compromise formation, an institution per se may be objectionable or open to condemnation from an absolutist perspective—or one may seek a self-negating "institution" as in certain forms of anarchism. Whether a particular compromise in the more ordinary sense is acceptable or not requires further argumentation and the decision cannot be made on the basis of a defense of the status of, or processes within, an institution as a compromise formation.

culation derived from accounting and observe that the obligations of the ethical agent have "incalculable" dimensions and are never exhausted by the agent's subjective consciousness of them. But accountability may nonetheless allow for counting on others, and one's willingness to count on others or have them count on oneself may be in part related to fallible knowledge of the way people (including oneself) have behaved in the past and the more or less justifiable expectations one may have about them with reference to the future. This is a type of institutional "calculation" that has a role in ethical relations and that, without obliterating the role of excess, change, risk, and chance, resists the total divorce of ethics from desirable normative limits, cognition, justifiable expectation, or fallible knowlege with respect to others. Moreover, in his notion of the university as a "shifting disciplinary structure that holds open the question of whether and how thoughts fit together," Readings does not raise and explore the crucial question of articulatory practices that, without reaching definitive closure, may relate areas of thought and specialization in nontotalizable ways.

I would now like to turn, however inadequately, to the crucial, long-term problem of specialization on which Readings touches and at least raise the question of articulatory practices that relate areas of thought without necessarily closing the question of whether and how they fit together. Such a problem could be more comprehensively addressed only if it were systematically related to various sectors within the university (including, notably, the natural sciences), to the differential relations between sectors of the university and the worlds of business and government, and to the problem of structural change in the economy and society, including the interaction between national economies and globalizing, including transnational, forces. Even without such an account, however, one may specify certain goals or desiderata whose implementation in any effective and cogent fashion would depend on these daunting, larger considerations. My own reflections are by and large focused on, but not entirely restricted to, the humanities and dimensions of the social sciences—but in ways that may also raise questions for one's very conception of the natural sciences, for some of the issues I raise could well be argued to be relevant to them as well.

I would suggest that we are faced in the contemporary academy with at least three types of specialization, each of which may detract from the humanistic goals of furthering both self-understanding and critical inquiry into culture and society, including the university itself. Indeed each type is tempted to see itself not as a problematic part of the university but as a whole unto itself. Specialization in the larger context of the division of labor is of course related to questions of identity and experience—how one is defined by others and conceives of oneself as well as how what one does can be related to other activities. One crucial issue here is how exclusive and exhaustive an identity provided by an occupational or disciplinary orientation is and whether (or precisely how) it may be open to other identities, both professional and other than professional (for example, that of a public intellectual). This question becomes acute beginning in graduate school, but preprofessionalism may carry it back into undergraduate education, where courses may be chosen in accordance with expectations (however accurate) of future professional or occupational demands.

Preprofessionalism might be seen as the first and most familiar type of specialization and is by now widely decried. It is a form of "vocationalism" in the narrow sense of adaptation of one's college education to the putative demands of a future job in the so-called outside world. The specter of preprofessionalism haunts most academics, especially in colleges of arts and sciences. As Readings and others have insisted, the university has become central to a complex, skill-dependent society and economy both through the certification or credentialing of students as potential professionals and through information processing, the collection of databases, research, and development. In this sense, the boundary between the inside and the outside of the academy is permeable, at times permeable enough to generate problematic conflicts of interest and commitment. In significant ways, as Readings contends, the modern university is like a multinational corporation, and its links to big business may well increase as administrators search for and tap sources of funding to replace diminishing governmental allocations. And faculty members, especially in certain areas such as biotechnology, computer science, and engineering, may form links to business or even create business enterprises, whose relations to their role in the university can be very difficult to adjudicate.

The second type of specialization often fails to recognize itself for what it is and may even be identified with a valid liberal arts education. I am referring to the tailoring of undergraduate education to the specifications of future academics themselves. University and college teachers are tempted to consider all undergraduates—or at least the undergraduates at whom they direct their teaching—as homunculi who ideally will come to resemble themselves. This approach sees the world in terms of its own professional interest or occupation writ large. In fact advanced academic specialization places the academy in a position comparable to that of other sectors of the occupational sphere. Training to become an academic may often be as preprofessional as training to become a doctor or lawyer.

A third type of specialization, to my knowledge first discussed at length by August Comte in the nineteenth century, is the prerogative of what might be called the specialist in generalities or in general culture. This is how Comte saw the sociologist. But sociology has gone in the direction of very advanced if not extreme specialization, and the dubious distinction of specializing in generalities perhaps more aptly designates a field such as intellectual history or, in certain ways, cultural studies.

There is, I think, a limited role for this paradoxical kind of specialization in a complex society. It provides at least some rudimentary liaison or mapping function that helps students to find their way about a complex intellectual terrain. But it should be recognized as one special focus among others, and its limitations are obvious. It is in good measure a propaedeutic to other, more concentrated fields and critical practices, in one or more of which even the intellectual historian or cultural analyst must achieve competence if he or she is not to be reduced to the perpetually introductory role of a cultural MC.

If one agrees that one is confronted with three more or less competing kinds of specialization—broadly occupational, academic, and the paradoxical, synoptic specialization in generalities—the problem seems obvious. How does one relate the disparate parts?

At least a beginning is made when one realizes, with Readings, that one indeed confronts a problem with no simple answers and, more importantly, that the parts do not—even ideally—add up to a perfect whole. And there is always the possibility that, in seeking a whole that is larger than the sum of its parts, one may end up with one that is less than their sum. At best one may develop articulatory practices whereby the parts can enter into a more genuinely informative exchange with one another, and those working in a given area can raise more provocative questions for others who, in the best of possible worlds, have at least a basic sense of where these questions are coming from. In this sense, the challenge for those concerned about a broad, liberal arts education is to work through the existing parts (or some subset of them) in order to elaborate a significantly different, more interactive relationship among them and perhaps a different configuration of the fields of knowledge. There is no "quick fix" such as that provided by a core curriculum or a list of common readings in the classics that can adequately answer this challenge. This is of course not to deny all value to a core curriculum, especially one that assures basic competence in skills such as writing, reading, and mathematics. But it is to note its limitations and the need for specific mediations among areas of specialization, mediations that require intimate knowledge of the areas to be related. It is also to insist on the ways in which the university is not like a business enterprise, task force, or team that has clear-cut but restricted goals such as implementing a delimited agenda, selling a product, maximizing profits, abetting efficiency, eliminating all seeming redundancy, beating out competitors, or even generating more "interesting" differends. Following a narrowly conceived business or task-oriented model can lead to patently absurd conclusions, such as the idea that historians should not study literature or art, that literary critics should engage only in formal textual analysis, or that the study of Freud should be restricted to psychology departments (despite the fact that the latter may not pay any attention to Freud or psychoanalysis).

Can the humanities (as well as the interpretive areas of the social sciences) offer a more or less distinctive perspective here? To the extent that they can, it is for a rather strange reason: it is because they are—and in some ways have long been—experienced as being in a state of crisis. As I intimated earlier, the long-standing, recurrently repeated "crisis" metaphor can of course be misleading, either because it induces the complacent banality of crisis management or because it is taken to apocalyptic or postapocalyptic extremes that magnify it out of all proportion. Still, the sense of crisis has recently been fed by diverse and at times divergent forces, some of which I have already mentioned: the high cost of a college education, the perceived imbalance between research and undergraduate teaching at major universities, the relative inaccessibility of recent theoretical tendencies, the antipathy to a narrowly preprofessional education, the refinement of specializations to self-referential or conceit-laden extremes, the sense of aimlessness and a supermarket mentality in the liberal arts, and the realization that the neo-Kantian, neo-Humboldtian, and neo-Arnoldian ideals cannot be—perhaps never were—worthy objects of pursuit. The occurrence of more extreme, traumatizing events, or the recognition of the chronic character of certain of them, can only exacerbate a state-of-crisis or state-of-emergency mentality.

A point that directly affects humanists is that the kind of academic preprofessionalism that sees undergraduates as embryonic literary critics, historians, or philosophers is itself under siege. The untoward reason is that the humanistic disciplines themselves have been faced with forceful challenges to their own definitional self-images. It is today difficult to say precisely what a literary critic, historian, or philosopher is. Only those who adamantly resist more contemporary challenges can believe that they can stipulate with apodictic certainty or even with serene self-confidence what clearly and distinctly does or does not constitute a valid definition of a humanistic discipline, its legitimate pursuits, and its practitioners. Indeed the fragility of disciplinary definitions often breeds intolerance and a penchant for ostracism in those who desire a secure professional identity and identity-forming disciplines at any price. This state of affairs makes it difficult both to give sound advice to undergraduates who want to go on to graduate school and to graduate students who want a strong professional formation (essential for viability on the job market) but are wary of too narrow an identity as a practitioner of a specific discipline.

Literary criticism in particular has recently not been a well-defined discipline with established protocols of inquiry and a coterie of classically educated gentlemen for whom canonical texts function as the verbal analogues of school ties. It has become an arena for a lively and puzzling contest of contemporary critical discourses and at times disconcerting intellectual styles. Other areas in the humanities, such as history and analytic philosophy, have remained more secure or at least more complacent in their implicit or explicit self-definitions. But they have not entirely escaped self-scrutiny and the questioning of established procedures. Along with Readings's *University in Ruins*, at least two other well-known books are of interest here: Peter Novick's

That Noble Dream and Gerald Graff's *Professing Literature.*[23] These books trace somewhat parallel developments in professional history and literary criticism, and quotations may be drawn from each to indicate that the current indictments of the putative chaos and disarray in humanistic studies have their uncannily exact replicas in the past—a point that challenges the pertinence of a stark contrast between the present and "the past we have lost." The current crisis did not originate ab ovo in the 1960s. It has recurred periodically in the past, and its current configuration has both particular inflections and the inescapable distinction that it is particularly significant to us because we are in fact living through it. But our immersion in it should not lead us to resort to false genealogies that picture a unified past and either demonize or idolize the 1960s—genealogies that serve as myths of origin or, at best, critical fictions, for restricted and perhaps misleading retrospects and responses.

One feature shared by Novick and Graff is that they tend to treat their particular disciplines in overly intramural terms and do not focus more insistently on a problem Graff explicitly recognizes: the way the interaction among disciplines has been and continues to be crucial for the self-definition of any given discipline or department. Curiously, despite his awareness of the problem, this intramural tendency may be more pronounced in Graff's actual analysis than in Novick's. Novick does not thematize consistently or treat in a sustained manner the problems of interdisciplinary interaction, ranging from active mutual influence to insulation and exclusion. But, motivated in part by the traditional historiographical ideal of exhaustiveness and all-inclusiveness, he does note the way the work of nonhistorians (such as Thomas Kuhn or Clifford Geertz) has affected historiography. To some extent their own methodologies indicate how Novick's and Graff's books are—perhaps necessarily—symptomatic both of the problems they treat and of the disciplinary formations of their authors. Nonetheless, within their own parameters, they are (like Readings's book) thought-provoking studies and provide much useful information and many arresting insights, especially when they are read in tandem.

[23] Peter Novick, *That Noble Dream: The "Objectivity Question" and the American Historical Profession* (Cambridge: Cambridge University Press, 1988). Gerald Graff, *Professing Literature: An Institutional History* (Chicago: Chicago University Press, 1987). Page references, included in the text, are to these editions.

Novick has written an impressive, magisterial survey of the U.S. historical profession since its inception. He offers substantial documentation to illustrate the steadfast commitment over time of mainstream professional historians to the profession's elusive founding ideal of objectivity. I would instead term this ideal "objectivism," for one may criticize it yet defend objectivity in a delimited, self-critical sense. This sense would imply the need to counteract projective reprocessing or rewriting of the past and to listen attentively to its "voices," notably when they pose a genuine challenge, thereby resisting one's desire to make them say what one wants them to say or to have them become either straightforward evidence for a thesis or vehicles for one's values and political agendas. The "objectivist" ideal, which is open to criticism in important ways, brings with it an unqualified correspondence theory of truth, an exclusively representational conception of language, a restriction of history to reconstruction of the past, the objectifying status of transcendental (often securely ironic) spectator (or bystander) for the historian, a "research imperative" that in its exclusive or even dominant role downplays the significance of theoretical reflection and critical self-questioning, an occlusion of the problem of the voices or subject positions of the historian in a contemporary context of inquiry, and a set of more or less tacit conventions governing allowable modes of historical discourse. These conventions tend to foster repression or denial of the role of transferential relations between historians and both other investigators and objects of investigation. But they allow for—even prompt—a relatively uncritical return of the repressed as these relations are intermittently acted out rather than explicitly thematized, critically confronted, and to some extent worked through. Moreover, the desire for a secure disciplinary identity may induce disciplinarian behavior, typically with one dimension of, or approach to, historical studies (say, social or cultural history) deceptively being positioned at the center of the discipline and other approaches marginalized, made dependent, or declared to be passé (at times the status imputed to critical-theoretical analysis and self-reflexive intellectual history, especially when directed at historiography itself).

I would simply note in passing that the concept of transference facilitates a rethinking of the problems of subjectivity and objectivity in historical inquiry, and transferential processes may be seen as occuring in multiple contexts: in the relations between people (notably instructors and graduate students) as well as between present inquirers and the dead whom they re-create and study; in the relation to institutions and "cathected" abstractions such as the university or the nation; and in the more general, basic tendency to repeat, in our own discourse or approach, aspects—including aspects we explicitly criticize—of the phenomena we study. In my judgment, transference occurs willy-nilly, and the problem is not whether it occurs but how one comes to terms with it through processes of repression, dissociation, denial, symptomatic acting-out, and more or less critical working-over and working-through. Working-through should not be understood in purely personal or experiential terms; it requires an attempt to situate problems in broader contexts and macrohistorical processes that provide some critical perspective on personal experience and contemporary concerns.

In conventional historiography, which is at times loathe to thematize and explicitly confront these problems, the privileged space for transference is, in variable ways, the more personal and subjective preface, epilogue, or other marginal portion of, or addendum to, a work (including the letter, both private and public), while the principal text is presumably governed by norms of strict objectivity and conventions of impersonal prose narration and analysis. Although Novick expresses his personal views and his doubts about certain conventions in paratexts, such as his preface or occasional footnotes, their quarantined status inhibits the exploration of related questions in the main argument. In the principal text, he by and large adopts the prevalent narrative (or subject) position of the ironic observer or bystander who is panoptically situated above the fray. Thus he begrudgingly conforms to professional expectations (much to the satisfaction of those who relish the performative contradiction between his objectifying conventional practice and his sometimes excessive, even relativistic criticism of objectivity).[24] Novick also tells the tale of periodic critics who pose somewhat more basic challenges to conventional procedures and the ideal of objectivity, for example, Charles Beard and Carl Becker in the interwar period—some of whose arguments are echoed in the work of more recent critics such as Hayden

[24] See, for example, Thomas Haskell, "Objectivity Is Not Neutrality: Rhetoric versus Practice in Peter Novick's *That Noble Dream*," in *History and Theory: Contemporary Readings*, ed. Brian Fay, Philip Pomper, and Richard T. Vann (Malden, Mass.: Blackwell, 1998), 299–319.

White. Certain recent critiques often seem (like their predecessors) to be locked in a strategy of reversal, for example, by opposing subjectivist, constructivist, or particularist relativism to objectifying universalism. But they are of course marked by a more insistent concern for the problem of language if not by a "linguistic turn." Novick thinks that recurrent critiques are useful and provocative, but he somewhat pessimistically and fatalistically feels that—even when they attempt to question the cogency of limited strategies of reversal—they will have little real and thoroughgoing effect on an essentially conservative profession. He himself tends to characterize the modern period of questioning and self-questioning in largely negative terms, and the vitality of critical contestation remains a rather confined, subdominant theme in his own reaction to recent developments. He in brief leaves one with the image of repeated *Frondes* that never add up to a revolution or even to durable structural reform and more accurate self-understanding.

Gerald Graff's approach is significantly different and more directly committed on an argumentative level, and it includes a fruitful recommendation. Graff attempts to indicate how recent experimental overtures, while at times going to questionable extremes, nonetheless reinvigorate the humanities in ways that are not altogether unprecedented. His central insight is that the quest for consensus often masks hegemony and leads to an obfuscation of the conflicts that not only typified the discipline of literary studies in the past but that continue to agitate and enliven it today. And he recommends that these very conflicts become a focal point in the educational process itself. In some sense, the problem becomes part and parcel of its own (partial) solution at least insofar as one foregrounds and attempts to work through it. One has here the logic of the antidote. (One may at times see a similar logic in Readings but he often seems to prescribe overdosing on the antidote through an excessive response to excess rather than attempting to work and play out a viable relation between excess and limits.) As Graff puts it:

> A university is a curious accretion of historical conflicts that it has
> systematically forgotten. Each of its divisions reflects a history of
> ideological conflicts that is just as important as what is taught within
> the divisions yet is prevented from being foregrounded by the divisions
> themselves. The boundaries that mark literary study off from creative

writing, composition, rhetoric, communications, linguistics, and film, or those that divide art history from studio practice, or history from philosophy, literature, and sociology, each bespeak a history of conflict that was critical to creating and defining these disciplines yet has never become a central part of their context of study. The same is true of the very division between the sciences and the humanities which has been formative for both yet has never been an obligatory context for either. (257–58)

Graff continues:

At issue in the teaching of literature, then, and in the formation of a literature curriculum, are how much of the "cultural text" students must presuppose in order to make sense of works of literature, and how this cultural text can become the context of teaching. That there is no agreement over how the cultural text should be understood, or whether it should come into play at all in the teaching of literature, seems to me an argument for rather than against a more explicitly historicized and cultural kind of literary study that would make such disagreements part of what is studied. The important thing, in any case, is to shift the question from "Whose overview gets to be the big umbrella?" in which form it becomes unanswerable, to "How do we institutionalize the conflict of interpretations and overviews itself?" To emphasize conflict over consensus is not to turn conflict into a value, nor certainly is it to reject consensus where we can get it—as would the silly recent argument that identifies consensus with repressive politics. It is simply to take our point of departure from a state of affairs that already exists. (258)

Readings finds Graff still too consensual in providing a new rendition of the liberal idea that one should at least agree to disagree. And Graff would obviously not agree with Readings's insistent substitution of dissensus for consensus. But Graff is close to Readings when he ends this passage by echoing Jacques Derrida's remark that one must begin where one is, thus stressing the importance of a critique that both situates itself in immanent fashion within given contexts and attempts to be situationally transcendent in working through present problems toward more desirable possibilities. In Graff's discussion, this methodological point does, I think, open up a suggestive line of thought. It resonates with the idea that the study of the very constitution of a canon should complement and supplement the critical reading of both canonical and noncanonical artifacts. Graff also leaves us in generative doubt about the extent to which traditional procedures in the teaching of literature (for example, close reading) are to continue in more or less transformed fashion or whether there should be a more basic reconceptualization of literature departments as halfway houses to programs in critical cultural studies that systematically transgress the boundaries between established disciplines such as history and literature.[25]

Significant supplements to the works of Graff and Novick, which take the argument in somewhat different directions, may be found in two related contributions to a recent volume on the role of the university in the larger society, focusing on the humanities and, more particularly, literature: *The Institution of Literature*.[26] In his contribution, "The Life of the Mind and the Academic Situation," Jeffrey J. Williams focuses on the role of professionalism in the university in relation to forces and possibilities in the larger society. In contrast to both those who more or less lucidly insert themselves within a restrictive professional frame of reference (such as James Phelan) and those who indict professionalism and defend the amateur (such as Edward Said), Williams tries to work out a model of a critical professionalism consistently aware of links between the academy and the larger society.[27] Indeed Williams not only insists on situating tendencies in the academy in the context of larger currents (such as professionalism itself) but cogently demands that any concern for ethics or psychology (such as empathic response) be explicitly connected to sociopolitical analysis and concrete proposals for change. As he puts it:

> I would stress this liminal opening that the university and
> professionalism present; the university is frequently deprecated as an
> ivory tower, but in reality comprises a significant contemporary public

[25] In her *Academic Instincts* (Princeton: Princeton University Press, 2001), Marge Garber offers a spirited defense of cultural studies that may be contrasted to Readings's negative assessment of it. Albeit with an affirmation of nonpartisanship and an aversion to taking sides, she in certain ways joins Graff in defending an approach that explores disputes in the academy without pretending to transcend them.

[26] Ed. Jeffrey J. Williams (Albany: State University of New York Press, 2002).

[27] See James Phelan, *Beyond the Tenure Track: Fifteen Months in the Life of an English Professor* (Columbus: Ohio State University Press, 1991); Edward Said, "Secular Criticism," in *The World, the Text, and the Critic* (Cambridge: Harvard University Press, 1983), and *Representations of the Intellectual: The 1993 Reith Lectures* (New York: Pantheon, 1994).

sphere that is open to relatively large numbers of people, where one can address and debate issues that inform social and political policy and actions. As Henry Giroux points out, we are already in a public sphere by virtue of being in a classroom. Beyond the classroom, the university presents a significant public forum, as Edward Said reflects in an interview: "But there's no question that, in some ways, neither Chomsky nor myself would have had the audiences we've had without the university. A lot of the people who listen to us when we speak . . . are university students. The university provides one with a forum to do certain things." Further, the professional base of the university garners a certain social legitimacy and position from which academic-intellectuals can cross over to larger media channels and other public venues, as oppositional intellectuals like Said, Chomsky, Cornel West, Patricia Williams, and many others have. This crossover, however, should not only be to make our professional discourse more publicly accessible, as Michael Bérubé advises, but also to open that discourse to public and worldly concerns. . . . Rather than seeing professionalism as a danger, as Said does, or as a quarantine, as Phelan does, this alternative vista offers a kind of press pass to the public sphere and public policy—which in my view constitutes not only a choice but an obligation of intellectual life. (219)

While Williams moves from work within the university to considerations bearing on the larger public and social world (as I tend to do), Evan Watkins, in the contribution that ends the collection ("Educational Politics of Human Resources"), begins with an understanding of the larger socioeconomic context that shapes or even determines tendencies within the university. He runs the risk of recapitulating and remaining largely within these larger contextual forces, but his own argument is that the larger context is indeed the world in which we live and that our only viable option is to become more aware of its nature and of the professional and market-oriented options available to those of us in the academy. Hence he takes Readings's orientation one step further, turns his back on the putative ruins, and boldly enters the world he finds has taken possession of a university it has reconstructed in its own image.

Watkins sees a full-scale integration of the academy into the corporate economy in a fashion that goes well beyond the training and certification of youth for entry into the job market. This integration is both diagnosed and managed by "human resources" analysts, and it seems that humanists must also recognize that they too are Kentucky-fried as more or less coordinated managers of human resources for a diversified, often niche-oriented economy.

> The emphasis on knowledge growth and knowledge workers that shapes corporate direction will also affect public policy with regard to educational institutions. To the extent that human resources management is itself a set of educational practices, I think it altogether likely that programs for educational reform will reposition those of us who teach in the humanities as an extension and corroboration of the intellectual work practices of human resources management. On the one hand, this means that like human resources professionals, humanities intellectuals would acquire a new status as economic agents. Rather than simply "taking care of the kids," humanities instruction becomes a valuable contribution to an economic productivity that depends on human resources, and "the kids" appear as a pool of well-trained and flexibly skilled adults. On the other hand, however, the attention to culture in the humanities would itself take on new meanings as an economic activity. In the new terms of corporate organization cultural practices after all are everywhere linked to the realization of corporate goals. (268)

The corporate concern for culture in production and marketing is related to an optimal utilization of human resources, rather than to any ethical or political interest in affirmative action, and it is likely to lead to the employment of skilled minority workers. Watkins's orientation takes him to the point of elaborating a model of the corporate rather than the state citizen—a corporate citizen molded by a new form of the university of (corporate) culture and human resources management. "The 'corporate environment' ... offers a way of rethinking a great many fundamental premises of liberal democracy as now recentered around the *corporate* citizen rather than the citizen of the State. That is, managing diversity as a cultural education is also a political education in citizenship, and ultimately corporate selection practices thereby identify the process of incorporation into a body politic" (281).

Watkins concludes by formulating the implications of corporate citizenship and human resources management for the humanities and for political action as well.

Understanding literary and cultural studies as a profession inserted within the multiple, diverse market field of professional service providers functions like Gramsci's redefinition of the "intellectual," enlarging both positional reference and representational affiliations. Which is not quite the same as training more English majors, but has everything to do with the specific linkages of economic professionalization and political incorporation. For the idea of "The Market" has become more than an economic fiction. It is a politics of colonizing control and "management," against which the proliferation of self-designated professions and the mazy intricacies of the "informal sector" from which they emerge function as a reminder that actual markets are always collision zones of political struggle. . . . [It is not] possible to escape the often contradictory imperatives that come with a professional, academic position. But the encounters with multiple publics in such positions nevertheless encourages new forms of tactical maneuver where what we learn as educators is not only a matter of cultural resistance. Equally important, as professions multiply before our eyes, we learn how to leverage economic practices into a weapon in the struggles for political change. We learn possibilities for making use of an economic agency. (285)

Here Readings's interstitial, mobile, nomadic resister becomes not quite a professional revolutionary but a professional manager who is savvy about operating in an institution that is lucidly and somewhat reductively seen by Watkins in corporate and political terms. Still, the concluding invocation of militant language cannot disguise the absence of anything comparable to Gramsci's call for an alternative hegemony based on a different form of civilization that might recapture and redefine aspects of the cultural past. We seem to be left with a conception of politics and of academic practice as tactical maneuver in which we learn how better to leverage market positions and economic practices. This lesson is no doubt useful in certain circumstances, for example, the unionization of graduate students or a change in requirements for tenure. But it does not do enough in helping one to envision and effect changes that are not entirely encompassed by a market-oriented conception of activity both within and without the academy. And it may not be beside the point to note that the very language in which the argument is formulated (of which I have tried to give some sense in extended quotations) is itself often overly within the restricted frame of reference it is analyzing, sharing both its seemingly expert jargon and its somewhat bewildering abstraction if not nebulousness. Watkins's well-informed article has, I think, the uncanny effect of engendering an experience of enlightened disempowerment: it seems both to convey general, even world-historical, knowledge as well as apprehensive concern about larger forces and to undercut or disorient understanding related to desirable possibilities of action, especially in the academy and its bearing on the larger society. His alternatives, while seemingly more realistic and "in the know" than Readings's, offer little critical purchase for practical reason and political response. And any residual postapocalyptic sense has itself been dispersed and thoroughly professionalized. Watkins's perspective, while appearing as the sobering chaser to Readings's heady account, also seems like the photographic negative of Habermas's view, which was discussed at the beginning of this chapter. And the constructive incentive, even the somewhat unrealistic idealism, of Habermas's vision is replaced by a dispirited understanding of the nature and fate of the university in our time. The views I shall express in conclusion cautiously seek possibilities between utopian and dystopian extremes.

How can the sense of crisis in the humanities, which has by now become almost too familiar (and, for Readings, should be replaced or at least displaced by the notion of ruins), be turned in desirable directions? Or, to phrase the question in other terms, how can the aporias of the globalized university be approached not only as impasses but as demands for openings that suggest different possibilities? I would propose—at least for purposes of discussion—three areas in which the sense of crisis may prompt one to reinforce countercurrents to dominant or prominent features of Readings's university in ruins (or of its flip side—Watkins's university of accomplished resource management) and to arrive at a conception of at least certain possibilities in the humanities as well as in the relations between the humanities and other areas, including the professions.

First, one may distinguish between the narrow kind of specialized, preprofessional humanistic education I mentioned earlier and the necessary and legitimate increase in complexity and difficulty that comes with the elaboration of newer methodologies and critical approaches to problems. It is too easy to assume that, while the sciences advance and become more intricate, the humanities must remain fixated at the point of some idealized vision of the way things were, if not sometime in the nineteenth century, then at least a generation ago when one was privileged to sit, with other burgeoning "New York intellectuals," at Lionel Trilling's knee. It is also too facile to think that, while preliminary training is necessary for work in the sciences, anyone with a little flowery rhetoric and a desire for self-expression may competently engage in writing or criticizing literature. The humanities may differ from the sciences in that it is more difficult if not impossible to organize them pedagogically in stages leading from the simple to the complex. But this does not mean that differences in education and training do not make a difference. Education in the humanities is a little like learning to swim. A freshman and an advanced graduate student jump into the same pool. Both may read Heidegger or try to understand the nature of the Nazi regime. But, if education does what it is supposed to do, the relation between sinking and swimming varies significantly in the two cases. Expressed less metaphorically, one's ability to formulate issues and relate problems should improve in both coherence and thought-provoking complexity. What should not be lost in the movement from beginner to advanced student is the desire to make larger connections, at least by learning how to generalize within cases, that is, to elicit the implications of what one reads or studies for processes of critical thought in other areas.

Second, there should be—and I think there is increasingly—a desire not simply to conjoin or confuse methods but to work out articulations that may cut across disciplines in the investigation of problems or problem areas. This desire may be termed cross-disciplinary, indeed at times transdisciplinary, rather than interdisciplinary insofar as one is not content to take up disciplines in their existing state and somehow combine them. One of the most misleading beliefs in the academy is that if you get, for example, a historian and a literary critic to coteach a course, the result will be cross-disciplinary historical criticism. The problem is, unfortunately, more basic. One has to work out a reconceptualization of investigation in ways that connect concerns that were disjoined in the initial definition of disciplines (for example, archival or ethnographic research, close reading, and critical theory addressed to an assumed conceptual framework and its relation to the material being investigated). Indeed problems that are themselves cross-disciplinary bring out in accentuated form the need for newer articulations that do not entirely conform to existing definitions of disciplines or of departments that often lay claim to disciplines, indeed articulations that may indicate the possibility of more fruitful disciplinary and departmental formations. One might reformulate certain of Readings's own arguments in somewhat more modest yet more institutionally pertinent terms to contend that significant problems in the humanities and social sciences tend to be cross-disciplinary and at times transdisciplinary, and the issue is how they relate to existing disciplines and may lead to their questioning and reformulation.

Here a basic distinction may need to be rethought: the distinction between the core of a discipline and its externalities or merely peripheral, parasitic elements. What is marginalized or seen as merely external is at times the larger setting in which an activity has social and cultural significance, notably including the culture of, and modes of identity formation within, various disciplines themselves. Often marginalized along with a concern for the larger setting is a critical, self-questioning approach to disciplinary practices and what is taken for granted in them. There are, for example, good reasons to explore critically the relations among historiography, literary criticism, philosophy, and social theory. All these disciplinary areas confront the problem of how to read and make use of texts and how to articulate the relationship between accurate reconstruction of objects of inquiry (including objects reconstructed on the basis of inferences from textualized traces of the past) and an engagement in more or less responsive exchange with them. Yet these disciplines have significantly different cultures: analytic philosophy and history for example, are more theoretically conservative than literary criticism, where people, with whatever degree of preparation and success, may be more inclined to pursue problems or lines of inquiry because they are thought-provoking even when they unsettle clear-cut classifications.[28] Other obvious areas both receiving and calling for more extensive

[28] One should not romanticize, exoticize, or idealize literary criticism, as Richard Rorty is at times inclined to do. Not only do conventional methods and exclusions retain an important role here, but literature departments (like other departments) may be preoccupied with boundary maintenance and professional identity and may a resist hiring or even working closely with colleagues not having a delimited professional formation, typically understood as an advanced degree conferred within a certain sort of department or program.

connection are engineering and urban planning or biology and ecology. The current interest in hybridized, multigeneric forms, in "nomadic" discursive formations and intellectually displaced life styles, or in what have been misleadingly called "blurred" genres attests to the desire for newer connections—connections that may prove fruitless but may also open onto more viable modes of articulation. Indeed if a multiversity is to be more than a collection or an amalgamation of schools and disciplines, it must further the exploration of ways and means of connecting various pursuits, including the professions, the sciences, and the humanities.

One may also mention how the humanities have taken over and reinvigorated problems or areas of study abandoned by the social sciences in their attempt to become professionalized and "scientized." Both psychology and sociology (even in certain respects analytic philosophy) have at times jettisoned certain important traditional concerns and turned a deaf (at least tone-deaf) ear to recent tendencies (such as hermeneutics, Frankfurt school critical theory, and poststructuralism) that can have a rejuvenating or fruitfully critical relation to tradition and the texts that convey it. Indeed the contemporary social sciences, to the extent they emulate a certain (perhaps misleading) idea of the natural sciences, have tended to believe that whatever is valuable in past theorists has been integrated into the present state of the discipline, thereby eliminating the need for a close reading of their texts and a self-questioning, critical dialogic exchange with earlier approaches that may still have something to teach us. If a student wants a course on the work of Emile Durkheim, Max Weber, or Sigmund Freud, the chances are that she or he will find it not in a department of sociology or psychology but in history, German studies, science studies, a humanities center, or an English or French department. Moreover, certain problems (such as the relation between theory and practice or the self-reflexive implications of observer-participation) have tended to migrate into the humanities because of the inhospitable environment for them in important if not dominant sectors of the social sciences. This migration has taken place with respect to almost the entire field of psychoanalysis, which has undergone a major renewal and at times reconceptualization in departments of literature and history. Moreover, the humanities retain the ideal of relating the parts that are left separate when a discipline becomes extremely professionalized and specialized, and humanistic studies are dedicated to keeping questions alive that have a bearing on public life, notably including ethicopolitical questions.[29]

Third, there is the gadfly (or nomadological) element—the activity in the interstices or on the margins of existing disciplines, where the riskier ventures are encouraged even if they may not have immediate payoffs. This activity may be most cogent and most challenging to practitioners of various disciplines when the one who undertakes it has a thorough understanding of the disciplines being interrogated, including what counts as a significant problem within a given disciplinary matrix. In other words, the most telling critiques may emanate not from "Thought" but from thought that involves thorough familiarity with, and the attempt to work through assumptions and procedures of, disciplines in a manner that broaches problems not adequately housed within any given discipline—problems that are themselves cross- or even transdisciplinary. Such critical inquiry may of course take place within departments as well as in interdisciplinary programs. I earlier intimated that departments of literature have, in the recent past, probably been the primary loci for the elaboration of diverse and divergent perspectives that have had an influence even in more traditionally defined fields such as history and philosophy. And some of the strongest departments at major universities have been most open to different and at times opposed perspectives. An active tolerance for diversity, even a willingness to hire colleagues who can pose a genuine challenge to one's own point of view, have proven to be sources not only of heat but of light and genuine stimulation. By contrast, excessively homogeneous departments with

[29] I would also make special mention of the large number of very talented undergraduates who are motivated to apply for entrance to graduate programs in the humanities in spite of the poor job market. The fact that so many gifted undergraduates apply for graduate work in the humanities belies the idea that the humanities are in decline or have betrayed their vocation. Indeed the truly disapppointing things about graduate education today may have little to do with a university in ruins or with a lack of direction in the humanities. On the contrary, disappointment has much to do with the fact that there are many impressive applicants who must be denied admission to programs for which they are well qualified. It is also related to the fact that there are many recent PhDs who either do not find a position or have to settle for one that is makeshift, temporary, or incommensurate with their abilities. My own work with graduate students as well as my role in directing the Society for the Humanities at Cornell and the School of Criticism and Theory has brought me into contact with many scholars, especially younger scholars, who both stimulate an

rigid criteria of identity often have evanescent moments of glory. In any event, to the extent they are insular or self-involved, they contribute relatively little to neighboring disciplines or the university at large.[30]

I mentioned three types of specialization: occupational preprofessionalism, academic preprofessionalism, and the specialization (or professional "expertise") in generalities. In addressing the constructive possibilities of a sense of crisis in the humanities—the way crisis need not be exaggerated to apocalyptic proportions but may itself be a problematic sign of vitality, I mentioned the emergence of necessary, thought-provoking complexity,[31] the need for specific connections among complexities, and the role of the gadfly element. We thus end with neither a revivified old world nor a brave new world—each of which might turn out to be a Frankenstein monster.

The relation between the academy and the larger society on the model I have sketched involves an essential and significant role tension between scholarship or teaching and critical intellectual activ-

---

awareness of the remarkable talent going into academic life and the disturbing way in which this talent may not find suitable outlets in the current academic market.

[30] Here one may note the increase in the number of humanities centers together with the important role they play on campuses as gathering places (perhaps corrals) for gadflies, sites for cross-disciplinary work, and coordinators of events in the humanities. The number of humanities centers has increased rather dramatically in the last decade or so, and universities that do not have them often find that the creation of such a center is a top priority of humanists on campus. These centers are necessarily somewhat decentered in that they seek cross-disciplinary perspectives that may appear "blurred" or unfocused with respect to existing disciplinary and departmental lines. Yet, as I have already noted, some of the most important problems in the humanities and social sciences cannot be clearly assigned to one or another existing discipline or department. And some of the most interesting work in these fields is by scholars who do not fit neatly within existing departments, whether or not such scholars spend their professional careers within a given department or lead nomadic professional lives that take them from department to department or make them members of a number of departments. Moreover, the value I have attributed to articulatory practices does not prohibit the pursuit of lines of inquiry that cannot at present be articulated with others. Rather it implies the importance of pointing out the problem of articulation, even when significant linkages may not be found, and holding open the possibility of future linkages.

[31] I have in mind the complexity of a significant novel or a philosophical or historical text rather than, say, income tax forms, although the latter in their complexity certainly call for critical analysis. More generally, I am referring to the type of complexity that attempts to do justice to difficult problems rather than the formal, procedural, or instrumental complexity of finding increasingly intricate or involuted ways of applying an interpretive template, reading technology, or fixed idea (such as libido, desire, power, or trauma in certain of their uses).

ity. This tension requires, in my judgment, the creation of another category in the evaluation of a faculty member's performance and the appreciation of his or her experience—a category whose importance for the life of a university or college is underestimated at present. The three standard categories are research, teaching, and service. These often define the academician's professional or disciplinary identity, and they are the categories invoked when a department discusses the promotion or appointment of a colleague. The additional category I would propose is critical intellectual citizenship related to the role of the public intellectual (a category Readings enacts in his own way without thematizing).[32] This category refers to one's participation in the limited public sphere that exists in the academy and that is both found and generated in such events as conferences and public lectures. Active involvement in such events, especially events outside one's own speciality, obviously takes time from other activities, but it may also reinvigorate them and provide a forum for exploring ways of connecting work in the academy both across disciplines and to activites in the larger society. Such involvement is important for both faculty and students. Indeed it takes place in sites that allow somewhat different and possibly more basic and mutually challenging interchanges than those ordinarily offered by, or appropriate in, the classroom. The issues raised in these sites may also intersect with social, political, and cultural concerns in larger national and transnational public spheres.

To argue for the importance of critical intellectual citizenship is to affirm a conception of the university as offering a locus of discussion and debate about issues that are not confined to one discipline or area of expertise. It is also to stress the importance of providing forums for discussing policy issues that are often seen in extremely restricted, short-term, or inhibited ways in both the government and the media. But it is not to denigrate the importance of scholarship and teaching

[32] Jeffrey J. Williams's defense of what he terms secular professionalism (related to his conception of the university as a public franchise) may be compared to what I discuss as intellectual citizenship. See also Williams's discussion of public franchise (not reducible to corporate franchising on the McDonald's or Kentucky Fried model), in "Franchising the University," *Beyond the Corporate University: Culture and Pedagogy in the New Millennium*, ed. Henry Giroux and Kostas Myrsiades (New York: Rowman and Littlefield, 2001), 15–28. See also the valuable analyses in Bruce Robbins, *Feeling Global: Internationalism in Distress* (New York: New York University Press, 1999) and Bruce Robbins, ed., *The Phantom Public Sphere* (Minneapolis: University of Minnesota Press, 1993).

or to believe they should simply be superseded by policy-oriented discourse or political activity. Scholarship and teaching are the academic's business and, in the best of circumstances, his or her calling. One may criticize the view of the academic as a specialist who seeks self-replication in all students, as the priestly custodian of redemptive values, or as the self-promoting entrepreneur—even the leveraging tactician—of marketable products. But one may nonetheless insist on a tense relation between scholarly or pedagogic pursuits and broader sociocultural and intellectual concerns that take one beyond one's special area of expertise. The student looks for an engaging course of studies in college and anticipates a career. That career in most cases will not be in the academy. Yet a liberally educated person should be an intellectual as well as someone with the skills to enter the job market—an intellectual in the specific sense of one who has a relation of proximity and distance toward what she or he does and can through that relation raise at times critical questions for her- or himself and for the larger society. Scholar-teacher and student meet not only on the level of skills or credentialing but through a role that Jean-Paul Sartre defined well when he observed that an intellectual is someone who does not simply mind her or his own business. How not to mind one's own business is as important an issue as how to be competent enough to mind it well, and it need not imply a conception of the intellectual as appropriating the voice of others, speaking from on high, or seeking secular redemption.

I would conclude by observing that the humanities or the academy in general cannot be seen either as the privileged cultural or political force that will utterly transfigure society or as a discursive ivory tower offering an escape from it. But my critique of Readings and, more importantly, of larger tendencies in which I think he participates, does not imply that I am satisfied with my own explicitly modest and cautionary analyses and counterproposals. The latter at best contain elements that I find worth putting forward and defending—elements that bring into pedagogical and institutional focus problems that have concerned me throughout this book.

Epilogue

There have been some significant changes in the context of critical and self-critical thought in the last generation. About fifteen or twenty years ago it seemed plausible to look beyond the discipline of history to find tendencies to import into it in somewhat qualified form in order to raise questions for conventional or dominant historical procedures. Hence, with responses that ranged from a good-neighbor policy to a variation of the Cold War, if not a perception of an "axis of evil," one looked to formalism, structuralism, poststructuralism, literary theory, or what is more generally termed critical theory to locate levers that might displace certain disciplinary and, for some, overly restrictive tendencies in historiography. Recently one has looked to such noteworthy developments as postcolonial theory, queer theory, and critical race theory. But I think the import/export model no longer works that well. Nonetheless, historiography has often confronted critical challenges through very selective incorporation, and recently there has even been a backlash in a neopositivistic, narrowly empirical, antitheoretical, or at best domesticating direction, in which leftist and neoconservative tendencies may converge. Here some markers of the turn away from or even against theory are Gérard Noiriel's *Sur la "crise" de l'histoire*,[1] Richard J. Evans's *In Defense of History*,[2] and Keith Windschuttle's unforgettable *The Killing*

[1] (Paris: Belin, 1996).
[2] (New York: W. W. Norton, 1997).

of History: How a Discipline Is Being Murdered by Literary Critics and Social Theorists.[3] Russell Jacoby has been lambasting academic intellectuals and excoriating theoretical orientations in a manner that at times runs together neoconservatism and seeming leftism—a strange intellectual phantasmagoria in which Theodor Adorno becomes the specular image of Leo Strauss. The antitheoretical, left-right convergence is especially evident in the collection (including an essay by Jacoby) edited by Elizabeth Fox-Genovese and Elisabeth Lasch-Quinn, *Reconstructing History: The Emergence of a New Historical Society*[4]—a series of manifestos that are dedicated to the editors' fathers (as well as a grandfather) and are presumed to serve the interests of an intellectually conservative historical society.

Despite the obvious limitations of the import/export model of exchanges in the academy, the development within literary studies of cultural studies and the new historicism has suggested possible interactions with, even linkages to, historiography that warrant greater attention by professional historians. Unfortunately, there has at times been active resistance or dismissive denigration. The relatively subdued role of theory in cultural studies might seem to make it appealing to more traditional historians, but it has also tended to include features that are not congenial to many in the profession, such as a largely ahistorical or synchronic focus (particularly in the study of mass media and consumerism) and monolingual and noncomparative emphases (whether in terms of American, English, French, or German cultural studies). Hence it has been subject to criticism both by critical theorists and by theory-averse historians. More than cultural studies, the new historicism has been marked, often in manifest fashion, by recent critical theories, notably varieties of poststructuralism (with Foucault and deconstruction often having pride of place). But its reliance on the telltale anecdote, at least as an inaugural gesture in inquiry, and its typical use of a montage technique in juxtaposing texts or signifying practices from across the sociocultural map, have made its sense of context often seem idiosyncratic if not arbitrary to historians. These limitations have been widely noticed and do not eliminate the more valuable dimensions of work in both

---

[3] (Paddington, Australia: Macleay Press, 1996).

[4] (New York: Routledge, 1999). Jacoby's essay is "A New Intellectual History?" (94–118); reprinted from *American Historical Review* 97 (1992): 405–24, which also includes my critical rejoinder.

cultural studies and the new historicism.[5] Moreover, cultural studies looking to the so-called Birmingham school, which included such figures as E. P. Thompson, Raymond Williams, and Richard Hoggart, not only had a reference point in which the historical dimension (including extensive archival work) was pronounced but one that became a model of research for many historians, especially those who turned historical inquiry in the direction of experience and culture, especially popular culture. And the new historicism has had mutually beneficial interactions with historiography and its professional practitioners such as Thomas Laqueur and Carla Hesse, as well as some not at Berkeley or involved in the journal *Representations*.

Here an interesting phenomenon is the discussion, in the pages of *American Historical Review*, of the book *Beyond the Cultural Turn*, edited by Victoria E. Bonnell (a sociologist) and Lynn Hunt (a historian and president of the American Historical Association in 2002–3) and containing contributions from other notable sociologists and historians.[6] It may be misguided to place too much emphasis on this book, which resulted from a conference and has the usual divergence and unevenness in its contributions. But the fact that it was selected for special attention by *American Historical Review* gives it a particular status and makes it a focus of attention. In the *AHR* the book is discussed by Ronald Grigor Suny, trained as a professional historian but now in a department of political science, Patrick Brantlinger, a professor of English with a marked interest in history and culture, and Richard Handler, an anthropologist with an affirmed affiliation with the work of Franz Boas.

There is an obvious interdisciplinarity in the selection of commentators as well as in the choice of an interdisciplinary book for focused discussion about current trends in historiography. But, while there is some attention to the role of literary studies and critical theory (particularly pronounced in Brantlinger's contribution), the more decided emphasis is on the relation of history to (or simply inclusion in) the social sciences, and there is arguably a de-emphasis in the cast of

[5] See, for example, the interesting retrospect and prospect in Catherine Gallagher and Stephen Greenblatt, *Practicing New Historicism* (Chicago: University of Chicago Press, 2000) as well as the references in Patrick Brantlinger, "A Response to *Beyond the Cultural Turn*," *American Historical Review* 107 (2002): 1500–1511, to which I refer below.

[6] *Beyond the Cultural Turn* (Berkeley: University of California Press, 1999); *American Historical Review* 107 (2002): 1475–1520.

disciplinary or subdisciplinary fields: intellectual history, including its increasingly close interaction with both cultural history and critical theory, is not presented by the editors as a subdiscipline in dialogue with social and cultural history, although its somewhat liminal status in the historical profession might make it a likely candidate for an approach to inter- or cross-disciplinarity that looks within, as well as across, disciplines.[7] This selectivity may to some extent be contrasted to the approach of the book edited ten years earlier by Lynn Hunt that acts as a foil for *Beyond the Cultural Turn: The New Cultural History*.[8] In the earlier book intellectual history was at least accommodated under an expanded conception of cultural history. One reason why the relative de-emphasis in the later book is both worrisome and telltale is that intellectual history has been a significant conduit for more theoretical and self-critical tendencies within the historical profession, at times to the point of providing it with a gadfly element or a source of fruitful self-questioning.[9]

---

[7] One may note the similarity to Carolyn Steedman's orientation, discussed in the Introduction. *Beyond the Cultural Turn* includes an afterword by Hayden White. White, however, is not concerned about specific differences, or the interplay of subdisciplines, within professional historiography and their implication for the relations between history and other disciplines. His discussion both remains within the terms set by earlier contributions to the volume and turns to a broad discussion of the "more general issues—philosophical, theoretical, ideological, and methodological" on which he thinks the essays in the book bear (315). One may also note the presence of Jerrold Seigel's essay, "Problematizing the Self," which largely follows a relatively atheoretical "history-of-ideas" approach, reshaped and reinvigorated in light of Geertz's work. Its interpretations or readings of figures such as Nietzsche, Heidegger, Foucault, and Derrida are made to fit the theme of the "self," and its largely negative assumptions concerning poststructuralism, or even varieties of critical theory in general, are close to those of the editors. In any case it is difficult to see its relation to the emphases of the editors' framing introduction, especially with respect to the need for a reassertion of the social in the face of a cultural turn. It is noteworthy that there is only a single reference to White's afterword in the essays of Suny (1499) and Handler (1520) and none in any of the review essays to Seigel's contribution.

[8] (Berkeley: University of California Press, 1989).

[9] Bonnell and Hunt at times make mitigated defenses of theory. But they insist that "even the more theoretical essays included here have a resolutely empirical cast" (23). And despite their own effort to question the desirability of the theory/practice divide, their concluding words function to reinforce it: "Change, when it comes, will no doubt follow from something other than theoretical presciption. It will come out of new practices, embedded in the social world in ways that we cannot see" (27). Why reduce theory to prescription or ignore the role of theoretical practices that may well be bound up with other practices, including forms of research and "embedded" social action? Practices (including linguistic practices) are important, but they should not

In their introduction to the volume, Bonnell and Hunt indicate the reasons for the putative cultural turn in history inaugurated by two landmark texts of 1973: Hayden White's *Metahistory: The Historical Imagination in Nineteenth-Century Europe* and Clifford Geertz's *Interpretation of Cultures: Selected Essays*. They also see the limitations of the import/export model, and, along with some of their contributors, believe that the influence of Geertz and White may have been too great, or at least too uncritically and selectively adopted, in areas of historiography (a point they justifiably apply more to the reception of Geertz than to that of White). But they do not trace the reception of Geertz's and White's texts in various disciplines, which might provide a more concrete and critical estimate of their actual role as well as of significant divergences from their approaches with respect to the nature and implications of a putative "cultural turn." Indeed they may amalgamate too much under the banner of Geertz and White as well as assimilate, or at least approximate too readily, other theorists such as Foucault, Derrida, and Bourdieu. As Bonnell and Hunt at times recognize, schematic lumping may obscure the finer discriminations in recent developments, as well as the more thoroughgoing critiques of various figures and tendencies, both within and across disciplines.[10]

Bonnell and Hunt formulate in the following terms the reasons for the "turn" to culture and the need for an *Aufhebung* of cultural and social orientations:

> Frustrated with the limitations of social history and historical
> sociology—frustrated, that is, by the constraints of a commonsensical,

---

uncritically become a new ground or final instance. Especially when "practice" is opposed in misleadingly binaristic terms to "theory," one may not leave sufficient space for critical reflection about either practice or theory.

[10] For a critique of Geertz, in a widely read book published more than a decade before *Beyond the Cultural Turn*, see Vincent Crapanzano, "Hermes' Dilemma: The Masking of Subversion in Ethnographic Description," in *Writing Culture: The Poetics and Politics of Ethnography*, ed. James Clifford and George E. Marcus (Berkeley: University of California Press, 1986), 51–76. For my own at times convergent critique, published shortly after (and without knowledge of) *Writing Culture*, see *Soundings in Critical Theory* (Ithaca: Cornell University Press, 1989), chap. 5. See also the related argument in my "Is Everyone a *Mentalité* Case? Transference and the 'Culture' Concept" included as chapter 3 in *History and Criticism* (Ithaca: Cornell University Press, 1985).

usually materialist notion of the social—social historians and historical sociologists began to turn in a cultural direction and to look at the cultural contexts in which people (either in groups or individuals) acted. More and more often, they devised research topics that foregrounded symbols, rituals, discourse, and cultural practices rather than social structure or social class. As we have seen, they often turned to anthropologists for guidance. This linguistic turn was further fueled by the emergence first of structuralism and then of its successor, poststructuralism. (8)

The authors indicate their concern about the implications of this "turn" from the social to the cultural as well as their desire for a renewed sense of disciplinarity:

> To make a long and complicated story overly schematic, the cultural turn threatened to efface all reference to social context or causes and offered no particular standard of judgment to replace the seemingly more rigorous and systematic approaches that had predominated in the 1960s and 1970s. Detached from their previous assumptions, cultural methods no longer seemed to have any foundations. (9–10) . . . Dialogue among the disciplines depends in part on a strong sense of their differences from each other: exchange is not needed if everything is the same: interdisciplinarity can only work if there are in fact disciplinary differences. Thus a renewed emphasis on the disciplinary difference, or "redisciplinarization," seems to be in order. (14)

It is difficult to know how to evaluate claims and contentions made in so sweeping a manner that they escape the very standards of judgment that the editors opine have been placed in jeopardy by the cultural turn. A close analysis of some prominent texts or artifacts, while not offering the representative range necessary for broad (and perforce contestable) generalizations, would at least have provided the discussion with greater specificity and critical edge. Did the interest in "symbols, rituals, discourse, and cultural practices" really come with the sacrifice of attention to "social structure or social class"? Did this process occur in the work of William Sewell, who is one of their primary reference points and a prominent contributor to the volume? His *Work and Revolution in France: The Language of Labor from the Old Regime to 1849* (1980) would seem to be a relatively successful instance of a viable integration of culture and society in an approach to problems.[11] Nor would the editors' plaint apply to E. P Thompson, whose *Making of the English Working Class* (1963) serves as a crucial text in *Beyond the Cultural Turn*, for, as one of the contributors, Richard Biernacki, acknowledges, Thompson's work "bridged the older social and the newer cultural history," used particulars "to illustrate the premise that the economy becomes a historical force only as it is encoded in culture and interpreted in experience" (65), saw culture as indispensable but not totally autonomous (66), and even offered "compelling evidence of culture's dependency" with respect to "the needs of capital" (67). I would add that Thompson's own "turn" to culture and experience was directed at a more fine-tuned analysis of class and social structure and, if anything, came with a reliance on

---

[11] Both William Sewell, in "The Concept(s) of Culture," and Richard Biernacki, in "Method and Metaphor," their contributions to *Beyond the Cultural Turn*, focus on practice. Sewell actually attempts to define culture in terms of practice, which he distinguishes from culture as a system of symbols and meanings. The latter definition stems from Geertz and was presumably hegemonic in the 1960s and 1970s. The "concept of culture as practice . . . has become increasingly prominent in the 1980s and 1990s" (43). Sewell further specifies culture as practice in terms of Ann Swidler's notion of "a 'tool kit' composed of a 'repertoire' of 'strategies of action' " (45). Hence "culture is not a coherent system of symbols and meanings but a diverse collection of 'tools' that, as the metaphor indicates, are to be understood as means for the performance of action" (46). One may accept the former assertion but find the latter one excessively restrictive and even misleading as well as ideologically invested in an inexplicit manner. Culture as a collection of tools would overly circumscribe the notion of performativity and even seem to go in the direction of a narrowly instrumental conception, indeed converge with aspects of the type of "rational choice" theory that someone like Suny would like to escape, or at least counteract, by invoking a broad-ranging concept of culture. Biernacki distinguishes practice from the semiotic, which he equates with verbal sign systems. He sees practice as another dimension of Geertz's thought that the latter termed "the informal logic of actual life" (quoted 75). Practice in this sense is still symbolic (or signifying) but is implicit in action and "not articulated discursively." It constitutes a "tacit know-how" in bodily movements (for example, the making and operating of instruments), an "ethos or style" (for example, in this-worldly asceticism that outlasts the Protestant ethic), and a circulation of "messages apart from the signs those practices use" (77) (for example, the experience of reading a newspaper as part of the creation of an anonymous "imagined" national community). Biernacki also refers to the interesting case of double-entry bookkeeping that was, in "the era of capitalist takeoff," applied by accountants in deficient ways, which indicates that its role was not purely instrumental, in terms of profit making, but "fit into a broader ethos of calculation, abstraction from context, and spatial representation of information independent of the culturally framed goals and ultimate meaning of conduct" (76). Despite the vagueness of certain of his formulations, Biernacki recognizes that language uses may themselves be articulated in terms of implicit practical schemas that do not always conform to what people say about what they are doing in language, and he, like Sewell, points

empiricism and a somewhat deceptive resistance to theory. In addition, Thompson's approach to religion was at best shortsighted and insensitive, and it fell within what one might argue has been a broader neglect of the significance of religion and its secular displacements (including ritual) in modern thought (continuing a trend that looks, very selectively, for guidance in the Enlightenment).[12] Moreover, even Biernacki, who recognizes that "the celebrated turn to cultural history rested on unacknowledged continuity" (including continuity with earlier tendencies in social history and sociology), simply assumes that the only alternative to essentialism or foundationalism is radical constructivism, without noting the interdependence and mutual reinforcement of this pair of binary opposites.

Even if certain historians believe they turned from society to culture, one might want to test that belief against their actual practice in order to arrive at a better understanding (or "theory") of that practice. And can one vertiginously conflate the turn to anthropology, the cultural turn, and the linguistic turn (not to mention the turn to theory) even if one takes Geertz as one's representative figure? Even those who continue to stress the importance of language use, including its role in critically thought-provoking signifying practices, might nonetheless see this conflation as especially dubious in the light of the widespread, long-standing emphasis on performativity (including bodily gestures or movement) not only in language narrowly construed, but also in theater, dance, music, and painting as well as in sociocultural rituals, festivals, and activities of all sorts. Moreover, Derrida's famous or notorious notion of textuality (dating from *Of Grammatology*, first published in 1967) did not apply only to language

---

to performative uses of language that cannot be reduced to representational ones. It should be obvious that "practice" in the above senses undercuts the opposition between culture and society. A further problem is how various types of signifying practice relate to one another, including (I would add) the extent to which theories actually inform the practices (including language uses) to which they refer or have other purposes and functions (for example, self-legitimation, effects of sublimity, or an attempt to attain purity and to transcend implication in the empirical and referential).

[12] For a discussion of *The Making of the English Working Class* that recognizes its importance yet points to its limitations in the treatment of women, see Joan Wallach Scott, *Gender and the Politics of History* (New York: Columbia University Press, 1988), chap. 4. Scott's book, which insistently combines social and cultural history, might be cited as another example of the questionable status of the idea of a movement from the social to the cultural after the 1970s.

in any delimited sense but was extended to all instituted traces in a manner that made it converge in important ways with multiple signifying practices. Is Geertz's relatively commonsensical notion of text (as written, spoken, or read—indeed scripted—language analogized to culture) similar to Derrida's, and does it have the same critical implications? How can one refer to the significance of Foucault for both research and self-understanding and unproblematically assert that "'redisciplinization' seems to be in order"? And is the only alternative to sharp if not decisive disciplinary boundaries the notion of a bland, homogenizing sameness? Where is the complicating notion of "differences within" disciplines that was a hallmark of poststructural thought? And do conceptions of hybridity or *métissage* have no valid application to disciplinary practices? If one has a clear-cut, uncontested idea of disciplinary identity, how does one avoid the overly disciplinarian notion that a department controls a set of problems and procedures of inquiry or "owns" a discipline and its practitioners (who, to be authentic, must "belong" to the department)? One may raise these questions while still recognizing the value of training in those practices of a discipline that have a pragmatic coherence and might be best studied through the ethnographic methods made familiar by science studies.

Cavils about specific arguments or points may be an endless and fruitless task. Still, what is open to question in the editors' rhetoric is an ideological imperative based on a sense of loss, indeed of a past we have lost and must struggle to get back again if only to include it in a higher-order synthesis. This past itself, despite its felt constraints and frustrations, was presumably the site of rigorous standards, foundations, and disciplinarity. These plaints are of course familiar as the neoconservative fallout of the culture wars, and it is disconcerting to see them regenerated in a relatively unself-conscious fashion in a work of serious scholarship.[13]

The orientating framework of *Beyond the Cultural Turn*, with its exclusions, de-emphases, or begged questions, is in certain respects

[13] In important ways, *Beyond the Cultural Turn*, particularly as framed by its editors, is close in incentive to *Telling the Truth about History* (New York: W. W. Norton, 1994) by Joyce Appleby, Lynn Hunt, and Margaret Jacob. The latter book bases its argument on the opposition between a lost past in which there putatively was "a single narrative of national history that most Americans accepted as part of their heritage" and a present time of troubles in which "an increasing emphasis" is placed not on culture in general but on multiculturalism—"the diversity of ethnic, racial, and

echoed in the introductory words provided by the editorial staff of
The American Historical Review:

> One of the most dramatic shifts in our discipline between the 1960s and
> the 1980s was the increasing number of professional historians who
> began to describe themselves as "new social historians" and see their
> work as borrowing from or brushing up against one or another social
> science discipline. Then, beginning in the 1980s, the percentage of
> professional historians who claimed an affiliation with the "new
> cultural history" started to grow markedly. And this in turn led to
> novel ideas about connections between history and neighboring fields,
> including branches of the humanities such as literary criticism. . . . The
> review essays that follow were commissioned with an eye toward
> expanding the discussion beyond the disciplines of the coeditors
> [Bonnell and Hunt], in an effort to see how the relationship between
> the "social" and the "cultural" and recent changes in historical practice
> look when viewed from other intellectual borderlands. (1475)

Despite the absence of statistics to back up the impressionistic generalizations and, more importantly, of inquiry into what historians
using certain labels were actually doing, these introductory words
enunciate a new noble dream. The dream would have been less exclusionary if it had taken up some of the elements insufficiently evident
in the book but pointed to in the review essays themselves, notably
the role of critical self-reflection as it bears on differences within—not
simply between or among—disciplines. In the introductory comments in the *AHR*, the statement of "trends" is itself not simply
descriptive but performative and even normative, especially when it
appears in the pages of what is widely taken to be the official journal
of a professional discipline in the United States. These initial words
are not only stating what has presumably happened but lay out an
agenda (one in which the humanities would appear to be found in
neighboring fields rather than in part constitutive of the complex,

---

gender experience" accompanied by "a deep skepticism about whether the narrative
of America's achievements comprises anything more than a self-congratulatory
masking [of] the power of elites." The authors even wax (post)apocalyptic in asserting that "history has been shaken down to its scientific and cultural foundations at
the very time that those foundations themselves are being contested" (1).

internally dialogized, "identity" of professional history itself as both a social-scientific and a humanistic discipline). The variable relation of the agenda to the interests and orientations of the historians and sociologists who contribute to the volume under discussion is an unmarked feature of the proceedings that is obvious but merits mention.

The review essays are in important respects quite different from one another, but, especially in the cases of Brantlinger and Handler, they diverge in certain ways from the agenda enunciated by the editors of *Beyond the Cultural Turn* and repeated by the staff of the *AHR*. One feature the review essays nonetheless share is the sense that "beyond" in the title of the book is closely related to "before," and the seeming movement—or at least the call for a movement—beyond the "cultural turn" may be indicative not simply of continuities but of uneven developments or at times a possible move backward, notably toward a form of social history that was undertheorized or based on questionable assumptions. These assumptions involved an overly sharp divide between society and culture (often seen as epiphenomenal) and a marginalization of approaches (including variants of intellectual history) that stressed the less "ordinary" or more exceptional products of cultural activity and the way in which texts (or signifying practices), while certainly informed by multiple social and cultural contexts, might also rework or pose challenges to those contexts. Such texts or artifacts simultaneously demand a more-than-contextualizing or objectifying response from the reader (whether in terms of society or culture), including the historian sensitive to the problem of his or her implication in problems under study and aware of current contexts of inquiry and debate.[14] Indeed it seems that the

[14] The essays by Suny, Brantlinger, and Handler play off against one another in thought-provoking ways. Suny is justifiably concerned with the turn to "rational choice" theory in political science and the procrustean manner in which it eliminates a multiplicity of concerns that are pronounced in cultural history. Hence his primary incentive is understandably to show the interest of a broad-based study of culture, prominently including a stress on the importance of experience. But, seen from within historiography and critical theory, Suny's approach is normalizing or conventionalizing in that it is irenic and insufficiently addressed to significant problems, including the very understanding of culture and experience. Such problems are more at issue in Brantlinger's contribution, which both notes the questionable denigration of cultural studies and the new historicism in *Beyond the Cultural Turn* and explores the virtues and limitations of contextualization with respect to "worklike" cultural artifacts that may challenge their contexts of production or reception and are themselves more or less significant historical events. He also pointedly raises the question of

editors of *Beyond the Cultural Turn* and some of its contributors are inclined to resist certain transitions in historiography, notably those giving it a more accentuated theoretical, self-reflexive, self-critical, responsive, and internally dialogized dimension signaled, for example, by the problem of transferential relations to both objects of study and other inquirers as well as the need to work through those relations in as viable a manner as possible. Moreover, psychoanalysis, in its relation to self, society, and culture, has at most a very restricted place "beyond the cultural turn" that may turn away from too many problems on the pretext of turning toward new, or at least more "real" or "fundamental," ones.

I think we are at the point where critically constructive exchanges have become possible between different historians, say social, cultural, and intellectual historians, as well as between historians and those in other departments or disciplines (including anthropologists and sociologists, not only on ethnographic methods in microhistory but, for example, on the issue of transferential relations to the other, including the question of who is or is not deemed a worthy interlocutor or critical voice and not simply an informant, object of study, or outsider from another discipline). But this possibility may be aborted through born-again positivism, disciplinary retrenchment, and a more or less informed aversion to critical-theoretical reflection. It may also be aborted through disciplinary identity politics. Here, for example, the historian may legitimate an aversion to theory by means of an implicit or explicit reliance on an invidious notion of the "working historian" or an understanding of history as a theory-averse, craftlike "practice" one simply learns by doing. Yet any field, including its craftlike dimensions, becomes poorer if it is not

---

whether "thick description" (the widely accepted term put forward by Clifford Geertz, who remains the anthropologist of preference in *Beyond the Cultural Turn*) is less a theoretical concept than a description of—even a "pragmatic excuse for"—what historians and anthropologists generally do (1503). Handler objects to the divide between culture and society, which becomes a pretext for a return to a presemiological and perhaps precritical social history. He defends a sociocultural approach that fruitfully questions the binary opposition between "material" and "symbolic" culture, but he may not be sufficiently alert to the problematic dimensions of radical constructivism or its conflation with the study of semiotic processes in general (whose complex, internally divided, and at times opaque dimensions are not sufficiently addressed in a constructivism that sees processes of "construction" in overly intentional, conscious, determinate, goal-oriented, and, in any case, anthropocentric terms).

quickened by critical reflection and internal self-questioning, including at times the internalization or recognition as relevant of questions coming from other fields. But, by the same token, critically constructive exchanges are not well served by insistent theoreticism or high-altitude theory that self-referentially feeds on itself, construes historical phenomena as mere instantiations of transhistorical processes, and may even disparage historical research.

The important critique of monolingualism and the insistence on anticipating with caution and respect that the other may well speak a language that I may not fully master or even understand should be extended beyond the area of so-called natural languages, such as Spanish, Urdu, or Tewa, and applied as well to languages within and across natural languages, including both vernacular variations and the various languages of critical theory. One insufficiently recognized and even validated form of linguistic imperialism and ethnocentrism is the belief that various uses of languages should be translated without significant loss or remainder into the language recognized as transparent, normative, or ordinary (in effect normalizing) within a field or discipline. Such a belief may implicitly attest to the assumption that theory is unnecessary—a mere obfuscating jargon or alienated and alienating affectation. Without denying the value in what Gramsci or E. P. Thompson saw as the lived and at times powerfully articulated philosophy of the oppressed, we face the challenge of exploring the possibilities and limits of mutual translation between various uses of language, including the way critical theories may test not only one another but also "ordinary" language and its built-in assumptions, as well as the way translations in the direction of the "ordinary" may at times bring back to earth—for a periodic reality check, refueling, or even a parodic thump—theories that fly too high, are self-referentially involuted, or rashly all-consuming.

Even more important, it is necessary to insist on the lack of fit between significant problems and professional disciplines that attempt to "house" or at times own them. Problems such as the parameters of experience or identity and the role of trauma or violence are cross- or transdisciplinary in that they cut across disciplines and may be addressed—or marginalized and not sufficiently addressed—in various disciplines.[15] They may at times give rise to

---

[15] See the fruitful, cross-disciplinary engagement with the problem of violence and visual culture in Martin Jay, *Refractions of Violence* (New York: Routledge, 2003).

more or less evanescent subdisciplines such as "trauma studies." But the basic point is that the nonfit between significant problems and disciplines is not a reason for either the marginalization of problems or the cashiering of disciplines. It is a reason for exploring problems in their complexity, even if this takes one beyond recognizable disciplinary boundaries or into neighboring, even "alien," disciplines (for example, neurophysiology or narrative medecine in the case of trauma studies). It is also a reason for recognizing and affirming the flexibility and openness of disciplines as well as the realization that a contribution to them, or at least an initiative worth taking seriously in them, may be made by someone who is not within a given department or professional guild. Even more basically, it is an occasion to recognize and try to render enabling the exchange between various discourses (including "theory" and "ordinary" languages) and between problems and disciplines (including different, tensely related tendencies within disciplines).

I have referred to the sacralization, or rendering sublime, of trauma. A similar tendency exists with respect to violence, which is the typical way of breaking the psyche's protective shield or forcefully transgressing normative limits and thereby causing traumatization. Hence trauma and violence may be linked conceptually and evaluatively in a manner that construes them as ecstatic experiences or bases of *jouissance*, indeed the constituents of the nonsymbolizable "real." This tendency is especially prevalent in apocalyptic and postapocalyptic thinking. And, at least in its modern figuration, violence has been replete with sacrificial motifs and seen as a redemptive or regenerative force for the individual and the group. René Girard argued that what was sacred or sacralized in sacrifice was violence itself. He thought he was making an earthshaking, transhistorical, anthropological discovery of "things hidden since the foundation of the world."[16] He may simply have been situating his thought in a broad intellectual and cultural current of modernity and articulating one of its crucial but extremely problematic components. With varying degrees of critical distance on the nexus linking violence, trauma, sacrifice, the sacred, and the sublime, this current includes figures as different as de Maistre, Hegel, and Nietzsche. What I would point out is

[16] See *Things Hidden since the Foundation of the World,* trans. Stephen Bann and Michael Metteer (1978; Stanford: Stanford University Press, 1987) and *Violence and the Sacred,* trans. Patrick Gregory (1972; Baltimore: Johns Hopkins University Press, 1977).

the dimension, coming into prominence in the twentieth century, wherein critical distance is reduced to a minimum or disappears and violence is justified or glorified as a transformative force. In this sense violence is not seen as always problematic and at best only partially justifiable in terms of the context and the ends toward which it is directed but as something that runs counter to or even transcends instrumental reason and constitutes an apocalyptic, redemptive power. Hence it is indeed sacred or sacralizing or, in more secular terms, a glorious bearer and giver of an exhilarating, unrepresentable experience presumably beyond experience and transcendently out of this world. Perhaps the most dire and dreadful anti-Enlightenment inclination—one that may begin with a critique of instrumental rationality but at times shades into an at best equivocal evocation, "sublimation," or even glorification of violence and trauma—is to render sacred or sublime what attracts and repels and what one does not fully understand.

One finds an unabashed apology for violence in Georges Sorel's *Reflections on Violence*, a work that Zeev Sternhell has seen as crucial for fascists despite its affirmed "leftist" anarcho-syndicalism and pro-letarian leanings.[17] The crucial point is that Sorel's apology focuses on violence as a regenerative or redemptive force that will transfigure civilization, mark the return of heroic values, and end the reign of bourgeois complacency and instrumental or calculative rationality. Its vehicle, the proletarian general strike, is termed a "complete catas-trophe" (147) and is left utterly void of content. The specification of alternative institutions or practices is intentionally avoided in favor of tactics and calls to action. The note of the sublime is struck repeat-edly in the book, especially in its concluding pages. Its final words are: "It is to violence that Socialism owes those high ethical values by means of which it brings *salvation* to the modern world" (295). In Sorel there is a linkage among the sublime, the quasi-religious, art, and work in that violence will usher in the reign of creative, productive work in the context of self-sacrificial, transcendent values. Moreover, he postulates a dichotomy between justifiable proletarian violence (the good object) and state or bourgeois violence (the bad object). The latter was presumably manifest in the Terror during the French

[17] Sorel, *Reflections on Violence*, trans. T. E. Hulme (1915; New York: Peter Smith, 1941); Sternhell, *Neither Right nor Left: Fascist Ideology in France*, trans. David Meisel (1983; Berkeley: University of California Press, 1986).

Revolution and is supposedly worlds apart from the violence and terror of the proletarian general strike, which is the wellspring of transfiguration and salvation. Yet the proletariat itself seems like little more than the bearer of or cipher for violent transformation, and Sorel's later turn in an antisemitic and nationalistic direction was motivated by the same set of redemptive desires as were found in his earlier apology for apocalyptic violence and the anti-statist myth of the general strike. What is especially striking about his *Reflections on Violence* is the unmediated combination of high-altitude theory untested by experience, including an abstract apology for violence, and petty journalistic detail agitated by vitriolic polemic against enemies, particularly Jean Jaurès, who embodied the reasonable, reformist socialism that was anathema to Sorel's all-or-nothing, dogmatic implacability.

Sorel was quite important for the early Walter Benjamin of the "Critique of Violence," which is a critique only at most in a neo-Kantian sense and which conveys a rather uncritical, quasi-religious, "sublimating" apology for a certain sort of violence.[18] Active in it is the binary opposition between mythical, state, preservative, representational violence, which is bad, and divine, absolute, pure, redemptive violence (linked to the proletarian general strike), which is good. Good, or more precisely, sublime or quasi-sacred violence (in a sense, inaugural or originary violence situated beyond good and evil) is unrepresentable and performatively undermines the entire system of representation. This is not the place for a more extended analysis of Benjamin's tangled discussion, but it may be noted that Derrida provides a discussion of it that manifests a kind of *fort/da* attraction and repulsion with respect to Benjamin's line of thought, sympathizing with if not emulating it at points (notably with respect to an originary, revolutionary *coup de force*) and then drawing back, especially when analogies are made to fascism.[19]

[18] "Critique of Violence," in Walter Benjamin, *Reflections: Essays, Aphorisms, Autobiographical Writings*, ed. Peter Demetz, trans. Edmund Jephcott (1920/21; New York: Harcourt Brace Jovanovich, 1978), 277–300.

[19] On these questions, see my "Violence, Justice, and the Force of Law," *Cardozo Law Review* 11 (1990): 1065–78, which was written as a response for a conference at the Cardozo Law School, where Derrida delivered an earlier version of his essay not including the addenda referring to Nazism and the Holocaust. (The fact that the latter are addenda postdating my essay is not mentioned in the issue of the *Cardozo Law Review* in which the essays appear.) Derrida's essay, "The Force of Law: The 'Mystical' Foundation of Authority," may be found in the aforementioned volume of the

Sorel does not seem to be a crucial reference for Georges Bataille, although Bataille was familiar with Benjamin's thought, and Bataille explicitly yet tortuously engaged the problem of the relation between fascism and his own apology for violence in the traumatic context of sacrifice, useless expenditure (*dépense*), and the uncompromising critique of instrumental rationality (including for a time a defense of *surfascisme* or the escalating appeal to fascist procedures, including violence, presumably in opposing fascism). Bataille had the virtue of bringing out the limitations of instrumental rationality and economism as well as the persistent role of sacralizing and sacrificial forces, including their often covert or encrypted appeal in modernity. But, as intimated earlier, his rereading of Durkheim and Mauss, influenced in part by both surrealism and his reading of Nietzsche, tended to reverse Durkheim's and Mauss's emphasis on the role of legitimate limits as resistances to transgression and excess. Instead he formulated a view of social existence that stressed the value of excess, including violent and sacrificial excess, in which limits threatened to become little more than inducements to transgression.[20] In any event, Bataille was important in bringing a set of considerations into postwar French thought and modern European thought more generally, not only for René Girard but for many others (including Foucault).

The dubious sides of excess, transgression, and the apology for "sublime" violence were of course manifest in their role in fascism and Nazism. Despite the questionable nature of his own theoretical and ideological frame of reference, in which unfettered Deleuzian desire seems the only viable option to fascist rigidity, Klaus Theweleit provides valuable analyses of the violent, misogynistic, antisemitic fantasies of the Freikorps, notably in the writings of such important figures as Ernst Jünger and Ernst von Salomon.[21] It would be desirable to carry such analyses into the discussion of later fascists and Nazis, especially in light of the overly restricted tendency to see the Holocaust predominantly if not exclusively in terms of instrumental

---

Cardozo Law Review (920–1045) and in *Deconstruction and the Possibility of Justice*, ed. Drucilla Cornell et al. (New York: Routledge, 1992).

[20] See the selections in the appropriately entitled *Visions of Excess: Selected Writings, 1927–1939*, ed. Alan Stoekl, trans. Allan Stoekl with Carl R. Lovitt and Donald M. Leslie Jr. (Minneapolis: University of Minnesota Press, 1985).

[21] *Male Fantasies*, trans. Erica Carter and Chris Turner in collaboration with Stephen Conway, 2 vols. (1978; Minneapolis: University of Minnesota Press, 1987, 1989).

rationality, the machinery of destruction, and industrialized mass murder.[22] It would also be desirable to carry forward lines of inquiry already under way that examine the hypothesis that the Nazi genocide may have displaced or at least paralleled practices that were prevalent and, for many, acceptable in the colonies when applied to people of color. There are hints of this view in the work of Frantz Fanon, although there is also the questionable tendency to dichotomize between good and bad violence and to justify anticolonial violence undertaken by people of color not simply strategically but as therapeutic and transfigurative in terms at times uncomfortably close to the views of Sorel or the early Benjamin. But it is important both historically and critically to understand the way colonial violence of the sort Fanon attacked was at times of genocidal proportions and may well have been analogous to, or even one basis for, later initiatives that have been seen, at times in too unqualified a form and too much within an exclusively Eurocentric context, as unique, totally unexpected, and unprecedented.

Here I would mention what I think is an insufficiently known book, a mixed generic initiative that is not a work of history but includes very significant historical material and valuable critical analysis: Sven Lindqvist's *"Exterminate All The Brutes."*[23] The book is subtitled "One

[22] Theweleit asserts: "To examine fascist oratory in terms of the rhetorical strategies of Hitler or Goebbels alone would be to distort the picture. All fascist phenomena are phenomena of groups, strata, organizations. It does make sense, on the other hand, to direct attention to the 'Führer' from the perspective of fascism in general; almost every phenomenon examined in this book can be found in either *Mein Kampf* or Hitler's speeches. Hitler is not some unique monster, but rather the most significant condensation of the drives motivating the average soldier male after 1914." *Male Fantasies,* 2: 118n.

[23] Trans. from the Swedish by Joan Tate (1992; New York: New Press, 1996). On related problems, see Richard L. Rubenstein, *The Age of Triage: Fear and Hope in an Overcrowded World* (Boston: Beacon Press, 1983) and *Genocide in the Modern Age: Etiology and Case Studies of Mass Death,* ed. Isidor Walliman and Michael N. Dobkowski (1987; Syracuse: Syracuse University Press, 2000). See also Joan Dayan, *Haiti, History, and the Gods* (Berkeley: University of California Press, 1998). In an argument that may be read as paralleling Lindqvist's, Dayan traces the background of Sade's work to practices of slave owners in Haiti, notably with respect to the *Code Noir.* She comes to the conclusion that Sade was not anomalous. He was imaginatively yet realistically importing into Europe "sadistic" practices common in the treatment of slaves in Haiti and elsewhere. The works of Rubenstein, Lindqvist, Dayan, and others give additional meaning to Walter Benjamin's famous statement that every document of civilization is also a document of barbarism, although (as Rubenstein insists) the reference to barbarism may function deceptively to divert attention from the darkness at the heart of civilization and "modernity" themselves.

Man's Odyssey into the Heart of Darkness and the Origins of European Genocide." Lindqvist sets out ostensibly on a quest to find the sources of Kurtz's scribbled last words in Joseph Conrad's *Heart of Darkness* (quoted in the title of Lindqvist's book) and locates them in Conrad's familiarity, both through journals or newspapers and his own experience, with extreme and typically excessive practices in the colonies. In Lindqvist, an apparently literary project does not need to be juxtaposed or forcibly yoked to historical material; it can be accomplished only by attention to such material—in fact it leads unavoidably to it. Conrad's novel is bitterly realistic in a manner that does not detract from its aesthetic value but situates it with respect to a long history of colonial violence typically construed as a transfiguring if not redemptive force for disseminating (or imposing on others) the putative values of civilization and culture. Kurtz's words, or uncanny variations of them, are found in the mouths of numerous Europeans in the colonies or their supporters in safe positions at home. Lindqvist sees in these words and related violent, even exterminating actions the "origins of the European genocide" or at least one important basis for it. One such phenomenon was Germany's genocidal war against the Herero in the early twentieth century, but the latter finds its place in a larger constellation of colonial violence and genocidal practices that was not restricted to Germany. Lindqvist does not intend a normalizing comparison that would make the Holocaust any less unacceptable or difficult to deal with. But he does find it necessary to approach it with an awareness of its historical antecedents and relation to prevalent tendencies that for him should not be acted out or glorified but, insofar as possible, critically understood and counteracted. As he cogently puts the point in his preface: "Each of these genocides had, of course, its own unique characteristics. However, two events need not be identical for one of them to facilitate the other. European world expansion, accompanied as it was by a shameless defense of extermination, created habits of thought and political precedents that made way for new outrages, finally culminating in the most horrendous of them all: the Holocaust" (x).[24]

[24] While there may well be significant parallels or relationships, at points Lindqvist may make too great an approximation if not conflation of genocide in the colonies and the Nazi "extermination" of the Jews (for example, 158–60). One difference is that at least assimilated Jews, as in some sense enemy brothers, posed an internal threat to Nazis in a way Africans in the colonies did not. Moreover, African troops could be

Lindqvist's *"Exterminate All the Brutes"* might be read as a succinct companion piece to Claude Lévi-Strauss's *Tristes Tropiques*, which was published over a generation earlier.[25] Both books combine historical reflections on the colonial past, a contemporary anthropological quest, and personal, experiential interludes. (Especially prominent in Lindqvist, who published his book at the age of sixty, are apprehensive intimations of the inevitable approach of death.) Both books also convey to the reader what I earlier termed a feeling or sense of enlightened disempowerment. This may well be the most prevalent postapocalytic affect among informed intellectuals, especially as they address the ruin-strewn, unsettling, at times genocidal course of modern history. Here the most well-known icon of enlightened disempowerment may be Walter Benjamin's traumatized or shell-shocked angel of history (a mutation of Hegel's owl of Minerva):

A Klee painting named "Angelus Novus" shows an angel looking as though he is about to move away from something he is fixedly contemplating. His eyes are staring, his mouth is open, his wings are spread. This is how one pictures the angel of history. His face is turned toward the past. Where we perceive a chain of events, he sees one single catastrophe which keeps piling wreckage upon wreckage and hurls it in front of his feet. The angel would like to stay, awaken the dead, and make whole what has been smashed. But a storm is blowing from Paradise; it has got caught in his wings with such violence that the angel can no longer close them. This storm irresistibly propels him into the future to which his back is turned, while the pile of debris before him grows skyward. This storm is what we call progress.[26]

---

seen as "loyal *askari*," figured in terms of a positive military epithet that was unacceptable if applied to Jews—even "exotic" eastern Jews—under the Nazis. And Jews were not killed only or even primarily to expand Germany's *Lebensraum*. If *Lebensraum* were the primary consideration, Jews would have been treated more consistently in a selective manner similar to the treatment of Slavs, for example, with those in economically valuable occupations used as slave labor. A further question, especially in the case of Germany, is whether at least certain exterminatory "habits of thought" with respect to military or paramilitary action were already in place in the course of events in Europe and did not have to be invented in the colonies. (My colleague, I. V. Hull, is currently undertaking research on the latter question.)

[25] *Tristes Tropiques*, trans. John and Doreen Weightman (1955; New York: Atheneum, 1984).

[26] "Theses on the Philosophy of History," thesis 9 in *Illuminations*, ed. Hannah Arendt (1940; New York; Schocken Books, 1969), 257–58.

Lévi-Strauss's angel comes clothed in ironic nostalgia and lamentation for vanishing life forms that the anthropologist carefully preserves in amberlike prose and structural models. In Lindqvist, the angel provides a less veiled or clouded account of disaster and is agitated by anger and frustration. Still, even the near nihilistic despair (or perhaps what might be termed the history rage) of the narrator may generate the insistent sense that—hope against hope—there is still a role for Benjamin's weak messianic power, now distinguished from longings for redemption and directed toward a critical approach to history aware of the inquirer's constitutive implication in present problems and limited future possibilities. The sentiments of the present narrator are evidently closer to Lindqvist's than to Lévi-Strauss's or to the more exalted reactions of such recent postapocalyptic prophets as Agamben.[27]

I would add that research on, and thinking about, the Holocaust is itself not narrowly confined to the Nazi genocide but has significant and mutually informative relations to research and thought on other genocides or limit events. And disciplines such as history, literary criticism, psychoanalysis, and social theory (as Lindqvist's thought-provoking book makes manifest) have interactive relations to one another that become particularly demanding and possibly fruitful with respect to problems, such as violence, trauma, and genocide, that cannot be confined to any one of them. But exchanges take place not only abstractly between disciplines, subdisciplines, theories, and problems, but between people, including both colleagues and students. In these exchanges in the classroom, the meeting room, and the conference hall, the possibilities and limits of disciplines and subdisciplines may be explored in a particularly telling manner. One may even confront the issue of whether certain sets of problems or approaches are better located in a discipline other than the one that is currently their primary site. And the relation between teacher and student poses in an accentuated fashion the need for "translations" between levels or dimensions of discourse, at least if one does not see

[27] For a pronounced, world-historical expression of the postapocalyptic mood of enlightened disempowerment, which despite its very contemporary array of references is in many ways in the tradition of Schopenhauer and Spengler, see John Gray, *Straw Dogs: Thoughts on Humans and Other Animals* (London: Granta Books, 2002). Gray's valuable attempt to question the invidious opposition between humans and other animals itself threatens to be undermined by his gloom-and-doom, pessimistically fatalistic view of humans and their future on the planet.

the learning and use of theoretical discourses as a process of initiation that depends on an elitist practice of inclusions and exclusions. Democracy in the classroom need not be leveling in order to confront the problem of making complex theories accessible enough to facilitate a mutually challenging and testing relation between them and the varied vernacular discourses of everyday life (which themselves should not be reduced to a normalizing notion of "ordinary" language).

In these multiple, at times agonistic but at best enlivening and self-critical, exchanges, theory at its most thought-provoking—importantly including forms of psychoanalytic theory—has, I think, at least five significant and valuable contributions to make, and I shall conclude by enumerating them for critical consideration: (1) it renders explicit what might be called background assumptions or preconceptions; (2) it thus opens these assumptions to critical examination that tests and may, in varying degrees, validate or invalidate them; (3) it creates space for, and may legitimate, different practices, including research practices (such as close reading or its analogue in micrological thick description) that never totally coincide with it; (4) it may have a mutually interrogative relation to historical research or specific problems in analysis in which each term in the exchange (theory and history or specific problems) questions and may lead to reformulations in the other; (5) in its more speculative form, it explores conceptual possibilities that may be misleading but also, at their best, may loosen the grip of existing assumptions and either legitimate them or prepare the ground for alternatives. In the above senses, theory is an attempt to understand better what one knows or thinks one knows. It must be informed but cannot be reduced to information or simply found by "grubbing" in the archives. It is an attempt, however nontotalizing and self-critical, to turn erudition into learning.

INDEX

Abraham, Nicolas, 81n, 108n
Adorno, Theodor, 12, 122, 143n, 212,
    216, 250
Agamben, Giorgio, 12–15, 17–18, 75, 76,
    104n, 111, 113n, 120n, 139n, 146,
    153n, 155–194, 195, 202, 208, 224,
    269
    The Coming Community, 160n, 191n
    Homo Sacer, 163n, 164, 177n
    Means without Ends, 173
    Remnants of Auschwitz, 12–13, 75, 111,
        139n, 155–194
Alcoff, Linda Martin, 35n, 42n, 67n
Althusser, Louis, 7n, 219
Améry, Jean, 188
Antze, Paul, 106n
Appleby, Joyce, 66, 157n–158n
Arendt, Hannah, 163n
Aristotle, 22, 164n
Arnold, Matthew, 213
Augustine, 49

Badiou, Alain, 110
Baer, Ulrich, 6n
Bakhtin, M.M., 21n, 36n, 48
Balibar, Etienne, 179n
Ball, Karyn, 110n, 188n
Barbie, Klaus, 107n
Barthes, Roland, 80
Bataille, Georges, 6n, 111n, 147n, 153,
    153n–154n, 164n, 265
Beard, Charles, 234
Becker, Carl, 234
Beckett, Samuel, 13, 123, 127n, 137, 139,
    187
Bellamy, Elizabeth J., 106n

Benigni, Roberto, 100–102, 104, 137
Benjamin, Walter, 54, 117, 160n, 167,
    188, 193, 201–202, 264–266, 268–269
Berger, James, 18n, 43n, 63n, 108n, 165n,
    195n
Bersani, Leo, 211
Biernacki, Richard, 255–256
bin Laden, Osama, 97n
Binetti, Vicenzo, 155n
Blanchot, Maurice, 137, 139, 149, 152,
    157
Bloom, Allan, 209, 213
Bloor, David, 201n
Boas, Franz, 251
Bohrer, Karl-Heinz, 113n
Bomba, Abraham, 129, 131n
Bonnell, Victoria E., 251–254
Borch-Jacobsen, Mikkel, 91, 94
Bormann, Martin, 5
Borowski, Tadeusz, 113n
Boucher, Jill, 63n
Bourdieu, Pierre, 253
Brantlinger, Patrick, 251, 259, 259n–260n
Braudel, Fernand, 26
Brison, Susan, 110–111, 124
Brown, Wendy, 110
Butler, Judith, 35n, 155n

Camus, Albert, 194n
Carruthers, Peter, 63n
Caruth, Cathy, 87n, 106n, 111n, 112,
    118–123, 120n, 124, 128, 134, 138
Celan, Paul, 123, 137, 138–140, 189
Céline, Louis-Ferdinand, 163n
Chambers, Ross, 125n–126n
Chomsky, Noam, 215

Clendinnen, Inge, 134
Clinton, Bill, 85
Cohen, Stanley, 134n
Comte, August, 229
Conrad, Joseph, 267
Crapanzano, Vincent, 253n
Crimp, Douglas, 134
Cvetkovich, Ann, 127n

Davis, Colin, 122n–123n
Dawidowicz, Lucy, 108
Dayan, Joan, 266n
Dean, Carolyn, 109n, 135n
de Certeau, Michel, 3, 141, 185n
Delany, Sam, 53–54
Delbo, Charlotte, 121n, 128, 138
Deleuze, Gilles, 13
de Maistre, Joseph, 262
de Man, Paul, 41, 49, 74n, 80, 123, 152
Demjanjuk, John [Ivan], 107n
Derrida, Jacques, 14, 18n, 22, 24, 26–29,
    32, 33, 47, 49, 50, 80, 149–150, 152,
    153n, 157, 199, 212, 216, 226, 236,
    252n, 253, 256–257, 264
de Sade, Marquis, 266n
de Saussure, Ferdinand, 36n
Diamond, Nancy, 217n
Donaldson, Laura E., 186n
Douglas, Lawrence, 107n
Douglass, Ann, 107n
Downs, Laura Lee, 36n
Duras, Marguerite, 138
Durkheim, Emile, 33, 48, 49n, 153,
    153n–154n, 196–198, 200, 244, 265

Eichmann, Adolf, 107n, 184
Evans, Richard, 66, 249

Fanon, Frantz, 215, 266
Faurisson, Robert, 149n
Felman, Shoshana, 65, 120n, 123, 170, 174
Ferenczi, Sándor, 89–91
Festus, Pompeius, 164
Flanzbaum, Hilene, 43n, 108n
Foster, Hal, 106n
Foucault, Michel, 14, 24, 83–84, 141,
    153n, 163n, 164n, 166, 250, 252n,
    253, 257, 265
Fox-Genovese, Elizabeth, 250
Frank, Anne, 66, 137
Freud, Sigmund, 22, 24, 25, 45n, 58, 74,
    87, 89, 90, 93–94, 101, 102, 119, 230,
    244

Friedlander, Saul, 3n, 106, 177, 184n
Fukuyama, Francis, 1n
Fuss, Diana, 37n

Gallagher, Catherine, 251n
Garber, Marge, 237n
Geertz, Clifford, 102, 232, 252n, 253,
    255n, 256–257
Gilroy, Paul, 118n
Ginzburg, Carlo, 3
Girard, René, 154n, 262, 265
Goethe, Johann Wolfgang von, 102
Goldhagen, Daniel Jonah, 61, 75
Graff, Gerald, 232, 235–237
Graham, Hugh Davis, 217n
Gramsci, Antonio, 240, 261
Gray, John, 269n
Greenblatt, Stephen, 251n
Guillaume, Pierre, 196n

Habermas, Jürgen, 198–200, 219, 241
Halbwachs, Maurice, 93, 109n
Hames-Garcia, Michael R., 35n
Handler, Richard, 251, 252n, 259,
    259n–260n
Hartman, Geoffrey, 106n
Haskell, Thomas, 234n
Hegel, G.W.F., 22, 80, 262
Heidegger, Martin, 4, 12–14, 22, 25, 33,
    50, 58, 133n, 152, 162, 168, 182n,
    185n, 190, 193, 196–200, 208, 242,
    252n
Heller-Roazen, David, 155n
Herf, Jeffrey, 113n, 154n, 202n
Hesse, Carla, 251
Hilberg, Raul, 136n
Himmler, Heinrich, 140n, 146, 154n,
    181, 183–185
Hirsch, Marianne, 108n
Hitler, Adolf, 154n, 198, 224
Hoggart, Richard, 251
Horkheimer, Max, 216
Hull, I.V., 268n
Humboldt, Wilhelm von, 213
Hunt, Lynn, 66, 156n, 251–254,
    257n–258n
Huntington, Samuel, 97n
Huppert, Elisabeth, 129n
Husserl, Edmund, 4, 22, 30

Jacob, Margaret, 66, 201n, 257n–258n
Jacoby, Russel, 250
Jaurès, Jean, 264

Jay, Martin, 36n, 261n
Jones, Paula, 85
Jünger, Ernst, 113, 265

Kafka, Franz, 123, 137
Kannsteiner, Wulf, 109n
Kant, Immanuel, 49, 148n, 175, 184, 213, 223
Kaplan, E. Ann, 206n
Karlin, Danny, 20n
Kearns, Thomas R., 107n
Keller, Helen, 63n
Kellner, Hans, 138
Kierkegaard, Søren, 49
Klages, Mary, 63n
Klemperer, Victor, 55n, 139
Klüger, Ruth, 158n
Korman, Gerd, 170n
Kristeva, Julia, 122n, 163n
Kuhn, Thomas, 232

Lacan, Jacques, 70, 112n, 123n, 187
LaCapra, Dominick, 3n, 9n, 12n, 18n, 27n, 28n, 30n, 36n, 47n, 49n–50n, 55n, 61n, 65n, 66n, 67, 71n, 72n, 74n, 75n, 84n, 88n, 95n, 109n, 110n, 116n, 121n, 125n, 127n, 130n, 137n, 141n, 145n, 148n, 149n, 152n, 154n, 165n, 167n, 168n, 174n, 188n, 193n, 194n, 197n, 200n, 201n, 253n, 264n–265n
Ladurie, Emmanuel Le Roi, 3
Lamarck, Jean-Baptiste, 107
Lambek, Michael, 106n
Lang, Berel, 138
Langer, Lawrence, 3n, 168n
Lanzmann, Claude, 65, 81, 115n, 120n–121n, 129–130, 131n, 145
Laqueur, Thomas, 251
Lasch-Quinn, Elisabeth, 250
Lash, Joseph P., 63n
Latour, Bruno, 201n
Laub, Dori, 65n
Lefebvre, Henri, 4
Lerner, Paul, 107n
Levi, Primo, 76, 113n, 128, 136, 139, 157, 161, 166, 167n, 168, 170, 174, 178–181, 185, 187–189
Levinas, Emmanuel, 4, 122n, 191, 226
Levine, George, 206n
Lévi-Strauss, Claude, 268–269
Leys, Ruth, 83–93, 107n, 112
Lifton, Robert J., 98

Lindqvist, Sven, 114n, 266–269
Lukács, Georg, 48
Lynch, Michael, 201n
Lyotard, Jean-François, 12, 13, 14, 49, 111, 148, 150n, 170–171, 174, 177, 212, 216, 223, 226

Maechler, Stefan, 125n
Mahoney, Richard J., 206n–207n
Maier, Charles, 108
Mann, Thomas, 33, 102
Marcuse, Herbert, 212
Marx, Karl, 48, 162, 212
Masson, Jeffrey Moussaieff, 63n
Mauss, Marcel, 265
Mayer, Arno, 108, 195n
Melville, Herman, 20
Merleau-Ponty, Maurice, 4
Messer-Davidow, Ellen, 206n
Michaels, Walter Benn, 42–43, 108
Michale, Mark S., 107n
Michelet, Jules, 24
Mill, John Stuart, 224
Mineta, Norman, 97
Moeller, Susan, 134n
Mohanty, Satya, 37n, 40, 43n, 67n, 108n
Morrison, Karl F., 135n
Morrison, Toni, 43, 100, 108, 132
Mowitt, John, 109
Moya, Paula M.L., 35n, 37n
Mozart, Wolfgang Amadeus, 63

Naïr, Sami, 129n
Nancy, Jean-Luc, 212, 224, 225
Newman, Cardinal, 202, 214
Nietzsche, Friedrich, 121n–122n, 252n, 262, 265
Noiriel, Gérard, 66, 249
Nolte, Ernst, 188
Norris, Andrew, 164n–165n
Norris, Christopher, 27
Novick, Peter, 42–43, 66, 93–95, 107, 231–235, 237

Olson, Alexandra, 217n
Omar, Mullah, 97n

Parker, Hershel, 20n
Pascal, Blaise, 49
Paxton, Robert, 67n
Pelikan, Jaroslav, 213
Phelan, James, 237
Plato, 22

Powers, Richard, 63n
Probyn, Elspeth, 128n

Raczymow, Henri, 114, 130
Ramadanovic, Petar, 123n
Ranke, Leopold von, 26
Rauch, Angelika, 56n–57n
Ravetto, Kriss, 131n
Readings, Bill, 13–15, 17, 18, 80n, 165n,
    195–196, 201–203, 207–227, 228, 229,
    232, 236, 237n, 241, 243, 247, 248
Rentschler, Eric, 7n
Resnais, Alain, 138
Richman, Michelle, 153n–154n
Robbins, Bruce, 247n
Rorty, Richard, 243n
Rosenbaum, Thane, 100, 108n
Rosenberg, Alfred, 154n
Roth, Michael S., 36n
Rothberg, Michael, 70n, 106n, 109n,
    158n
Rousso, Henry, 67n, 94–95, 108
Royle, Nicolas, 165n–166n
Rubenstein, Richard L., 266n
Rudner, Rita, 59
Rumkowski, Chaim, 188

Said, Edward, 237
Santner, Eric, 52n, 106n
Sanyal, Debarati, 194n
Sarat, Austin, 107n
Sartre, Jean-Paul, 4, 21n, 57, 160n, 173n,
    187, 248
Sawyer, R. Keith, 207n
Schaffer, Simon, 201n
Schlosser, Eric, 165n
Schmitt, Carl, 123n, 166
Schreber, Daniel Paul, 52n
Schulte-Sasse, Linda, 7n
Scott, Joan, 35n–36n, 38, 53–54, 256n
Segev, Tom, 94–95
Seigel, Jerrold, 252n
Sewell, William, 254, 255n
Shapin, Steven, 201n
Schopenhauer, Arthur, 269n
Sloterdijk, Peter, 219
Smith, Bonnie G., 24, 33
Sommer, Doris, 38n
Sorel, Georges, 55n, 153n, 263–266
Spector, Scott, 7n
Spengler, Oswald, 97n, 269n

Spiegel, Gabrielle, 109n
Spiegelman, Art, 33, 95, 194n
Starr, Peter, 154n, 224n
Steedman, Carolyn, 24, 26–33, 252n
Sternhell, Zeev, 198n, 263
Strauss, Leo, 250
Suny, Ronald Grigor, 251, 252n, 255n,
    259n
Swidler, Ann, 255n

Taylor, Charles, 65
Terada, Rei, 63n
Theweleit, Klaus, 55n, 73n, 113n, 265,
    266n
Thompson, E.P., 251, 255–256, 261
Toews, John, 35n, 38, 53, 60, 62, 64
Torok, Maria, 81n, 108n
Trezise, Thomas, 128n
Trilling, Lionel, 242

van Alphen Ernst, 106n
van der Kolk, Bessel, 87n, 119
Veysey, Laurence, 218n
Vidal-Naquet, Pierre, 196n
Vogel, Thomas A., 107n
von Salomon, Ernst, 265
Voss, John, 217n

Watkins, Evan, 238–241
Weber, Max, 73, 123n, 244
Weiskel, Thomas, 55n
White Hayden, 25, 27, 29, 73n, 77, 80n,
    123n, 235, 252n, 253
Wiesel, Elie, 170
Wilkerson, William S., 37n
Wilkomirski, Binjamin, 47n, 81, 108,
    114, 116, 118n, 125, 125n–126n, 126
Williams, Jeffrey J., 156n, 237–238, 247n
Williams, Raymond, 251
Windschuttle, Keith, 249
Wittgenstein, Ludwig, 177
Wood, Nancy, 106n, 138n, 188n

Yerushalmi, Yosef Hayim, 108

Zammito, John H., 35n–36n, 40n, 44, 54,
    63, 64, 67–68
Zelizer, Barbie, 106n–107n
Žižek, Slavoj, 7n, 9, 120n–121n, 123n,
    155n, 180n, 187, 219
Zundel, Ernst, 107n